Tagore
in Tripura

Praise for the book

'Khagesh Dev Burman's book *Tripuray Annya Rabindranath* (*Tagore in Tripura*) is a nicely laid-out compilation, which has thoroughly encompassed the relationship between Rabindranath and Tripura and established a precedent worthy of mention. The role played by Rabindranath during the regime of Maharaja Radha Kishore shows a hitherto unrevealed aspect of the poet. The chapter traces how the poet was also an able administrator, who saved a kingdom by counselling the king in running the administration. In the life of Rabindranath, this instance remains incomparable.

'Now, at this time, we accept with love and respect this offering made to us.'

—Anath Nath Das, scholar and writer
(review published in *Desh*)

'It is a matter of great wonder that even when Rabindranath was not internationally known, he was recognized as a "Great Poet" and accepted cordially by the royal family (across generations) with all due humbleness and courtesy. This book, inlaid with gems and jewels of the royal family of Tripura, has naturally become an item for collection and preservation. The book unfolds with *Bhagna Hriday* (*Broken Heart*) but in the end leaves the heart fulfilled. The various pictures in the book are a treat to the soul.'

—Barid Baran Ghosh,
author
(review published in *Anandabazar Patrika*)

'*Tripuray Annya Rabindranath* undertakes a different kind of research work on Rabindranath. Khagesh Dev Burman has dealt with the subject in this book with well-corroborated documents on how the ceaseless relationship of Rabindranath, over a period of sixty years, with four generations of Maharajas has glorified the history of Tripura. This valuable book is, no doubt, a product of the writer's hard diligence. Those interested in Rabindranath can find the answers to several of their queries in the book.'

—*Bartaman Patrika*

Tagore *in* Tripura

AN ENDURING CONNECTION

KHAGESH DEV BURMAN

Translated *from* the
Bengali by the author

HarperCollins *Publishers* India

First published in English in India by HarperCollins *Publishers* 2025
HarperCollins *Publishers India*, Cyber City,
Building 10-A, Gurugram, Haryana-122002, India
www.harpercollins.co.in

2 4 6 8 10 9 7 5 3 1

Copyright © Khagesh Dev Burman 2025
Photographs courtesy of the author

P-ISBN: 978-93-6989-525-0
E-ISBN: 978-93-6989-971-5

The views and opinions expressed in this book are the author's own
and the facts are as reported by him, and the publishers are not
in any way liable for the same.

Khagesh Dev Burman asserts the moral right
to be identified as the author of this work.

All rights reserved. No part of this publication may be reproduced,
stored in a retrieval system, or transmitted, in any form or by any means,
electronic, mechanical, photocopying, recording or otherwise,
without the prior permission of the publishers.

Without limiting the exclusive rights of any author, contributor or the publisher
of this publication, any unauthorized use of this publication to train generative
artificial intelligence (AI) technologies is expressly prohibited. HarperCollins also
exercise their rights under Article 4(3) of the Digital Single Market Directive
2019/790 and expressly reserve this publication from the text and
data-mining exception.

Typeset in 11/15.5 Adobe Caslon Pro
by HarperCollins *Publishers* India Pvt. Ltd

Printed and bound at
Thomson Press (India) Ltd

This book is produced from independently certified FSC® paper
to ensure responsible forest management.

HarperCollins *Publishers*, Macken House, 39/40 Mayor Street Upper, Dublin 1,
D01 C9W8, Ireland

To
my beloved wife, Sumita,
my sons, Rajnish and Gaurav,
and my daughters–in–law, Amrita and Leena,
whose desire to learn about Tripura knows no bounds.
Their love, affection and encouragement infuse me with life and
strengthen my will to live long among them.
All of them are my cherished possessions.

Contents

Preface ix

1. Rabindranath and Maharaja Bir Chandra Manikya 1
2. Rabindranath and Maharaja Radha Kishore Manikya 35
3. Rabindranath and Maharaja Birendra Kishore Manikya 109
4. Rabindranath and Maharaja Bir Bikram Manikya 149
5. Rabindranath and Maharaja Kumar Brajendra Kishore 188
6. Rabindranath and Colonel Mahim Chandra Deb Barma 205

Epilogue 221
A Glossary of the Manikya Dynasty of Tripura 223
Appendices 227
Bibliography 293
Notes 295
Index 299

Preface

I believe it is my solemn duty to write this book: firstly, to bring to light, as a son of the soil, the glory and pride of Tripura for its spiritual bond with the Nobel Laureate Rabindranath Tagore for a period of sixty years; secondly, to present an episode that remains unfamiliar, unknown and unexplored among followers, critics and scholars of Tagore; and, thirdly, and most important of all, to rediscover Rabindranath as a human being with his own set of strengths and vulnerabilities, which were never exposed anywhere other than in Tripura. This is a different Rabindranath and an untold story that the world does not know.

The relationship of Rabindranath with four generations of the Maharajas of Tripura began in the year 1882. When seeking refuge from the intense grief caused by the death of Maharani Bhanumati, his prime queen, Maharaja Bir Chandra found solace in Tagore's *Bhagna Hriday*, written when the poet was a teenager. Maharaja Bir Chandra was so deeply moved by the heart-rending poems of Rabindranath that he sent his minister, Radha Raman Ghosh, to Jorasanko, Calcutta (now Kolkata), miles away from Tripura, to bestow on him the honourific title of a 'Great Poet'.

Rabindranath unhesitatingly acknowledged that in this period, when he was struggling as an amateur poet and was yet to become famous, he had received cordial recognition as a 'Great Poet' only from Maharaja Bir Chandra Manikya of Tripura. He said, 'For the first time, I have received felicitation from the country.' After that, in praise of Maharaja Bir Chandra's farsightedness, he added:

> In my immature beginnings, his wisdom could foresee the picture ahead in the future and that was why he honoured me as a "Great Poet". The fame that I am getting in my life; he was the first person in the entire world who had predicted. A person who stays on the peak can see what is not normally visible to others; Bir Chandra identified what would make me distinctive.

He further termed the relationship with the father-like Maharaja Bir Chandra as historical and said, 'It is difficult to obtain in the history of literature an account of such a spontaneous and open friendship of a king with a tender-aged poet whose road to fame was totally uncertain and doubtful.'

After the death of Maharaja Bir Chandra, during the twelve years of Maharaja Radha Kishore's reign, like Kautilya, Rabindranath as a true friend took full responsibility of running the administration of the state. He proved his wisdom by counselling Maharaja Radha Kishore in all matters of administrative reforms: social, economic and political—ranging from cautioning the Maharaja against the antagonism of courtiers, unveiling of conspiracies, to aiding him in the appointment of ministers and solving family complexities and feuds. Tripura was singularly fortunate to have witnessed the most astonishing, multifaceted talent of Rabindranath. During Maharaja Radha Kishore's regime, Rabindranath was deemed as the one who enjoyed absolute authority in all fronts of the government. This relationship of two intimate souls led to the widespread development of Bengali literature, culture and science—towards which Maharaja Radha Kishore made generous financial contributions.

In fact, any donation given by voluntary self-denial and with immense pleasure is peerless. If the Maharaja had not financed the scientist Jagadish Chandra Bose's travel to England, the history of science in India would have been a very different story. In fact, the Maharaja has been instrumental in funding scientific and literary research in India.

Rabindranath knew what sacrifices Radha Kishore had to make. He was certainly aware that the royal treasury was draining; he himself had been directly involved in taking a loan of 15 lakh rupees from the bank—despite that, the Maharaja never hesitated to be as generous as possible to turn Rabindranath's dreams into reality.

On 7 Poush 1308 Bengali Era (January 1901), Rabindranath established Brahmacharya Ashram and a school at Shantiniketan. The poet told the Maharaja that he had no monetary capability to run the school; it could be possible only by the Maharaja's favour. Apart from yearly assistance of 1,000 rupees, the Maharaja gave his word to provide help as and when required. These regular donations and occasional extra amount donated in critical times saved the institution from disaster. All these assistances continued for more than half a century. As long as Tripura was a princely state (up to 1949), the next generations of Maharajas also did not break the promise. All the Maharajas had sent good numbers of students to Shantiniketan with a stipend so that the institution would not need to bear any expenses for the students of Tripura. If not for the assistance of Tripura, Shantiniketan would have faced a sudden death in its embryonic period and failed to flourish to the levels it has today.

The shadow of grievances that was cast in the minds of the courtiers and the people of Tripura regarding the charities of Maharaja Radha Kishore Manikya, and the involvement of Rabindranath in all acts and deeds of the state, soon broke out into the open. In their opinion, the first duty of the king was to develop his underdeveloped kingdom. Tripura needed help rather desperately from outside. Prosperous and advanced Bengal did not require charity from Tripura, which was then very much below the poverty line. Above all, the handover of absolute power to a minister from outside the state (at the insistence of Rabindranath) led to agitations within the kingdom. The people of Tripura did not like the idea of Tagore converting their Maharaja into a magnificent cipher; they raised their voice against the move and labeled Rabindranath as 'selfish and ambitious'.

An infuriated Rabindranath now emerged full-scale on the political stage to counter the charges levelled against him. In doing so, an entirely different Rabindranath came forth: (the form in which Bengal had not seen him, not to speak of the whole world, that appeared only in the small state of Tripura) a shrewd, pragmatic, partisan Rabindranath hitherto unknown, unseen. He wanted to see Tripura as an ideal native state and, for that matter, he did not give a damn about any resistance.

The sincere friendship that had grown with the royal family of Tripura from 1882 made Rabindranath feel as if he had become equally involved in all their joys and sorrows. He could not remain stoic in their calamities as is evident from a letter that reveals his sympathies:

> I feel God has conferred on me a vow that the system in the kingdom of the Maharaja will have to be settled. My heart is eager to take leave from service, but I have clearly understood that this work must be accomplished by me. I am religiously bound by it—even the Maharaja will not be able to set me free

from this. In the midst of all my present problems relating to property, the thought of the Maharaja's kingdom is by no means leaving me. It is not for the Maharaja only; I shall have to apply my mind to his work to release me from anxiety. The connection that my grandfather had to the history of Tripura; I shall have to maintain that. For that purpose, by the will of God, the late Maharaja had tied me with Tripura.

Rabindranath came to Tripura five times during the reign of Maharaja Radha Kishore and once each in the times of Maharaja Birendra Kishore and Maharaja Bir Bikram Manikya. Never had he returned empty handed—the bounties as promised continued unabated with further additions by the subsequent Maharajas.

In world history, this sort of incident had never happened. The celebration of Rabindranath Tagore's eightieth birth anniversary was held in the royal durbar (royal court in the Ujjayanta Palace) and for felicitating him with the royal honour of 'Bharat Bhaskar'. It was a matter of immense pride for Tripura that the love and affection of Rabindranath for the state did not deter him from performing the last ritual duty of his life despite his severe illness. Tripura was always treated specially by the poet.

The subject matter of this book also corroborates and evaluates royal heritage, aristocracy, splendour, literary activities and the merits and demerits of the Maharajas of Tripura. They were not only patrons of art, literature and culture; many of them were successful artists. The Maharajas of Tripura never tolerated the slightest disrespect towards the Bengali language, the royal language of Tripura. The comment of Radha Kishore, here is worthy of mention: 'I love the Bengali language as my life.'

The contribution of Tripura towards the development of Bengali literature is unparalleled. In fact, we have the example of *Rajmala*, the first book in Bengali that was written in Tripura. Let me quote Rabindranath, 'I have keenly observed deep respect and attachment for Bengali language and literature in this family. My relationship with this family has become strong and steady because of this common attachment.'

The humbleness, magnanimity, generosity of the Maharajas and, above all, their large-heartedness to appreciate the good qualities of others, attracted the admiration of Rabindranath so much that, full of reverence, he admitted, 'The lofty impression that arises in the mind after studying Indian Puranas and poems about the ancient kings, I have noticed them amongst the Maharajas of Tripura.'

Riches matter little, what matters is a big heart; for riches do not give birth to kind sensibilities—it is the heart where kindness blossoms forth. Referring to the benevolence of the Maharajas, Tagore wrote to Acharya Jagadish Chandra Bose about Radha Kishore: 'I have not seen such a bright role model of spontaneous generosity.' Rabindranath understood the ancient essence of Tripura from the core of his heart, its cultural heritage, royal splendour and 'elevation of mind'; therefore, the knot of the relationship never came loose and continued for sixty years till the poet's death. Tripura prompted him to unveil his unique talent and qualities of character that remained hidden from the rest of the world.

In literature, the art of letter-writing occupies a very important place. This book shows how letters function as invaluable pieces of historical evidence, and I find it astounding that the history of six decades of a kingdom can be retrieved just from epistolary exchanges. It is our misfortune today that letter writing is no longer in vogue, and for that we have lost, for good, one crucial facet of literary practice.

1

Rabindranath and Maharaja Bir Chandra Manikya

Maharaja Bir Chandra's period of reign: 1862-1896

The beginning of Tagore's relationship with Tripura: 1882

The glorious union of kings and poets is integral to the history of art and literature in India. From time immemorial, poets in royal durbars occupied the highest ranks. The witty and humorous poetry of Kalidas, Bharat Chandra, Vidyapati and Jaideva, among others, flourished under royal favour. In those days, the kings were only patrons of art and literature with no or little contribution to these fields. But the kings and queens of the Manikya dynasty of Tripura were exceptions. They were not only patrons of art and culture; many of them were successful artists. The members of the royal family were connoisseurs of Bengali art and culture. Tripura's horizons echoed with music and the recitation of poems, which flowed through the veins of its natives. For ages, the inner court of Tripura reverberated with discourses on music, drama, poetry, paintings, literature and culture.

There is an impassable distance between the practical life of a king and a poet. Their environments, lifestyles and mental attitudes make all the differences. Yet there exists an invisible resemblance, which acts as a bridge—the culture of the land—and both the poet and the king respond to it and engage with it, albeit in their own ways. In the context of Tripura, Rabindranath Tagore said, 'Culture and elevation of mind, which are the country's topmost human fortune; the kings had once considered them as the main feature of royal splendour.'

The relationship of the great poet with Tripura germinated out of severe grief caused by death. *'Mrityu Amrita Kore Dan'* ('Death confers immortality'). But again, the pang of separation is so unbearable that people burst into tears and seek shelter. They find shelter in poetic justice. This was what happened to Maharaja Bir Chandra Manikya. The Maharaja, stricken with grief at the death of his first queen, Bhanumati Devi, had visualized the image of his inexpressible mental sufferings, which he underwent at that time in the book of verses, *Bhagna Hriday*, penned by teenage Rabindranath Tagore. Distressed in those days by the woes of estrangement from his queen, Bir Chandra himself was writing poems to vent his agony. What an outpouring of feelings of estrangement the poems exude! Simply heart-rending! The language is Brajabuli. Roughly translated, it goes:

> Now a mild breeze is blowing,
> Scorching the heart of estranged lovers,
> Away from the beloved with eyes streaming with tears,
> The glowing springtime has arrived.
> The blooming of the flowers malati, golap,
> Sheoti, bakul, champak and juthi;
> The buzzing of bumblebees and the ceaseless

Dance of Sottish peacocks are viewed by the
Young women of Braja, cuckoos and the bees
While servant Bir Chandra sings.

Can you imagine the profundity of Bir Chandra's pain? *Bhagna Hriday* most probably was published in May 1881. Maharani Bhanumati died the following year. It seems that the book had reached Bir Chandra that same year. This proves once again that the Maharajas of Tripura were very interested in Bengali literature; otherwise, why would a royal family have in their possession a book of poems portraying a then unknown poet's childhood dalliance?

Rabindranath described his adolescent experiences in *Bhagna Hriday*. He was afflicted with the unbounded, disruptive madness of youth. He wrote:

On the whole, that was a period of my madness. I passed many a sleepless night at my own will. Not that there was any need of it but as sleeping at night was a simple matter, perhaps to upset that normal order, I intended to overturn the system ... On many occasions in summer, I used to roam alone in the dead of night on the roof of the second floor like a ghost without rhyme or reason, amid shadows cast by big trees grown in rows of tubs in motley moonlight. If anyone takes it as poetic license, they will be mistaken. There was a time when the Earth witnessed regular earthquakes and volcanic eruptions. In the present, when that kind of restlessness is observed, people are astonished. But in early years, when her crust was not that hard and the inside was full of gaseous materials, the Earth regularly had to bear unthinkable calamities. The events at the onset of youth were something like that. The ingredients that constitute life, if they're not properly formed, start creating disturbances.

The madness of a young Rabindranath had an infectious effect on the middle-aged Bir Chandra. The perceptions of love expressed in *Bhagna Hriday* was nothing but the burning passion of an adolescent. But it's a fact that in the case of maddening love, age is no bar. It is a state of being heavily stricken with grief. Rabindranath in his teens might not have had the true feeling of love, but as poets are seers, his poems elegantly expressed the agonies of separation. For instance, Rabindranath wrote a tune for the following song—'*Eh bhara badar, maha bhadar, shunya hridaya more*' ('In this heavy rain, this great downpour, my heart lies empty')—and sang it to Kadambari Devi, his sister-in-law. His condition was also no less miserable. The feeling of estrangement pained him; emptiness had crept into his heart and soul. And this same feeling of estrangement had hit the lonely heart of Bir Chandra so hard that he had a feeling of deep sympathy for the poems of *Bhagna Hriday*.

Bhagna Hriday is about the delight of adolescence and the agonies of love. One of the poems '*Ektuku chhoya laagey, ektuku katha shuni*' ('Just a little touch, just a few words I long to hear') reveals its unspoken agonies. Rabindranath wrote a few chapters of this book at the age of seventeen or eighteen and left for England. He wrote, 'I have started writing another book of poems in England. I have completed it on my journey back and after coming back to my country.'

Students of literature know that Rabindranath had a very intimate relation with his elder brother Jyotirindranath and his wife, Kadambari Devi. They had spent so many days together, especially in the garden houses at Srirampur and Chandan Nagar. The loneliness of Kadambari elapsed and was filled up by the songs and poetic recitations of young Rabindranath. She was well educated, a good listener and a voracious reader. There was no hide and seek in their intimate relationship.

In the inner mahal of the Tagore family, Kadambari Devi was known as 'Heyketi'. This name was given to her by Rabindranath to highlight the bantering relationship of an elder brother's wife with her brother-in-law. Prabhat Kumar Mukhopadhyay wrote:

Kadambari Devi's feminine heart was a confluence of three rivers. She rendered respect to the poet Biharilal, love to Jyotirindranath and affection to Rabindranath, and she made them all her own. That is why the relatives used to call her three-headed Heyketi.

No doubt, Rabindranath dedicated *Bhagna Hriday* to Kadambari Devi as a present. A long poem containing thirty lines in five stanzas was dedicated to *'Srimati Hey'*. Sajanikanta Das[1], thus, raised a question, 'Who is this "Hey"?' This 'Hey' was none other than Kadambari Devi.

Love does not expect any return. It gives everything and becomes a pauper. In love-poems, the strain of offering one's own self makes one melancholic.

The poems of *Bhagna Hriday* set ablaze the heartstrings of sorrowful Maharaja Bir Chandra and created a sort of endless crescendo. Self-dedication gave him peace and tranquillity. The essence can be reclaimed from the third stanza of the long lyric *'Uphar'* that opens the poems in the book:

Probably Devi, thou know not, tied with an invisible knot
I went far and near, but that attraction persists.
Its immobile strength hast strayed me not
Otherwise, my heart like a torn comet
Would've failed to ascertain the right way
Under the endless sky.

Rabindranath had unhesitatingly come out with an outburst of personal emotion in the last stanzas of the poem and bowed down to '*Srimati Hey*' in a posture of self-surrender:

> Under the sunshine of love, with my heart and soul
> The last song I sang, Devi, standing on this side
> Seeks shelter in the shadow of thy mind
> Donate him please a drop of thy tears
> Goodbye to-day, shall I see thy again—
> Will then my heart sing with thy ray of affection?

Bhagna Hriday was a medium through which started a longstanding relationship of sixty years between the Maharajas of Tripura and Rabindranath Tagore. The relationship continued till Tagore's death. His self-revelation in Tripura was not only as a poet but also as a human being of a versatile character. This is an unknown Rabindranath Tagore and an untold story, which people outside Tripura are not aware of.

Bir Chandra perceived the poet of *Bhagna Hriday* as a great man. Having found his refuge from grief in the book, the Maharaja had sent his minister, Radha Raman Ghosh, to Jorasanko, the Tagore family's ancestral home in Calcutta (now Kolkata) and confer on Rabindranath Tagore the royal honour of a 'Great Poet'. It created a tumultuous affair in the Tagore family. Rabindranath, then a young man of twenty-one, listened shamefacedly to what Radha Raman Ghosh said as a conveyer of the message from Maharaja Bir Chandra. Let us hear from Tagore about that day:

> In those days, very few people knew about me and my writings. My identity was confined to only near relatives and friends. Once at that time a messenger from Maharaja of Tripura, Bir Chandra

Manikya Bahadur, had sought an interview with me. I was very young, and I welcomed him with a lot of hesitation. Most probably, many of you know his name—he was Radha Raman Ghosh. The Maharaja had sent him from far-off Tripura especially to convey the message that he wanted to felicitate me as a poet. For this unexpected incident, the young poet had no end of surprise.

In his reminiscence that very time had cropped up again and again. In his last two months of life, while accepting the royal honour 'Bharat Bhaskar' from the Maharaja of Tripura, Rabindranath talked about those old times with Maharaja Bir Chandra.

> I was then young, and my writings were very few. Most of the readers of the country sarcastically labeled them as "child's pleasure". Bir Chandra knew about it and felt sorry. For that he had proposed to buy an independent press at 1 lakh rupees, where an ornamental edition of my book of poems would be published.

Rabindranath unhesitatingly acknowledged with gratitude that in this period, when he had not yet achieved any fame, he had received cordial recognition as a 'Great Poet' only from Maharaja Bir Chandra Manikya of Tripura. He said, 'For the first time I've received felicitation from the country.' After that, in praise of Maharaja Bir Chandra's farsightedness, he added:

> In my immature beginning, his wisdom could foresee the picture ahead in the future and that was why he honoured me as a "Great Poet" at that time. The fame that I'm getting in my life, he was the first person in the world who predicted it. A person who stays on the peak can see what is not normally visible; Bir Chandra likewise identified what would make me distinctive.

In the year 1882, when Rabindranath came to know Maharaja Bir Chandra, he was then only twenty-one years old; Bir Chandra was forty-five. Despite such an age difference, Bir Chandra, who appreciated the good qualities of others, never failed to pay due respect to the poet. That was why this difference of age, instead of creating a distance, gave birth to a close intimacy.

The recognition from Tripura had aroused an enormous curiosity in Kabiguru Rabindranath to know all about the native state. He grew keen to acquaint himself with the ancient history of the state. He came to know for the first time that the royal language of Tripura was not its dialect Kokborok but Bengali. In a non-Bengali state, the honour of Bengali as the royal language greatly astonished Rabindranath. In this context, an incident of 1884 is worth mentioning. This incident indicated how attached Ishwar Chandra Vidyasagar was to his mother language. In an article *'Tripuray Bangabhasha'* (Tripura's Bengali language), Colonel Mahim Chandra Deb Barma wrote:

> Ishwar Chandra Vidyasagar Mahashay, noticing a gold coin constantly oscillating with my gold chain, asked with a smile, "With your coruscating chain a gold coin is glittering; what is this coin?" He took it in his hand and read out, "Sri Sri Radha Krishna, Srijut Maharaja Govinda Manikya, and Sri Sri Maharani Gunabati Devya." He was thrilled after reading it and told the respectable persons present therein, "In this (coin) is imprinted the Bengali language. Does it mean that my Bengali language is the royal language?"

Mahim Chandra Deb Barma (Colonel), of the royal family, was at that time a class-fellow of Balendranath Tagore in Hare School, Kolkata. Mahim Chandra (1864-1923) became a bosom friend of Rabindranath. He wrote about it:

In those days, because of the poet Balendranath (and a classmate), I got the right to have an association with the Tagore family. The charge of dispatching new books published in Bengali to Maharaja Bir Chandra was given to a young humble servant like me. And in this connection, my acquaintance with Rabindranath had gradually evolved into a close friendship.

Mahim Chandra[2], thus, played an important role as a medium of connection between Rabi Thakur[3] and Bir Chandra and the subsequent Maharajas of the state. From Mahim Chandra, Rabindranath learned much about the history of Tripura and the role of Bengali as the royal language of the state. Apart from this, historian Kailash Chandra Singh, son of Golak Chandra Singh, the revenue secretary of Tripura, oversaw the zamindaries of the Tagores in Orissa. He also acted as an assistant editor at the Adi Brahmo Samaj from the year 1884. The history of the kingdom of Tripura and its royal dynasty was on his fingertips. He was the person who wrote *'Rajmala O Tripurar Itihas'* ('The Royal Chronicle of Tripura') and tried to give it factuality. Rabindranath, therefore, got two persons on hand, who could tell him the comprehensive history of Tripura. This communion only made him more interested. He used to treat Kailash Chandra Singh with great respect. In fact, Tagore wrote a novel *Bou Thakuranir Haat* (meaning Royal Hut of Daughter-in-law) based on an article *'Banglar Dadash Bhowmir Itihas'* (roughly translates to 'History of Bengali land', first published in Bharati, January 1880), written by Kailash Chandra Singh. In the books *Mukut*, *Rajarshi* and *Bisharjan* (meaning Crown, Kingdom and Immersion—respectively, all set in Tripura), Rabindranath had collected and used materials from Kailash Chandra's *Rajmala* and also from the documents provided by Maharaja Bir Chandra. *Mukut* was published in the magazine *Balak* (serialized from May to June 1885) which was based on historical tales of Amar Manikya. Later, it was given the form of a drama.

Now, let us turn briefly to the history of the Bengali language in Tripura. In a non-Bengali state, where the natives' mother tongue was primarily Kokborok (dialect), how did Bengali receive the honour of being the royal language? Let us hear what Rabindranath had to say:

> In this royal family, from time immemorial, the Bengali language had been receiving honourable treatment. In fact, the history of all countries reveal that the country's language is not only the mother tongue but also her royal language. As the duty of a king is to protect and preserve the subjects; so also, he has to protect the language. The kings of a country should not be moved by the splendour of foreign custom and forget about this noble responsibility. I have keenly observed the deep respect and attachment for Bengali language and literature in this family. My relationship with this family has become strong and steady because of this common attachment. I have seen very few letters written like that of Radha Kishore and Bir Chandra. Those letters were self-restrained, polite and savoury. Such an adroit use of the mother tongue is a part of their royal courtesy.

There would not have been any scope for me to write this book if the Bengali language would not have played its connective role in the relationship of the Maharajas of Tripura and Rabindranath. This Bengali language tied them with one string. To satisfy the curiosity of the readers, I have presented here a short history of the Bengali language in Tripura.

First, let us begin our discussion by raising the issue of dispute on the period of writing of *Rajmala*. *Rajmala* is Maharaja Dharma Manikya's immortal achievement. The period of Dharma Manikya's reign has also been disputed. According to *Rajmala*, the period of his reign was 1432-1462, whereas Dinesh Chandra Sen and Rama

Prasad Dutta marked it as the years 1407-1439 and 1458-1490 respectively. Historian Kailash Chandra Singh, who wrote *Rajmala O Tripurar Itihas* opined that Dharma Manikya ascended the throne in the year 1407. He did not ascertain any year or date about the end of his rule but had, however, mentioned that Dharma Manikya in May 1458, Monday, the thirteenth lunar day of the bright fortnight, donated twenty-nine *drone* (a drone is equivalent to a little over twenty-nine kilograms of corn) of rent-free corn field to Kautuk and seven other Brahmans by a royal edict inscribed on a copper plate. In that deed of grant, the writings proved that Dharma Manikya was the king of Tripura in the year 1458. He wrote: 'If my line of descent becomes extinct and the kingdom is subjugated by another, I would be the slave of his slave if he does not abolish this grant of rent-free land to the Brahmans.'

The year, date and day of that incident has been proved to be correct on count. On this ground, one may counter the claims of *Rajmala* being an imaginary tract for it is not possible to write a fictitious tale with such accurate details. And for this reason, I conclude that Dharma Manikya was a king in the fifteenth century.

Historians Dr Dinesh Chandra Sen and Kailash Chandra Singh admitted that Pandits Shukreshwar and Baneshwar wrote *Rajmala*, the ancient history of Tripura, after 1407. The problem started later when the historians claimed *Rajmala* as the ancient book written in Bengali. Reverend Long[4] wrote in praise of *Rajmala*:

> The *Rajmala* is a curiosity as presenting us with the oldest specimen of Bengali composition to the extent the first part of it having been compiled in the beginning of the fifteenth century, the subsequent portions were composed at a more recent date. We may consider this then as the most ancient work in Bengali

that has come down to us, as the *Chaitanya Charitamrita* was not written before 1557, and Kirtibus subsequently translated the *Ramayana*.

It is clearly mentioned in the prologue to *Rajmala*:

In the lineage of Trilochan there was a king, Maha Manikya, whose son Sri Dharma Manikya was famous for his pious disposition, righteousness and devotion to scripture.

Once, the Maharaja sitting on the sacred throne expressed his desire to hear the glorious achievements of the royal dynasty.

There is also no obscurity about the writers:

The name of the head priest of fourteen deities was Durlavendra who knew well the feat of the unending royal dynasty.

Baneshwar and Shukreshwar, the two Brahmins, were well versed with the esoteric scriptures of the Hindus.

Three of them said, "Raja, listen attentively to the proved history of your genealogy. It's a sin if scriptures are exposed in speech. The priest, therefore, tells it to the raja in the Tripuri language."

It is written at the end of the first chapter of *Rajmala*:

'*Iti Rajmalaung Sri Dharma Manikya Jignyasha Durlavendra Chantai, Baneshwar, Shukreshwar Dwija Kathanang Samapthan*' (The questions asked by Sri Dharma Manikya and answers given by Durlavendra Chantai, Baneswar and Shukreshwar end here in *Rajmala*).

Rama Prasad Dutta in his book *Tripurar Prachin Punthi Prasangey* had raised a question that Chantai might have told the history of the royal dynasty in the Tripuri dialect—but where was the proof that Baneshwar and Shukreshwar had translated it in Bengali? Besides *'Kathanang Samapthang'* ('the speech ends') meant it was delivered orally, not written. But again he, himself had referred to *Rajmala* written by Durgamani Ujir[5] where it was clearly mentioned that, 'There was an old *Rajmala*; its language was disjointed and obscene.'

One should keep in mind that India had no readymade history. It was written long after based on the Vedas, Puranas, Ramayana, Mahabharata, the ancient rock inscriptions and excavations done later. Nobody disbelieved the honesty of those historians who shaped Indian history. When *Rajmala* was written in the hills and deep forests of Tripura in the fifteenth century, were they aware of the fact that it was the first book written in Bengali? Is falsehood possible without any motive? If the references of different scriptures can give birth to history, why should one not acknowledge the mention of *Rajmala* written in Dharma Manikya's reign? The reason for non-acceptance is due to its having fallen into the jaws of death by the wheel of time. In the sixteenth century, at the time of Amar Manikya's reign, an old *Rajmala* was found where it was specifically mentioned that the writing of *Rajmala* in Bengali had started during the reign of Dharma Manikya.

Durgamani Ujir had also spoken about this old *Rajmala*, the language of which was 'disjointed and obscene'. Exactly, just so, *Rajmala* did exist in the fifteenth century. It cannot be denied that the old *Rajmala* was thoroughly repaired in the eighteenth and nineteenth centuries. The Bengali language of *Rajmala* was modernized in the hands of different writers starting right from the fifteenth century itself.

Leaving aside further arguments, I would emphatically say that the historical value of *Rajmala* is endless. Tripura was ruled continuously (barring a few years under Shamsher Gazi) by 184 generations of kings from AD 590 to AD 1949 (Tripura Era 1359). The annals of Tripura kings described them as Chandravanshi (Lunar) Kshatriyas. They were said to have descended from the Kurus. In that case, the Tripura kingdom was founded much before AD 590. Acharya Dinesh Chandra Sen wrote in his *Brihat Banga*: 'Of all the princely states in India, the Tripura dynasties are the oldest. In no other dynasty can we find the chronology of 184 kings starting from the ancient times.'

No royal dynasty ever in India had in its pride possession such a voluminous family history like *Rajmala* written chronologically in several parts. In *Rajmala*, the tales of kings and queens, princes and princesses, their lifestyles, manners and customs of the royal durbar (court), societies of Tripura, hostilities and warfare are embalmed in every detail. Taking a recourse to *Rajmala*, Rabindranath had written the books named *Mukut, Rajarshi* and *Bisharjan*. This testifies to the importance of *Rajmala*. A study of *Rajmala* reveals that Dharma Manikya got the Mahabharata translated into Bengali. A nation averse to history does not believe in preservation and, therefore, the book could not be recovered. Dharma Manikya's queen Nanua Devi, in whose name stands the Nanua Dighi (a large and deep tank) at Comilla, now in Bangladesh, was an expert in Bengali and Persian. In Persian, she wrote some stories and a book in Bengali.

Dharma Manikya was quite fond of learning. In his regime, the court pandits had written *Ramayana, Utkal Khanda Panchali, Jatra Karanidhi* and *Pret Chaturdashir Geet* in Bengali. He was an ardent supporter of the Hindu religion. He was a patron of Vaishnavism and the Shakta cult. One old book of Vidyapati was found in Nepal where in the commencement of a narrative, the name of Dhanya

Manikya is mentioned with great éclat (*Bari Kamala Kamal Rashiya Dhanya Manikya Jaan*). The lyric's language is Brajabuli—a kind of mixed language used originally by Vidyapati in his poems. In the opinion of Dr Sukumar Sen, this was one of the oldest poems in Brajabuli, written in Bengali.

In the period of Amar Manikya (1577-1586 AD), *Rajmala* was enlarged. There was no dispute about this *Rajmala*. Govinda Manikya, in 1669, had ordered a Bengali translation of *Brihannaradiya Purana*. The name of the writer was not known; only the last part of the book mentions '*Debai Pandit kahey*' ('Thus, says Debai Pandit').

Champak Vijay depicts a very difficult period in the history of Tripura. Prince Champak Roy took the help of some people to regain the throne of Ratna Manikya II (1685-1712 AD). One of them was commander-in-chief Meer Khan and the other was councilor Sheikh Mahaddin. Sheikh Mahaddin was the poet of the book *Champak Vijay*. Let me quote Dr Dinesh Chandra Sen: 'The facts stated in *Champak Vijay* turned *Rajmala* and *Krishnamala* lacklustre. We came across hardly any historical book in the Bengali literature of olden days and a few names of books of poems on historical events, which were devoid of reliable accounts.'

The advent of Shamsher Gazi was like a comet on Tripura's historical landscape. He captured the throne after defeating Indra Manikya in 1744. As the people vehemently refused to give him recognition as their king, he ruled the country in disguise under the name of Banamali Thakur, alias Lakshman Manikya, nephew of Uday Manikya. Prince Krishna Manikya fought against Shamsher for years but failed to defeat him. At last, when Meer Kashim became the Nawab of Bengal, he proclaimed Krishna Manikya as the king of Tripura. The biography of Shamsher Gazi, Sheikh Manohar's *Gazinama*, though not poetically beautiful, certainly presents an interesting historical account. This was the only break in the chronology of the Manikya dynasty. The refusal to recognize Shamsher Gazi as king exhibited the strength of character of the people of Tripura. Reverend Long therefore said, 'The people of Tripura, like the Sikhs, were a military race.'

Krishna Manikya was, in spirit, the Maharana Pratap of Tripura. Most of his life was spent in jungles fighting wars for regaining the throne. He had undergone a very strenuous life in the forest and hills. Maharaja Rajdhar Manikya (1785-1803), nephew of Krishna Manikya, had directed Pundit Ramganga to write a book of poems on the tales of heroism of Krishna Manikya. About *Krishnamala*, Dr Dinesh Chandra Sen said, 'It is an account of an eyewitness about one of the darkest periods in the history of Bengal.'

Due to the marital alliance with the Manipur princess, Rajdhar Manikya adopted the Vaishnavite religion as his way of life. *Geet Chandroday*, the largest edition of Vaishnav Padabali, was written by the court-poet Narahari Chakraborty. Apart from this, another book, *Geet Kalpataru*, was also compiled. One Muslim artist, Alam Karigar, undertook the task of illustrating this book. Janhavi Devi, the queen of Krishna Manikya, used to pursue literature devotedly. She wrote the Sanskrit adage engraved in the stone of Radha Madhav Temple at Akhaura.

Kaliprasanna Sengupta wrote:

Jagat Manikya, a great grandson of Maharaja Chhatra Manikya, executed the translation of *Kriyayogasara*, a part of *Padma Purana* in the form of poems. In this book, there were religious instructions about the process of creation, the excellence of Vaishnav, empirical nobility, the sublimity of the place where a river falls into a sea, the method of worship of Hari, the greatness of Vishnu, the majesty of God's domain, the glory of donation,

Brahmin's divine grace, the charm of Ekadashi and Tulshi, etc. Finally, the book ended with an account of the trend and the spirit of the times. Mukunda was the writer of this book. The particulars of his identity are not known.

The poems of middle age underwent a dramatic modernization in the regime of Maharaja Bir Chandra. Maharaja Bir Chandra, who gave recognition to the novice young Rabindranath as a 'Great Poet' was in fact the 'Bikramaditya' of Tripura. At the same time, he was not only a poet but also a connoisseur of fine arts, a musician and an artist excelling in photography and canvas paintings. Conventionally, he was not educated, but he was quite knowledgeable in Urdu, Sanskrit and Bengali. Kailash Chandra Singh, known as a staunch critic of Maharaja Bir Chandra, was bound to admit in his book *Rajmala O Tripurar Itihas* that,

> The Maharaja can speak fluently in Urdu, like it was his mother tongue. He is a pundit (maestro) extraordinaire in the art of music. He is very intelligent, artful and not addicted to drinking. So powerful is his wheedling language that even a person, who is malicious towards him, cannot help but change his view if he speaks with the king for some time.

Maharaja Bir Chandra was the first ruler who tried to modernize Tripura. In his autobiography *Abarjanar Jhuri,* Nabadwip Chandra Bahadur (father of S.D. Burman), the rightful heir of the throne had paid a glowing tribute to his uncle Bir Chandra who usurped the throne from him. The fact that he did not denigrate his uncle even once in his autobiography, but in fact, spoke highly of him; it clearly shows, then, that Kailash Chandra Singh's tirade against Bir Chandra owed to personal malice.

Now let us listen to what Nabadwip Chandra Bahadur had to say about his uncle Maharaja Bir Chandra:

On the death of father (Ishan Chandra Manikya 1850-1862), his younger brother and next king of Tripura, Bir Chandra Manikya, became our guardian. He was a man of culture with a heartfelt desire for higher knowledge and education. It was during his reign that the new light of western education entered the kingdom of Tripura. His excessive zeal for new-age education used to be debated in every household. After father's demise he arranged for our English education.

When even enemies were eloquent in his praise, it was nothing but natural that the poets, artists, musicians and politicians of India would assemble around him; in reality, that was indeed what had happened. In a place like Tripura, which was backward in education and culture, unlit by the rays of Western civilization, how could there be an assemblage of so many talented stars? It was simply unthinkable. Agartala, the capital of Tripura, was not even a town back then. The number of inhabitants would hardly be ten to twelve thousand. Who were the people then who adorned the royal court of Maharaja Bir Chandra? In the history of India, they were all worthy of eternal remembrance. They included the renowned politician and minister of Tripura, Dr Sambhu Chandra Mukhopadhyay, an eminent litterateur, master of Vaishnav literature and western philosophy; Radharaman Ghosh, writer and translator of *Srimad Bhagavat, Ujjal Nilmoni, Bhakti Ratnakar* and *Chaitanya Mangal*; Ramnarayan Vidyaratna, humourist and nature-poet; Madan Mitra, whose books *Kabita Kadamba and Bhubanmay* are still remembered. This list also includes magicians of music: the veena player Nisher Hossain from Uttar Pradesh; the pakhowaj player Panchanan Mitra, who later on became assistant personal secretary; sursingar and esraj player Haidar Khan from Gwalior; Kulandar Baksh, a Kathak dancer from Kashmir; dhrupad singer Kshetra Mohan Basu, whom witty Bir Chandra called by the name of 'Droupadi'; pakhowaj players Keshab Chandra Mitra, son of Sir Ramesh Chandra Mitra and Ram Kumar Basak of Dhaka, who charmed the Delhi-durbar; Kirtania (a singer of songs about Radha and Krishna) Pratap Mukhopadhyay and Madan Mohan Mitra; jaltaranga player Sarat Bain of Kalikachchha; the famous singer of Benaras Chand Bai; and, lastly, the title-holder 'Tanraj'—given by Bir Chandra—music maestro dhrupad singer Jadu Bhatta; classical singers Kashem Ali Khan, a descendant of Tansen, and Bholanath Chakraborty; sitar player Nabin Chandra Goswami, and violin player Haridas, to name but a few.

Had Maharaja Bir Chandra only played the role of a patron of literature, art and culture or was he also dramatis personae, a true practitioner engaged in these fields? He had an extraordinary poetic talent. His poetic compositions in the form of books were *Akal Kusum* (written on Maharani Manmohini Devi), *Hori* (songs on the *leela* of Krishna and Radha), *Jhulan* (a record of an outburst of grief at the bereavement of Maharani Bhanumati Devi), *Uchchhash* (a compilation of lovesick emotional poems), *Prem Marichika* (dedicated to Bhanumati) and *Shohag* (dedicated to Manmohini). As his heart-rending outbursts were unveiled in his passionate lyrics and poems written in Brajabuli and Bengali, so also his devotional mind had sunk deep into the *leela* of Radha and Krishna.

Nabadwip Chandra Bahadur, in his autobiography *Abarjanar Jhuri*, had mentioned some instances that magnify Bir Chandra's literary practice. In reply to the courtiers' comment that etiquette goes astray if an unrestrained literary discussion is conducted in front of adolescents, Bir Chandra had said:

Beauty is not easily consistent with ugliness. Fine arts and obscenity are contradictory to each other. One pushes the other, never pulls ... A straight face looks distorted in a mirror on account of the unskillful casting of glass. Whatever is there for enjoyment and for knowledge, people will crave for and know it. If you do not keep the path wide open for a learner, he surely will find a narrower path. It means a teacher's duty is to mould a learner while accompanying him on his way in broad day light. If that is not done, the students will without doubt take the route of lanes and bylanes in the light and shade of evening. What condition is more desirable? This is not the age to play hide and seek ... you find fault with the likings of leading poets—you get scared after going through the filthy language used in their creation of Gods and Goddesses.

The debate on decency and indecency will perhaps never end in literature. Bir Chandra's interpretation of it remains beautiful. He was an attentive and knowledgeable reader of contemporary literature. To bring it to light, Nabadwip Chandra wrote: 'Bankim Chandra's *Durgesh Nandini* was published just then ... Hearing slanderous criticism of the book by the courtiers, uncle said that this powerful writer will liberate the Bengali language as a debtor to Sanskrit. Pandit's Bengali, known as chaste Bengali, will perhaps not remain any longer.'

In order to emphasize how superior he was as a critic of poetry, I am tempted to quote here a lengthy passage from Nabadwip Chandra's *Abarjanar Jhuri*:

> He admitted in no uncertain manner that *Meghnad Badh* was a poet's fantastic creation—a true poetic beauty. But he had differences of opinion with others and, therefore, he gave a

lengthy statement which I did not forget at all. He said this excellent book, like pure gold, had become imperfect, especially where the poet could not restrain the inclinations of his instinct. Madhusudan's unreasonable partiality had forced Lakshman to enter the Nikumvila sacrificial alters leaving aside all his heroism. There, he sustained a blow by a canoe-shaped water container and a canoe-shaped small spoon, and he remained unconscious for a long time. It seems he was as if almost dead! ... He had simply mocked the personality of Ramchandra.

At the sight of Meghnad's wife in battle armour, Madhusudan's Ramchandra started reciting prayers in the name of Madhusudan (Lord Krishna). After getting over the initial shock, his (Ram Chandra) doleful utterance to his friend Bibhisan suggests how he immediately wanted to give up his desire of fighting, upon seeing Meghnad's wife in that dress. Was it the language of a hero fascinated by the elegance of a woman or a hero who was an indomitable, persevering inventor constructing bridges over the sea? Could it be the language of a hero who mobilized huge armed forces out of brutal forest dwellers? They had sent an inferior incompetent Lakshman to Lanka to kill Meghnad, the conqueror of Indra. Was there any poet who depicted an opponent of his hero as a useless one? In fact, this vice of Michael Madhusudan Dutt was like his virtue, a beauty forever.

It was this very Bir Chandra who could comprehend the 'distinctive' poetic sensibilities in a young Rabindranath. Only a poet can understand the innate nature of another. There is a saying that a shepherd knows his ewe. Bir Chandra always respected Rabindranath's talent. Bir Chandra, a gifted man, was famous not only in the country but also abroad. His name is still remembered with due honour as a pioneer of Indian photography. Today, when people fail to locate Tripura on the map of India, we should recall that the photographs of Maharaja Bir Chandra adorned the journals of France and America and received high applause 143 years ago. This special talent attracted an artist, named Apollonius, who came to Tripura from France and ended up becoming one of the photographers in Bir Chandra's royal court.

Bir Chandra Manikya was drawn towards photography while research for the modernization of this art was underway all over the world. At that point of time, it was astonishing to think that a king of a native state in India managed to keep pace with Europe in his endeavour to modernize photography. Tripura was almost cut off from the rest of India. Communication systems were severely underdeveloped. Even then, he used to bring books, journals and research papers from England, and he got them translated into Bengali by his personal secretaries since he was not conversant in English.

In an article, the Photographic Society of India commented on his experiments and research in the evolution of chemical processes in photography, keeping in tune with modern ideas and equipment:

> His enthusiasm in the art never lagged—as each successive improvement was introduced it was successfully taken up by the late Maharaja. Through all the stages of wet and dry colloidal plates, he had struggled with a success that was wonderful, considering the difficulties with which he had to work. With the introduction of gelatin dry plates, many of these difficulties disappeared, and this enabled His Highness to carry out his photographic work on a most extensive scale.

Progressive Tripura (1930), edited by Dr Apurba Chandra Bhattacharjee, gives a glimpse of Maharaja Bir Chandra Manikya's artistic contribution in the field of photography:

In the eighties of the last century, the Maharaja followed the rapid developments in photography with keen interest and was always found making photographic experiments in his studio especially equipped for scientific experiments. For the encouragement of the princes, nobles and the people of the state, he used to hold the annual Photo Exhibition at Agartala. His activities in connection with photo art attracted so much public attention that 'Practical Photographer', the photographic journal of America, published an illustrated biography of the Maharaja in one of its issues. Though in his early life the Maharaja spent much of his time in hunting, wrestling and all other games, in his latter age, he devoted his time and energy to photographic and other scientific experiments and also to painting. He appointed a French artist for painting the portraits of some of the deceased Maharajas.

From the year 1884, he made it a point to hold an 'Exhibition of Photography' in the royal palace, every year, organized by the Camera Club of Tripura. In the 'Calcutta Photographic International' exhibitions, many of his photographs were exhibited and earned high acclaims from the critics in 1891. He never believed in medals or awards, so he used to send his photographs to competitive exhibitions after their scheduled submission deadlines. Even then, the authority, realizing the proper worth of his photographs, used to hold a separate exhibition outside the purview of the competition. Let us go through the comments of the 'Photographic Society of India' in this context:

> There was a large table in the centre of the room strewn, like leaves on the stand—with the work of our talented confrere and member, His Highness the Maharaja of Tipperah. Unfortunately, for His Highness, these pictures reached the hands of the

Honourary Secretary too late for the medal competition ... It is hardly necessary to pick from them any particular work as exhibiting the qualities required in a medal picture. They were of very high merit, exceptionally so indeed, and their execution reflects the greatest credit on His Highness's skill as a photographer. I hope that His Highness may be induced to send us once more a selection of his works for our club Album.

[...] Late Maharaja's works in photomechanical printings are to be found ... as showing the high degree of perfection to which he had brought his photographic work ... such as they are, the typography, the antiquarian research and artistic skill are the result of indigenous effort in an ancient mountain kingdom beyond the border of British India.

Music maestro Bir Chandra gave tune to his own lyrics. His books are now not easily available. The Maharajas of Tripura were Vaishnavs. A devoted student of Vaishnav literature, Bir Chandra, drenched in the flavours of Vaishnav Padabali, would plunge deep into affaires de coeur of Radha and Krishna. In a love couplet, his devoted soul had been immersed in transcendentalism. Let us look at one of his lyrics:

> God like a hunter comes forward silently
> With a seven barralled gun
> His able aim misses no target
> Oh God! Emptiness pervades all over
> I'm standing all alone in darkness.
> How to sever the thread of karma (work)
> It's like a knot of thunder
> Take servant Bir Chandra at thy feet
> So long the days are in Sri Brinda grove
> Oh God! Let me serve thy divine pair.

This rhyme of self-surrender, Bir Chandra heard in the young poet's *Bhagna Hriday* which initiated an unbroken relationship between Rabindranath and Tripura.

Being recognized as a 'Great Poet' by the Maharaja in his youth, Rabindranath therewith formed an indissoluble bond with Tripura. After *Mukut*, he thought of the novel *Rajarshi* after a vivid dream. About this dream, Rabindranath wrote in *Jibansmriti*:

> After the publication of one or two issues of *Balak* (a magazine), I went to Deoghar for one or two days to see Rajnarayan Babu. At the time of returning to Calcutta, the night train was overcrowded, and I could not get proper sleep ... I thought if sleep was not possible, it was better to think about a story for *Balak*. My effort to think of a story did not materialize but sleep finally overcame me. I dreamt and saw on the steps of a temple, a girl, seeing the stain of a blood sacrifice, asking her father very eagerly in a pitying voice, 'Father, what it is? It's blood!' The father was distressed at the girl's sadness but at the outset tried to cover up the question somehow, pretending as if he was angry ... Blending this dream with the ancient history of Maharaja Govinda Manikya of Tripura, I started writing a story, *Rajarshi*, and published it serially in the magazine every month.

Rabindranath found scanty materials for *Rajarshi* from Kailash Chandra Singh's *Rajmala*—he adapted sections of the stepbrother Nakshatra Rai's hostility towards Govinda Manikya and the latter's defeat in war and becoming a fugitive at Chattogram. No other materials were available to him. That was why he gave up writing the book and left it incomplete. Later, he had a mind to complete it. Maharaja Bir Chandra could only provide the actual information about Maharaja Govinda Manikya. Thus, Rabindranath Tagore, for the first time, on 5 May 1886, wrote a letter:

> I have heard that your royal family and our family have been acquainted with each other for a long time. For this I've ventured to write this letter to the Maharaja. My intention is simply to remind him of our old association.
>
> Maharaja might have heard that I'm writing a novel named *Rajarshi* on the background of the royal history of Tripura. But I could not be true to history, because history was not available to me. I crave your indulgence for it. Although it is too late now, yet if the Maharaja sends me a detailed history of the reign of Maharaja Govinda Manikya and his brother, I will try my best to make the changes accordingly. It will be a great help to me if I may come to know in what condition and in what places Maharaja Govinda Manikya was at Chattogram during the period of his exile. I would be benefited if I could get the photographs of the old capital of Udaypur and other places in Tripura.
>
> I will consider myself fortunate if I get a response to this letter and an opportunity to converse with your majesty.

A scrutiny of this letter reveals that, in the exchange of their ideas and thoughts, this letter was the first step. In this letter, one should note Rabindranath's hesitation. Without mentioning his own relation with the royal family, he raised the topic of his family's earlier relationship in his letter. Here, it becomes necessary to mention that Maharaja Krishna Kishore Manikya, the grandfather of Bir Chandra, had sought the help of Prince Dwarkanath Tagore in some serious political issues. Prince Dwarkanath was then considered as a leader of the Calcutta society and also of India. With his cooperation, Maharaja Krishna Kishore successfully came back home.

In reply to this letter, Maharaja Bir Chandra wrote on 31 May 1886:

I'm very delighted to receive your letter. You've written that the main purpose of your letter was to recollect the relationship between our two families. I did not forget that happy association. I'm extremely felicitated and obliged that you've come forward again for its glorification.

I've already read both *Mukut* and *Rajarshi*. The lapse committed relating to historical events can be rectified by you without any difficulty. There is a custom among hill-born people that they compose songs and sing in their own languages (dialects), which are based on some special incidents that happened in the lives of the Maharaja's. So many narrations can be derived from these songs. I'm ever grateful to you for taking care of the history of Tripura in writing novels. Whenever you need help for your research, I'm ever ready to collect the materials from the aforesaid originals. This is my earnest desire that, in your commendable articles on various subjects, the interpretation of history should be proper and accurate ... I would send you a few photographs of Udaypur after writing an account on each of them. The ways the characters of Govinda Manikya and his brother Chhatra Manikya are depicted in *Rajratnakar* have already been copied. It will be sent after the completion of typing.

It does not escape one's notice that both Maharaja Bir Chandra and Rabindranath Tagore signed their letters at the end, after writing 'pranata'—the exact meaning of which is not 'humbly' but 'lying prostrate in obeisance'. Rabindranath, instead of writing his surname 'Tagore', wrote 'Debsarman' to harmonize with 'Deb Barma' and to indicate the pride of his high birth. Being a

Debsarman, he lay prostrate in obeisance before a Kshatriya king, and on the other hand, by repeating the same words at the end of his letter to a poet, like his son, Maharaja Bir Chandra had left an unprecedented example of appreciation of good qualities as a true Vaishnav. For this reason, Pramatha Nath Bishi in his article, '*Tripurar Bhasha O Sahitya*' ('Tripura's Language and Literature'), talks about the relation of Rabindranath with the royal family of Tripura: 'This sort of relationship between the king and the poet is rare in all times and in all countries. The cordiality and communion of Goethe with the Duke of Weimer, perhaps, may be historically similar.'

Based on documentary accounts sent by Bir Chandra, *Rajarshi* was completed, but the spontaneity of the first part was impeded in the following chapters. Rabindranath also admitted this fact: 'Actually, the novel had ended on the fifteenth chapter. In a land of agriculture, where the border line stood, no tilling was done and, therefore, weeds turned it into a jungle'.

Rabindranath as such attempted to write *Rajarshi* in the form of a drama. He came very close to historical truth. The characters like Rani Gunabati (the real name of Govind Manikya's main queen), Aparna, Chandpal, Nayan Rai etc., were new additions in *Bisharjan*. The play, *Bisharjan*, had gone through several changes. The edition now available is vastly different to the earlier versions. Maharaja Govind Manikya, following a custom, introduced gold and silver coins engraved with the phallic symbol of Lord Shiva on the one side and the name of the queen Gunabati on the other. The main God of the Tripuris was Shivrai alias Lord Shiva. Although the Tripuris adopted Vaishnavism from the days of Dharma Manikya, the worship of Lord Shiva and Goddess Kali remained altogether uninterrupted. It is, therefore, not possible to discern the worshipped deities of Govind Manikya from the engraved phallic symbol of

Lord Shiva. One can find it in the records—'*Sri Sri Radha Krishna Padey*' (at the feet of Radha Krishna) was inscribed brightly in silver and gold coins. To a Vaishnav, killing a living being is sin. Govind Manikya tried to abolish this custom from his kingdom. He wrote: 'In my Tripur kingdom/whoever does animal slaughter in the name of the Mother of living beings/in the guise of worship will be banished' (*Bisharjan*). Chantai (Head priest) had become extremely hostile against this pronouncement. In the introduction of *Rajarshi*, Rabindranath had written, 'The main story relates the opposition to the worship of brutal strength by non-violent love.' The story ends with the self-sacrifice of Jai Singh:

'Blue blood runs in this body
I shall give this blood
this should be the last blood Mother
quench thy endless thirst by this blood for the last time,
Oh! Blood Thirsty!'

It can be said without exaggeration that Rabindranath, beginning with the play *Bisharjan*, wanted to enshrine the religion of truth—which was nothing but humanism. The proximity with the four generations of the Maharajas of Tripura and their thinking of human welfare above rituals had greatly influenced Rabindranath. In his article '*Deshiya Rajya*' ('Princely state') he talked about the country's small state Tripura:

In the royal insignia of this Tripura, one sentence in Sanskrit is imprinted—"*kil bidurbiratang sarmekong*"—valour is the sole object. This saying is an absolute truth ... the soil of the country has to be given manure, and that manure is nothing but "*kil bidurbiratang sarmekong*" – know that valour is the only manure.

The subject matter of *Bisharjan* exhibits this valour as a manifestation of the qualities of *satvik* (goodness) and *rajas* (spiritedness or passion).

Rabindranath wrote his first letter to Maharaja Bir Chandra on 5 May 1886. After that, correspondences continued regularly, but as luck would have it, the letters were lost, like Bir Chandra's books of poems, due to negligence. So strange! Many of the letters of Rabindranath written to the four generations of Maharajas and others were recovered later from the custody of several persons, who were closely associated with the Maharajas in different capacities. Nobody knows how the letters had changed hands. But it did happen. For this reason, there occurred some apparent mistakes in the wheel of events, such as in Satya Ranjan Basu's article '*Tripuray Rabindra Smriti*' ('Tripura's Rabindra committee')—it was mentioned that the poet met Bir Chandra twice at Kurseong. The source of this was claimed to be a lecture delivered by the poet in Kishore Sahitya Samaj (Agartala). Prabhat Kumar Mukhopadhyay, the first biographer of Tagore (the book is *Rabindra Jiboni*), without verifying the fact from Satya Ranjan Basu, wrote with a footnote (the magazine *Rabi* and the lecture of Rabi Thakur in Kishore Sahitya Samaj were not supposed to be available with him): 'Most of the time of summer 1301 (Bengali Era) was spent in Calcutta, though he went to Kurseong in the meantime for a few days. The Maharaja of Tripura Bir Chandra Manikya invited him there to spend a few days with him'.

There is no documentary evidence at all regarding Rabindranath or Bir Chandra's visit to Kurseong in summer 1301 (1894).

It was a fact that Bir Chandra had to go to Calcutta every now and then to accomplish his royal duties, and for leisure and medical attention. His relationship with the poet did not cease with the mere appreciation of *Bhagna Hriday* and supply of materials for *Rajarshi*. It was solidified more and more as the days went by. It was published in *Indian Mirror* that Bir Chandra went to Calcutta on 1 January 1892 and on 9 December 1894. Mahim Chandra Deb Barma in his essay '*Tripurar Darbarey Rabindranath*' had written:

> Whenever Bir Chandra Manikya went to Calcutta, he used to call Rabi Babu to come to him. Although there was a wide age difference between the two, Bir Chandra loved to listen with parental affection to the recitation of poems and songs sung by handsome Rabindranath. Rabindranath used to feel a lot of embarrassment in reciting his poems ... But Bir Chandra's natural enthusiasm allowed Rabindranath to easily surmount his hesitation.

Rabindranath himself admitted, 'Maharaja Bir Chandra was a maestro extraordinaire of music. It can be easily understood how much hesitation I had as an inexperienced one to sing before him. I got the courage only for his indulgence and affection.'

Bir Chandra was not well for a long time. To recover his broken health, he decided to go to Kurseong accompanied by Colonel Mahim and his personal secretary Radha Raman Ghosh. He invited Rabindranath also to come along with him. In October 1896, the literary landscape of Kurseong was enlivened by their deliberations on poetry and philosophy. Radha Raman Ghosh was a pundit of Vaishnav literature.

It is quite astonishing that Radha Raman Ghosh took lessons on the philosophy of Vaishnav scriptures from Maharaja Bir Chandra for the first time. After his appointment, the Maharaja was amazed by his knowledge of western philosophy. The Maharaja said to him, 'Radha Raman, you've done enough deliberations on western philosophy. Now it's time to discuss philosophy in the Bengali language.' Without saying anything more, Bir Chandra handed him a copy of *Sri Sri Chaitanya Charitamrita*, requesting him to read it attentively. After a few days, Radha Raman declared that he could not find any philosophy in this book, but the Maharaja insisted that he read it ten times. Radha Raman's illusions eventually faded; he spent the rest of his life discussing Vaishnavite philosophy.

Now, let us read in the words of Colonel Mahim what Radha Raman Ghosh was in the eyes of Rabindranath:

> I heard Rabi Babu saying that he derived enormous pleasure having discovered a jewel in Bir Chandra's royal court. He was Radha Raman Ghosh. I was looking after Rabi Babu in Kurseong. Rabi Babu was all along busy in discussing Vaishnav Padabali and its philosophy with Radha Raman Babu. One day, I returned after taking some photographs of the place and found that Radha Raman Babu and Rabi Babu were deeply engrossed in discussion. At that time, there was much interest in comparing the writings of Emerson with Vaishnavite philosophy. I understood that Radha Raman Ghosh had got over him. Rabi Babu was so moved by the scholarship of Radha Raman that he expressed his eagerness to learn Vaishnavite philosophy. Whenever he went out for an evening walk, Rabi Babu spoke highly of Maharaja Bir Chandra and his companion Radha Raman. This shows that Rabi Babu had the ability to appreciate one's qualities.

That Bir Chandra was seriously ill was proved by the fact that he passed away within a month. His zeal for music and poetical compositions was so unrelenting that, once engrossed, he used to forget the world. He went to a health resort in Kurseong to recover, but he never did abide by the rules of hygiene. Colonel Mahim wrote about it thus:

It was past ten o'clock at night; Bir Chandra was then fully engrossed in discussing the inner beauty of music and poetry with Rabindranath. He wanted to find a way to fulfill his desire to publish *Vaishnav Mahajan Padabali* (an anthology of lyrics by great mediaeval poets who composed Kirtan songs about Radha and Krishna). After the discussion was over, the Maharaja used to get up and accompany Rabi Babu up to the stairs every night to bid good night. Rabi Babu knew that Maharaja Bir Chandra was unwell, but he still participated in the discussion with a smiling face, remaining stoic about his unbearable pain. One day, Rabi Babu told Bir Chandra he didn't need to burden himself accompanying him upstairs. Bir Chandra replied, "I'm afraid of laziness becoming an impediment to my duty. Please don't say no to me." Rabi Babu said, "I'm fortunate to have a glimpse of what an aristocratic family is truly like."

Acharya Dinesh Chandra Sen, the writer of *Bangabhasha O Sahitya* and *Brihat Banga*, was also overwhelmed by the touch of this glory. The printing costs of *Bangabhasha O Sahitya* was borne by Bir Chandra. In the introduction of the second edition of this book, Dinesh Chandra Sen wrote:

In the epilogue, I'm expressing my deep condolences for the death of the late Maharaja of Tripura, Bir Chandra Manikya Mahoday. He had borne the expenses of the first edition of this book. Amidst the different types of calamities I've faced, his sudden death four years back was one of them. In one corner of his deathbed, I noticed this humble book.

Let me inform you that Bir Chandra wrote a congratulatory letter to the unknown Dinesh Chandra Sen the moment the book was published. Several books on Vaishnavite literature, translated into Sanskrit, were published from Baharampur with the aid of Maharaja Bir Chandra. At that time, Bir Chandra had spent more than a lakh rupees to print *Srimad Bhagavat*, which he then distributed free of cost.

Bir Chandra could not go back to Tripura from Kurseong. He died in Calcutta on his way back to Agartala on 11 December 1896. Reflecting on the death of this father figure, Rabindranath wrote: 'Just before his death, when I was enjoying his hospitality, I had various discussions with him on literature at that time. He had resolved to collect the whole of Vaishnava Padabali as far as possible and to spend a lakh on publishing it. But his sudden death has left his missions unfinished.'

The sudden demise of Maharaja Bir Chandra Manikya did not hinder the deepening relationship between Rabindranath Tagore and the royal family of Tripura. The next Maharaja, Radha Kishore Manikya, had offered his friendship in this time of their shared grief. The rest is history.

2

Rabindranath and Maharaja Radha Kishore Manikya

Radha Kishore's period of reign: 1897-1909

After the demise of Maharaja Bir Chandra on 11 December 1896, Rabindranath wondered if his bond with the Tripura royal family might now be broken. The coronation ceremony of Radha Kishore, the elder son of Bir Chandra, was held on 5 March 1897. After ascending the throne, he found the royal treasury empty. He was entangled in family complexities and feuds, as well as in court cases relating to rights of succession. He was embarrassed to no end. Above all, within seven days after his coronation, an earthquake destroyed much of the palace. There were also severe administrative problems. In these conditions, an encumbered Radha Kishore set his mind to putting things in order. There was no communication with Rabindranath for a while.

Referring to this period, Rabindranath later recounted his feelings in his speech while receiving the title of 'Bharat Bhaskar', conferred upon him by Maharaja Bir Bikram, in the last days of his life:

I thought this death (Bir Chandra) had put an end to my relationship with the royal family. It was quite amazing that it did not happen. His father's respect and affection continued to flow without interruption, even in Maharaja Radha Kishore. In fact, at that time, he was preoccupied day and night with severe personal problems. But he did not forget me even for a day. Afterwards, I enjoyed his hospitality continually. And his love and affection towards me had never ceased, although various people in the king's proximity were suspicious. He was constantly in fear that some hidden disrespect might hit me hard. He even frankly said to me, "I wish you would come to me with a sound mind resisting the behavioral barriers put up by my courtiers." For that matter, during the short period he was alive, I did not pay any heed to the rising antagonism. It is difficult to find, anywhere in the history of literature, an account of such a spontaneous and open friendship of a king with a tender-aged poet, whose road to fame was totally uncertain and doubtful.

Radha Kishore met Rabindranath only once for a very short time in 1896. Mahim Chandra wrote about that meeting in his article '*Tripurar Durbarey Rabindranath*' ('Rabindranath in Tripura's Court'):

> Crown Prince Radha Kishore met Rabindranath in the durbar of his father in Calcutta only once, and for a very short time. The meeting did not last long; it was interrupted by the sudden appearance of a distinguished English officer. However, even just this momentary meeting drew them to each other. The way magnet attracts iron, a man of character had gravitated to another man of character.

As has been noted earlier, Radha Kishore had enormous economic, political and family problems, which could also be surmised from

Rabindranath and Maharaja Radha Kishore Manikya   37

the poet's observations. In such a perturbed condition, it was not possible for Radha Kishore to maintain contact with Rabindranath. As such, the poet had come forward at this stage with an offer of friendship. A news item of *Amrita Bazar Patrika* dated 14 February 1898 ran thus: 'The Maharaja of Tripura, for a while, was traveling to places like Agra, Delhi, Lucknow, Banaras etc.' The same newspaper dated 2 March 1898 said, 'He has arrived at Howrah station from Allahabad.' That very day, the Tagore family received and treated Maharaja Radha Kishore with great cordiality. Time being no problem in leisure, the Maharaja and the poet of the same age, in their conversations, tied the knot of friendship with a promise never to be severed.

This friendship revealed the character of Rabindranath in multifarious shades, and these details are known only in Tripura; the rest of the world has not the slightest idea.

In twelve years of Maharaja Radha Kishore's reign, like Kautilya, Rabindranath assumed full responsibility of running the administration of the state. He proved his wisdom by counselling Radha Kishore in all matters of administrative and economic reforms, the appointment of ministers and even for his family feud. Tripura was fortunate to have witnessed this astonishing side of the poet. The relation between Bir Chandra and Rabindranath was one of affection because of their difference of age. Radha Kishore acknowledged the poet as a friend. During Radha Kishore's reign, Rabindranath, in the eyes of many, was considered as one who enjoyed absolute authority on all fronts of administration. This relationship of two souls led to the victory of wider Bengali literature, culture and science.

Rabindranath, for the first time, got involved with the politics of Tripura when Maharaja Radha Kishore Manikya expressed his desire to induct his elder son Birendra Kishore as prince. Birendra Kishore was deigned as prince on 8 February 1899. The rule was that if the king nominated no prince, Bod Thakur had the right to become prince. As per the said rule, Bod Thakur Samarendra Chandra, the second son of Maharaja Bir Chandra, was supposed to be enthroned as prince. The agitated Samarendra Chandra had filed a complaint with the British Government and initiated a lawsuit in the British Court. Satya Ranjan Basu, in his article, '*Tripuray Rabindra Smriti*', noted:

> Mahim Chandra (Deb Barma), most faithful to Radha Kishore, was observing the situation after going to Calcutta. He was staying at the house of Rajendra Mukherjee as his guest. Rabindranath took up this matter as his own and did whatever he could for him. Mahim Chandra, in his letter to the Maharaja, mentioned this as being Rabindranath's own statement: "I do not know royal aristocracy—I only know this much, that there can be no indulgence for the sin of disrespecting a king ... I have no sympathy for him."

Ashutosh Choudhury, the Maharaja of Nator, and Anand Mohan Basu, bluntly refused to support Bod Thakur Samarendra. *Amrita Bazar Patrika* also withdrew its support. Satya Ranjan Basu said, 'It seems that Rabindranath played a vital role in maintaining contact and arranging deliberations.'

At that time, the poet was at Shilaidaha, though he used to come to Calcutta every now and then. In the opinion of Prashanta Kumar Pal, all these arrangements had been made through letters. It is a matter of regret that no letter could be traced.

In spite of all that, Samarendra Chandra remained very respectful to Rabindranath throughout. They met each other frequently since Samarendra used to live in Calcutta. He visited the Tagore family quite often. In the preface to his novel *Zebunnisa*, Abanindranath Tagore wrote that he was an excellent writer and photographer.

Compassionate to the cause of his own country and the eastern culture, Rabindranath, wore silk garments, manufactured by the Silk Industry institute, run by another patriot, Akshay Kumar Maitra; he also gifted silk garments to his friends to encourage the country's self-grown industry. While sending a present to the Maharaja, he wrote to Mahim Chandra thus:

> I'm sending through the hands of Sarbananda a sheet of woven silk fabric for the Maharaja. I do regularly purchase silk cloth to encourage the industrial institute. They cannot provide cloth in large quantities because of a lack of manpower. These cloths are not simply my presents to my friends; these are gifts of the country. I do, therefore, hope that you will not treat it with neglect.

At first sight, this present might appear negligible, but Radha Kishore treated it with great adoration. Mahim Chandra was a common messenger of the king and the poet. Rabindranath, instead of writing directly to the king, used to convey his thoughts, feelings and intentions to the Maharaja through Mahim Chandra. He was a deserving and trustworthy person to both the king and the poet. The British Government used to address Maharaja Radha Kishore only as 'Raja' and not 'Maharaja', as was followed in the case of former Maharajas, because of his patriotism. Radha Kishore had said, 'People of the state know me as Maharaja; if others don't acknowledge, is there any loss or gain?'

The company of Rabindranath also created doubts in the minds of the British. It could be easily inferred that the true friendship and inspiration of Rabindranath spurred Radha Kishore to rise against the British Government.

After receiving the 'gifts of the country', Radha Kishore met Akshay Kumar Maitra. At that time, Radha Kishore was introduced to many celebrities of Bengal; to name a few, they were Maharaja Jatindranath Thakur, Ashutosh Chowdhury, Jagadish Chandra Bose, Maharaja of Nator Jagadindranath Roy, Satyendra Prasanna Singh, Rajendralal Mitra, Dwarkanath Chakraborty, Rashbihari Ghosh, Nawab Bahadur of Murshidabad, Maharaja of Dwarbhanga, Nripendra Narayan–Maharaja of Cooch Behar, Nirmal Chandra Sen, Taraknath Palit, Lokendra Palit, Maharishi Debendranath, Dwijendranath Tagore, Satyendranath Tagore, Abanindranath Tagore, Gaganendranath Tagore, Sarala Devi, Ananda Mohan Basu, Sisir Kumar, Matilal Ghosh, Rajendranath Mukhopadhyay, and so on. The Maharaja had regular correspondences with all of them. Unfortunately, not a single letter could be traced now.

The new Viceroy of India, Lord Curzon, came to Calcutta on 3 January 1899. Naturally, all the kings of the native states assembled in Calcutta to have an interview with him. Maharaja Radha Kishore also came to Calcutta to settle the issue of the selection of the prince. The companionship of the Maharaja with the poet had deepened their intimacy. On 19 December 1898, Radha Kishore went to Jorasanko. After that, Rabindranath met Radha Kishore at his palace in Calcutta on 8 and 27 January 1899. On 17 January, Radha Kishore accepted the hospitality of the Tagore family. To reciprocate Tagore's hospitality, Radha Kishore invited the poet to visit Tripura. Rabindranath, for the first time, set his foot on the soil of Tripura, in March, at the time of the Dol Purnima festival[6].

What was the look of Agartala, the capital city, in those days? Satya Ranjan Basu had drawn a picture of it in his article '*Tripuray Rabindra Smriti*':

> The only way to come to Tripura was from the railway station, Mogra. You were to cross five miles either on boat or on elephant's back or by a palanquin. There was then no Akhaura

road or Akhaura station. In the capital, there were only two roads worthy of mention. Shakuntala road had gone by the western bank of the large and deep tank situated at the western part of the royal palace, named Ujjayanta Rajprasad (palace). From the gate of the present palace this road took a turn towards the south. To the east of this road was Sripat. This road reached the bazaar keeping on the south Maharani Tulsibati girls' school. The same road went up to Old Agartala and on the west it touched Mogra. The government employees and other inhabitants used to live on all sides of this road. There was a Manipuri locality behind the palace named Radhanagar. Another road from the western part of the palace, piercing the Manipuri locality, ran through the green forest like a snake and ended at old Kunjaban. Hither and thither of this road some neat and clean cottages having the colour of red ochre amplified the greenery all over. The natural beauty of the greenery had now elapsed due to modern civilization.

Coinciding with arrival of spring, Rabindranath came to Agartala as a royal guest. It was a welcome visit. Satya Ranjan Basu and Dwijendranath Dutta in their articles published in the book *Rabindranath O Tripura* had mentioned the date of visit as Sri Panchami Tithi, 1306 Bengali era (22 Magh 1306, 4 February 1900). But it was evident from the letter of Rabindranath dated 8 Falgun (February 1899), written to Shailesh Chandra Majumder, that the information was not correct. Rabindranath wrote: 'At the beginning of Chaitra mash (March), I have to go to Tripura to honour the invitation of the Maharaja of Tripura.'

From an account book of Tagore's, dated 20 March, it was found that lots of things were purchased to offer as presents to the Maharaja of Tripura. Sri Prashanta Kumar Pal, the writer of *Rabi Jibani*, had proved it beyond doubt by producing his letters, that Rabindranath was in Calcutta on the day of Sri Panchami, i.e., on 4 February 1900. For the delay caused in buying various items to be given as presents to the Maharaja, Rabindranath might have gone to Tripura not at the beginning of March but in the middle of the month, probably after the 20 February. Colonel Mahim Chandra wrote: 'That time Rabi Babu came for the first time to the capital Agartala. It was spring then. In the northern part of the capital, on a hillock at Kunjaban, the Basanta Utsav was held with pomp and grandeur. Rabindranath was elated at the sight of the equal treatment of the king and his subjects.'

In 1899, Dol Purnima was held on 27 March. From that very day onwards, Basanta Utsav was observed for years in Tripura. This fact also proves that Rabindranath went to Tripura after 20 March.

How was the preparation for the felicitation of the poet? Satya Ranjan Basu, who witnessed the event, wrote:

> The ceremony to pay tribute to the poet was celebrated on a hillock at Kunjaban. The stage for felicitation was made in the shape of a tang ghar (a high platform) of the original inhabitants of Tripura. The stage, made of thin bamboos and decorated with flowers and leaves, was marvelous. One could see how the surrounding low and high hills stacked in layers one above another faded away beyond the horizon. The canopy of the blue sky kissing the horizon provided a pleasant backdrop for the festival. These natural surroundings were enlivened by the dancing and singing of Manipuri artists in different groups. Bare bodies wearing orange-coloured dresses, orange chadars (sheets of cloth) hanging around the neck and head, with turbans of the same colour made for an enchanting sight. Even the audience, irrespective of men or women, were dressed only in orange. In this scenario, the Maharaja and the poet sat on durries on the stage.

This Basanta Utsav was a national festival of Tripura. Whenever Rabindranath came to Tripura, he got the taste of it. The songs of Dol, orange dresses, the rhythm of mridanga and the dance in Rash Leela, all enchanted him. In 1926, Rabindranath set foot in Tripura for the last time. The fascinating Basanta Utsav captivated his mind. It was not restricted to Dol Purnima only; in fact, with the advent of spring, Basanta Utsav started in full vigour in Tripura. Ultimately, Rabindranath introduced Basanta Utsav at Shantiniketan in the year 1923, following the tradition of Tripura. As a testimony of the fact that Basanta Utsav was celebrated in Tripura much before Shantiniketan, I would like to present a snippet from the annual administration report of 1903: 'The Basanta Utsav ceremony inaugurated by your Highness in 1312 Tripura Era (TE) was celebrated during the year under report with befitting éclat'.

In the context of the review of my book *Sachin Kartar Ganer Bhuban* (translated into English as *S. D. Burman: The World of His Music*), a critic of *Ananda Bazar Patrika* commented thus:

> For the first time in Dol the poet was there (in Agartala) and witnessed the festival. At Shantiniketan, Basanta Utsav was introduced in 1923; that was also not on the day of Dol. Is it not far-fetched that he (Rabindranath) introduced Basanta Utsav after twenty-four years of witnessing the dances and the songs of Dol in Tripura?

Many people, like this critic, might have a wrong notion. I'd like to remind them that the relationship of the poet with the Maharajas did not cease in the year 1899. The relationship started in 1882 and ended in 1941, with the poet's death. He came to Tripura for the last time in 1926. In this longstanding relationship of sixty years, how had a break of twenty-four years cropped up? Rabindranath was in constant touch with Tripura. The critic paid no heed to my comment that the enchanting beauty of Basanta Utsav had affected Rabindranath deeply. On other occasions, Rabindranath might not have come to Agartala on the day of Dol, but his enjoyment of Basanta Utsav was apparent from the descriptions of Satya Ranjan Basu, cited above. He was a witness of the Manipuri Rash festival, Basanta Utsav and Holi festival. During these festivals, the whole state of Tripura would be immersed in songs and dance. These festivities in Tripura inspired India's poet laureate to introduce Basanta Utsav or the spring festival at Shantiniketan.

The seed of any idea germinates in the soil of one's experience. It may take time to sow but as the root cause is the seed, it is essential. There was no iota of doubt that the idea of introducing Basanta Utsav at Shantiniketan was inspired by the Basanta Utsav of Tripura. The culture of Tripura revolved round Basanta Utsav. In any musical or dance function held either in public or in the raj durbar for the royal family, the influence of Basanta Utsav was unmistakable. Now let me tell you of an incredible coincidence. Like in Tripura, Wednesday was a holiday at Shantiniketan. Why Wednesday? In Tripura, Wednesday was a holiday because it was Maharaja Bir Chandra's birthday. But why was it so at Shantiniketan? The human mind preserves old memories of love and affection and yearns to express its gratitude. Not every incident can be corroborated by direct witnesses or by documentary evidence. Circumstantial evidence shows that Rabindranath probably wanted to repay his debt of gratitude towards a person who, for the first time in the world, had recognized him with the royal honour of a 'Great Poet'.

The earthquake of 1897 had reduced the palace to dust and, therefore, Rabindranath stayed as a royal guest in the newly built house of his friend Colonel Mahim. The rebuilding work of

Ujjayanta Palace was not yet finished. Shailesh Chandra Deb Barma, the grandson of Colonel Mahim and an ex-student of Shantiniketan, wrote an article, '*Rabitirtha Smriti*', in this context.

> I came to know from my grandfather that, on the occasion of Rabindranath's arrival in Colonel Bari(house), one of my grandmothers prepared a fascinating inflorescence. She decorated the bed and pillows of Gurudev with rich floral diagrams and ornaments of multiple colours. The artistic skill in the decoration of the head-pillow with multicolored flowers was simply enchanting. She had created a novel sort of art in painting the pillow all over; in the middle of the pillow, she'd written the name "Rabindranath Tagore" with flowers. That day, after getting down from the car with my grandfather, Gurudev was about to enter the west side room of the newly built house; but he stopped, overwhelmed by the smell of mixed spring flowers, and exclaimed, "Mahim thakur, what a beautiful smell!" After he entered the room, he was amazed by the scent of flowers all around, and he sat on a chair kept there. He was so wonderstruck by the charming floral decoration of his bed, particularly by the artistic beauty of the pillow, that he expressed his desire to be acquainted with the artist. Gurudev, after being introduced to grandmother, praised her profusely for her skill in the art of floral arrangement and thanked her sincerely. He did not sleep on that bed at night. He did not even sit on it lest the floral beauty get spoilt. He sat on an easy chair beside the bed and was gratified by the smell of the flowers and the beauty of the floral patterns. That night, grandfather had to arrange for another bed beside that bed. He was quite fascinated by the skill displayed in the arrangement of flowers in Tripura. Later, he asked grandfather to find a qualified artist to teach inflorescence to the students

of Shantiniketan. Grandfather tried his best but could not find anyone, and for that he expressed his regrets.

One fine morning in Colonel Mahim's house, Rabindranath was heard humming a song: 'Why didn't thou awake me before the night departed, my Lord! It's daytime, I'm flushed with shame.' As the rendition was heard in the poet's baritone, it was presumed that the song was written at Agartala itself. But it was not so; the song had its birth in the year 1897. This song was linked up with a funny incident. While in the colonel's house, the poet used to get up early in the morning and sit in the south veranda on an easy chair. The fluttering breeze of spring delighted Rabindranath. Colonel Mahim had the habit of getting up late in the morning. Rabindranath sitting in the veranda could hear his snoring howl like a violent storm. Meanwhile, the moment Mahim's wife opened the south door of her bedroom in the morning, she found Rabindranath standing in front. Looking at his friend's wife running away flushed with shame, witty, dulcet-voiced Rabindranath started singing: 'Why didn't thou awake me ...' That morning, Rabindranath viewing the beauty of women at *pukur ghat* (landing stage of a pond) sang another song: 'Why does your bangles jingle with great deception?'

During his stay in Tripura, Rabindranath came to know about the problems confronting Maharaja Radha Kishore at that time. Radha Kishore shared his thoughts and feelings with the poet without any hesitation. Both of them opened their minds to each other. Rabindranath was struggling to realize the dream of his life—to build Shantiniketan—and for that purpose he needed a lot of money; unfortunately, he was critically short of it. He also needed to find a way to solve the monetary problem of Acharya Jagadish Chandra for his scientific research. Radha Kishore's problems were related to state administration and family—firstly, appointment of efficient and loyal government officers and, secondly, qualified teachers for the princes and an efficient doctor for the inhabitants. Guided by a genuine love for his friend Radha Kishore, Rabindranath disregarded the coldness shown to him by the king's officers and courtiers; Radha Kishore's sincerity in friendship did not escape the poet's notice. That was why he openly admitted: 'He (Radha Kishore) had an extraordinary capacity to understand a person. I would be astonished at seeing it.'

After his return to Calcutta, Rabindranath's first priority was to find a qualified teacher for the princes. The poet had sought the help of Jagadish Chandra Bose. The combined efforts of both resulted in the appointment of Professor Nagendranath Basu and Mokshada Kumar Basu to take over the charge of teaching the princes. Prince Brajendra Kishore, who was like a son to Rabindranath, used to get very passionate while talking about Mokshada Kumar Basu's way of teaching.

Poet Hemchandra Bandhopadhyay became blind in the year 1897. He went to Kashi (now Varanasi), a cheap place for living and settled there to live the rest of his life. The intellectuals of West Bengal came to know about the wretched condition of Hemchandra and tried to collect money to help him. Rabindranath was one of them. At that time, Rai Bahadur Haran Chandra Rakshit wrote a letter to Durgadas Lahiri, editor of *Anusandhan*:

> Giving you a good news—just now I have received a letter from Rabi Babu. He says that the honourable Maharaja of independent Tripura, being pained at heart by the distress of Hemchandra, has agreed to grant 30 rupees per month for his lifetime, besides an honourary amount of 200 rupees. You might have understood that Kabibar (great poet) Srijut Rabindranath Tagore was its real cause; thinking about his conduct befitting a real poet, I have tears in my eyes.

However, this gift was not given at the request of Rabindranath; it was a spontaneous one. The unprecedented contributions of Radha Kishore, a devotee of literature, which he had silently left behind in the fields of literature, culture and science, had not yet been evaluated by posterity. He never wanted to be in the limelight. He wanted to keep his charitable deeds a secret because he thought it was his solemn duty to do so as a king. In this context, Mahim Chandra Deb Barma in his book *Deshiya Rajya* wrote:

> The Maharaja came to know through *Sanjibani* (a magazine) that the great poet (Hemchandra) was in distress due to his blindness and paucity of funds. He had immediately sent his proposal via Rabi Babu to Kabibar (Hemchandra), granting him 30 rupees per month from his own fund as a token of respect for his literary activities. He made an earnest request to Rabi Babu to take the responsibility to keep this news a secret.

The Maharaja no doubt wanted to keep this charity a secret; Rabindranath, however, could not help but announcing the magnanimity of his royal friend before the people of the country. Without writing directly to the Maharaja, Rabindranath by a letter informed Mahim Chandra:

> For the arrangement Maharaja had made to help Hem Babu, profuse thanksgiving is going on all around here. It is beyond my control to keep this matter a secret. Hem Babu is also very grateful for this act. Meanwhile by the grace of Maharaja, a part of the fame has also fallen on me. My father has granted 20 rupees per month and Gagan, ten rupees for Hem Babu.

Radha Kishore's outburst of passion after hearing the news of Hemchandra's relief on receiving the grants was recorded in Mahim's *Deshiya Rajya*:

> Although I am a small king of Bengal, if I presently allow him (Hemchandra) to embrace death like Michael Madhusudan in a charitable dispensary, then it will be a great misfortune for the country. All my courtiers will surely be condemned to hell; how far I have to go, I do not know. Your eyes and ears should not be kept shut in such a matter, and your mouth should always be wide open.

Noble work has its good impact. Following the instance of Maharaja Radha Kishore, others also offered help. Even the Bengal Government had granted twenty-five rupees per month for Hemchandra. Manmathanath Ghosh, the biographer of Hemchandra, specifically stated that Hemchandra had enough self-acquired properties. His luxurious sons lavishly spent most of the money sent to help him.

In September 1900, Radha Kishore thought of spending a few days in Darjeeling. In the meantime, he came to know that the poet had also decided to go there. The Maharaja requested the poet to stay with him. The poet gave his consent, writing a letter to Mahim Chandra. In reply to the said letter, Mahim Chandra wrote:

> I have received your two letters. The Maharaja is very happy to know that he would get your company. We have taken two houses named Wood Vine Villa and Lounge. We will start on the 7th by Chatga (Chattogram) Mail via Kushtia and reach Darjeeling on the 8th. We will leave the house on the 6th. Where and at what time will we meet each other?

On the same day (18 September) Maharaja had also written a letter to the poet:

> I am happy to learn from your letter written to Sriman Mahim that you are going to Darjeeling. I am not in a position to express how happy I would be on my stay there for a few days if I get your company in the glorious Himalayas. I suppose the impediments of Calcutta should not be there on the snow peaks ... Pay my respects to Maharishi. After I get to Darjeeling, I will write a letter to him.

This journey did not happen on account of unavoidable circumstances. Dwijendranath Dutta wrote: 'The journey of Maharaja to a foreign land was disrupted on the way to Goalnand due to the terrific stress of the storm.' Before going to Darjeeling again in May 1900, the Maharaja remembered the earlier occasion: 'I am afraid; there should not be troublesome hindrances like there were last time.'

In that year, Rabindranath's book of poetries, *Kahini*, was published. He wrote the last poem of *Kahini*, namely '*Karna Kunti Sangbad*', at the request of Jagadish Chandra Bose that describes Mother Kunti and her illegitimate son Karna's meeting in the eve of the great war of Kurukshetra. The tragedy of Karna's life was portrayed deftly by the poet:

> Mother, don't be afraid
> I tell you the Pandavas will win...
> Let the Pandavas become victorious and kings
> I shall remain in the company of the despondent and the unsuccessful
> For the sake of victory, fame and kingdom, oh!
> I shouldn't be deprived of the hero's happy journey after death.

When Rabindranath sought permission to dedicate *Kahini* to his royal friend Radha Kishore, he (Radha Kishore) wrote: 'You have expressed your desire to associate my name with "Kahini"—can I say no to it? I would be happy if you please send me ten or twelve copies the moment printing is over. I would distribute them to my friends here.'

Acknowledging the receipt of *Kahini*, Radha Kishore evaluated in his own way the talent of the poet:

> I have started reading *Kahini* in earnest. I could not go beyond half until now. The end of the year is near. Reading in a hurry is not right. One must savour the beauty of it. At least, this is what I do.
>
> Is there any significance in showering unnecessary appreciation merely for the sake of friendship? I must say that you're most adept at infusing your poems with solemnity. It may be your talent. I am delighted to grasp the sweetness with this solemnity. The expression and language befitting the hero and heroine are very appropriate. In the books written in modern times based on ancient history or otherwise, I did not find any skill in expression and language to preserve this befitting respect and solemnity. Your books, however, are refreshingly free of such flaws. With these qualities, the book comes to life.

Prince Birendra Kishore's marriage was fixed on 7 March 1901. In his invitation letter Maharaja Radha Kishore wrote:

> Amongst the friends who would make this auspicious ceremony joyous, I would be happy if some of them join the occasion. I would therefore, like to have you, Jyoti Babu, Gagan Babu, Ashu Babu and, if possible, Jagadish Babu. It is borne in my mind

that a laboratory is to be built for Jagadish Babu. I hope, in the aforesaid auspicious ceremony, you would definitely come, and at that time I would be ready to do whatever decision comes out of my discussion with you. I pray to God and wish Jagadish Babu a long life so that he enhances the glory of India.

The Maharaja was in Calcutta in December for the purpose of the prince's marriage. Rabindranath met Maharaja on 28 December. There were various discussions, but the point especially discussed was the impediments that Jagadish Chandra had to face in his scientific research. Jagadish Chandra was getting ready to go to England along with his new invention. The British objected to his use of the college laboratory for personal purposes. Their main objection stood on the ground that a scientist of Indian origin should not be allowed to become successful in the field of science and attain worldwide fame. He was, therefore, prohibited from using the college laboratory. Rabindranath was firmly resolved to build a science lab for Jagadish Chandra.

Before leaving the country, Jagadish Chandra invited knowledgeable, qualified and intellectual persons to get them acquainted with his invention. Colonel Mahim was also in Calcutta along with Maharaja. Rabindranath informed Mahim: 'Jagadish Chandra will be showcasing his invention at Presidency College tonight. If possible, try and attend.' In this matter, what Mahim Chandra had written highlighted the glorious personality and intellect of Maharaja Radha Kishore Manikya:

Taking this sheet of paper (letter of invitation), I came to Maharaja and asked leave for my departure. He said in a touchy tone, "You will go, but shall I not be able to go? I shall also go tonight." After reaching the laboratory of Presidency College at the right time, I saw an assemblage of qualified persons. Rabi Babu was delighted to see Maharaja and introduced him (this was the first and last direct meeting) to Acharya Jagadish Chandra Bose. Maharaja, in a sweet but sensitive voice asked, "Dr Bose, I am your pupil. Why don't you allow me to see the fun (experiment)? I have read the *Sanjibani Patrika*. I've read therein something about your new invention and scientific research." The Maharaja then sat amid the gathering and started viewing the experiments. Almost two hours passed. After the showcase was over, Dr Bose asked the Maharaja, "I spoke in English, have you understood anything?" Radha Kishore told him, "I don't know English, but if you allow me to take a look at your instruments, I will be able to check whether I've understood or not!" Jagadish Babu always exercised caution and prevented others from touching his instruments. But he took the Maharaja up to his instruments and looked at him questioningly. Picking up a book, the Maharaja put it in front of the instrument and then requested Dr Bose, "Now please give the shock; see, it's not responding." The Maharaja now overturned the book and requested to give the shock. The instrument immediately responded. Jagadish Babu exclaimed with delight, "Maharaja, I know you've understood. I couldn't make Lord Elgin understand; my MA students also failed to understand; you've left me to wonder."

A vital question automatically arises: what sort of Maharaja was he? Even small zamindars, the self-titled Maharajas go and come with courtiers all around. In any assemblage, they keep up appearances, like jewels, at the centre of anything. People in rows with folded hands welcome them. No one is allowed to speak without permission. They are accustomed to keep a distance from ordinary people. But here, the hero was merely a spectator. He was not given a seat different from the rest; in fact, he sat among the audience. Was he really a king or an ordinary man? Even ordinary people do not go to social ceremonies or meetings without an invitation as self-respect prohibits them from doing so. Why did this Maharaja attend a social gathering uninvited? Was it just curiosity that compelled him? No, it was not. Here lies the difference between the kings of Tripura, the second oldest kingdom of the world after Japan, and others. Remember, seriously ill, the old Maharaja Bir Chandra did not forget his royal duty to accompany young Rabindranath up to the stairs to bid him good night. Maharaja Radha Kishore was his worthy successor. Having the highest Vaishnavite humility and modesty, the kings of Tripura were an unprecedented example of how to appreciate the good qualities of others. They had never hesitated to felicitate qualified persons. Radha Kishore rather was touchy for not being invited. In their childlike pure hearts, they never allowed false vanity to have the upper hand and, therefore, felicitations of men of qualities were considered as an inseparable part of their royal duty. This is what we call a noble, royal heart.

The humbleness of the Maharaja touched everyone present. Rabindranath might have hesitated to invite him as the lecture would be delivered in English but his friend, inexpert in English, made Rabindranath feel proud and elated by his win over the intellectuals. Not a small achievement by any means!

Meanwhile, if Jagadish Chandra did not have a lab of his own, the invention of new theories of science would be hindered. Rabindranath, in utter grief, decided to collect 10,000 rupees out of the present requirement of 20,000 rupees from his friends and relatives, and the balance he intended to beg from the Maharaja of Tripura. Radha Kishore did not leave Calcutta at that time. He saw the poet coming in the dress of a beggar and told him: 'This dress does not suit you; your job is to play the flute, we, the devotees will carry the beggar's bag. The amount of money paid by the subjects supplies my royal food. Who in this world are bigger beggars than us? This beggar's bag suits only me and thus I must make it full.'

After a few months, the marriage of prince Birendra Kishore was scheduled to take place. The royal treasury was almost empty. Even in such a pathetic situation, Radha Kishore prioritized grander ideals over his personal problems. He said to the poet: 'At present, let one or two varieties of ornaments not be made for my would-be daughter-in-law, but in lieu of that the ornaments Jagadish Babu would bring from the seashore to adorn Mother India; are they not beyond compare?'

In fact, any donation given with pleasure in willful self-denial is the mark of true charity. The foreign travelling expenses of Jagadish Chandra, amounting to 10,000 rupees, if not paid by the Maharaja, would have stunted the progress of Indian science. There was no need of a separate lab for Jagadish Chandra then, but for his long-drawn stay abroad the necessary expenses had to be borne by Radha Kishore, who played a key role in India's scientific advancement.

It was a matter of regret that Rabindranath could not attend Prince Birendra Kishore's marriage. For some days, he had sent his family to Shilaidaha. He went to Shilaidaha on 27 February after receiving the news of his son's illness. Jagadish Chandra wrote to him on 2 March: 'I heard that you have to go to Shilaidaha for the illness of your family ... you are going to Tripura. Tender my respectful greetings to the Maharaja. I would have come if I could have got my leave sanctioned; I did not get the leave.'

Rabindranath unfortunately could not go to Tripura for his son's illness although he was willing to attend the marriage ceremony of the prince. He had sent cloths as a present through Pandit Baikuntha Bachaspati. Radha Kishore wrote to the poet on 24 March:

I am sorry that you could not attend the marriage ceremony as your son had suddenly fallen sick. However, I am not perturbed now after hearing the news of his being well. I have received your cloths as a present through Pandit Mahashay. The cloth befits my daughter-in-law. I have given it to badhumata (daughter-in-law) as your blessing. It has already been used by Srimati.

After the marriage of the prince, Radha Kishore being perturbed about the appointment of a suitable secretary for the prince and a personal lady teacher for the princess, sought Rabindranath's help. It was observed from the beginning that Radha Kishore used to take advice from Rabindranath both for political and family affairs. Rabindranath nominated Jatindranath Basu, MA Calcutta University, the son-in-law of Akshay Chandra Chowdhury, and he sent him to Agartala. Mahim Chandra, after his stay with Rabindranath at Shilaidaha, had returned to Agartala at the beginning of April 1901, along with Jatindranath Basu. In his letter dated 26 April, Radha Kishore wrote:

> I've met Jatindra Babu, I'm happy talking to him. Since you have personally selected and appointed the person for Sriman and Srimati, I have nothing more to say. Good results will come about if Jatin and his wife are employed for the same purpose. Jatindra Babu had already gone ... The arrangement for their house has been done. His work will start the moment he comes.

In the above letter, Radha Kishore expressed his desire to again go to Darjeeling. He informed the poet: 'I will let you know after fixing a date.' In reply, the poet wrote a long letter dated 3 May:

> The persons I've selected for the prince and princess are from a decent family of good repute ... I have counselled them

repeatedly about their responsibilities, yet for some habitual demerits, if they are found to be not a bit suitable for the posts, the Maharaja should not have the slightest hesitation in removing them at once. Kindly keep it in mind that compared to the bond of friendship, which I have with them, the welfare of the prince is much more important to me. In fact, it is very difficult to get a suitable educated gentle confidante Hindu lady for the princess. From the ordinary Brahmo Samaj, there are certainly good girls available, but in conduct and behaviour they may cause inconvenience in the inner mahal—for this reason, when it occurred to me that this is the only likely Hindu lady, I informed Mahim Chandra; I would be totally free from worries if they prove themselves suitable for the job assigned.

In middle of May, Jatindranath and his educated, cultured wife were appointed as the confidante personal secretary of the prince and the confidante teacher of the princess respectively. A highly educated litterateur, painter, architect and musician, Jatindra served Tripura effectively in various capacities for a long time. His books, *Shilaidahey Rabindranath* and *My Rabindranath: An Introspection* are still well received. His recorded folk song *'Ghatey Lagaiya Dinga'* ('The boat stands on the bank') remains very popular. Jatindranath's mother-in-law Sarat Kumari Chowdhurani, a writer, also stayed in Tripura for a long period and earned fame in the royal inner court and outside. Rabindranath and Jyotirindranath named Sarat Kumari as Lahorani. Long after leaving Tripura Sarat Kumari wrote to Maharaja: 'The days spent in Tripura are still vivid with all brightness before my eyes. Maharaja, the happiness I enjoyed in Tripura left me pained at the time of leaving it.'

Behold Rabindranath's discretion: it was very much in his mind that Brahmos might not be acceptable in a Hindu royal family. He was worried even after sending Jatindra with his wife. His worries ended on receiving a letter from the Maharaja:

> I've seen your letter written to Jati. I'm delighted to perceive your sincerity reflected in your directions elaborately given (to Jati) on the method of education for the benefit of Sriman (prince). It's difficult to get a friend in this world who can display such large-heartedness. It is commendable that, for the continuous help of a friend like you, Jati and his family are here at this time.

The Maharaja in his letter mentioned 'continuous help', which is integral to the foundation of a friendship based on faith; otherwise, it would not have been possible for Radha Kishore to not pay any heed to the antagonism of his courtiers. Many of them viewed their friendship with suspicion. Rabindranath knew about it. Radha Kishore requested him to ignore the opposition and come to him with an open mind. Rabindranath did so.

He went to Darjeeling at the request of the Maharaja on 21 May 1901 as a royal guest. They met each other at Kushtia. Before departure, the Maharaja wrote: 'I'm excited by the thought that my leisure time will become so much more pleasant with the combination of the glorious beauty of the Himalayas and your poems and music. Please bring your notebook of poetry and also one or two books along with you'.

The discussion between the poet and Maharaja at Darjeeling was about the collection of money for Jagadish Chandra's travel to England and his stay there. The British Government was insisting on admitting the princes of Tripura in Ajmer Mayo College. Radha Kishore did not want the princes to ape the thought and manners of the British.

It was decided that it would be worthy to receive advice from the Maharaja of Cooch Behar, Nripendra Narayan. There were the Lieutenant Governor of Bengal Sir John Woodburn, Raja Nripendra Narayan and many others from Calcutta at that point of time in Darjeeling, who were followers of British culture. Before the meeting between the two Rajas could take place, Rabindranath, though unwell, had to go to Shilaidaha to plan for the marriage of his daughter Madhurilata. He wrote a letter to Radha Kishore from Kushtia:

> I'm very eager to know what sort of meeting takes place with the Maharaja of Cooch Behar. If two Maharajas make a friendship, counselling will provide courage to both. I'm assured to think that if any dispute may arise between the state administration and the British government; the Maharaja would be able to come to a decision by discussing the matter with selfless, neutral persons who stand with the Maharaja as men of equal status.

In reply to this letter, Radha Kishore wrote:

> Today again, at three o'clock, there will be a meeting with LG. LG had accepted your and Cooch Behar's opinion about the education of my son. However, I had to make him understand a great deal. He advised me to appoint a good teacher from Cooch Behar. Accordingly, I've made a proposal to the Maharaja of Cooch Behar. Most probably, he'll send a letter to England (for this purpose).

While he was in Darjeeling, Rabindranath wrote a letter to Jagadish Chandra Bose requesting him to find a teacher for the princes of Tripura: 'I want to entrust you with a job. You're to select a good teacher from England and send him for the prince. The prince, staying away from Tripura, will be under his absolute control in the process of learning. It'll be better if the teacher is well versed in science.'

In reply to this letter, Jagadish Chandra wrote: 'You've written that the Maharaja desires to have a tutor from this country; yes, I can find a good man for this. But I think the teachers of the two countries differ greatly. Teachers of our country are satisfied at the progress of students, but if you take someone from this country, he may have other intentions.'

At last, the effort of Nripendra Narayan, the Maharaja of Cooch Behar, was crowned with success and one Mr T.R. Williams, MA (Oxon), a renowned educationist, came to Tripura from England to take charge of the princes. It was heard that he imparted education with an open mind, without being involved in the political, economic and social affairs of the state.

Acharya Jagadish Chandra Bose went to England in June 1901. Prior to his departure, the Maharaja had sent 10,000 rupees by money order to Rabindranath to finance Jagadish Chandra's travel. The Maharaja wrote: 'I do, therefore, intend to send the money order in your name.' After that, Maharaja handed over a cheque of 15,000 rupees to Rabindranath for expenses relating to Jagadish Chandra's work and stay in England. In this context, Rabindranath said:

> Radha Kishore listened to me and then said, with a slight smile, "I don't know specifically about Jagadish Chandra and his achievements. What I give, that will be given to you only; it's none of my business to know what you'll do with that." He handed over a cheque of 15,000 rupees to me, which I included in Acharya's travelling expenses. That day, at the time of my incapacity, I did my duty as a friend by the favour of another friend.

However, it transpired that, as resolved earlier, Rabindranath could not collect a penny for Jagadish Chandra's travel. He was supposed to raise a fund of 10,000 rupees out of total travelling budget of 20,000 rupees from his friends and relatives. The balance amount of 10,000 rupees, for which he appeared in the garb of a beggar before Maharaja Radha Kishore, had already been paid by cash for the said purpose in January 1901. He further paid 10,000 rupees by money order, which then covered the whole of the travelling expenses.

On 10 December, Rabindranath went to Tripura Palace at Ballygunge, Calcutta. The Maharaja was then in Calcutta. His reception function was held on 16 December. Jagadish Chandra was in England. The letter of Rabindranath written to Jagadish Chandra revealed Radha Kishore's magnanimity:

> The Maharaja of Tripura is now in Calcutta. I cannot express how elated he was by your success. Really speaking, he attracts my heart especially for the way he respects you from the bottom of his heart. On receiving your letter a few days ago, he was so elated as if he was specially honoured. He is eager to help you by any means.

The 'Bharat Sangeet Samaj' of Calcutta had arranged a function to felicitate Maharaja Radha Kishore Manikya on 16 December 1901. The play *Bisharjan* was staged on this occasion. Rabindranath played the role of Raghupati. Jagadindranath sang the song composed by Rabindranath for this occasion; the Maharaja of Nator played a pakhowaj in the background. He felicitated the Maharaja with a garland and sandal paste. The song was:

> King of kings, the laurel of victory is on thy fate,
> Men of merit and wit serve thy noble door,

They come with wonderful articles of worship,
Tender is thy moon-face that pours pathos.
Thy deft hands relieve sufferings of the distressed,
Thy assurance of safety dispels fear of the weak,
By the sunshine of thy qualities the world illuminates.

Rabindranath was excited by the opportunity to act before the Maharaja in the role of Raghupati. On 12 December, he wrote to Jagadish Chandra: '*Bisharjan* will be staged. I'll play the role of Raghupati.' He wanted to stop there but added in haste, 'The rehearsal of *Bisharjan* is pressing me hard, so goodbye.' He acted with such panache in the role of Raghupati that the editor of the magazine *Sanjibani* could not help but write a separate article lauding Rabindranath's performance. This is what the poet Jatindra Mohan Bagchi had to say:

> On the day of the auspicious arrival of Maharaja, the undernoted song was sung after due felicitation … "*Raj Adhiraj Taba Bhaley Jayomala*" (King of kings, the laurel of victory is on thy fate) … After that the Maharaja, befitting his status, in grave and thoughtful words, duly acknowledged the felicitation given. The play *Bisharjan* started thereafter … That was an exceptionally exciting experience of my life. I was overwhelmed with joy and wonder witnessing the performance of the poet in the role of Raghupati. That handsome, delicately slim Rabindranath had turned into a haughty hard Raghupati. The body was embellished with blood-coloured linen; the curly hairs were tied tight above the head in the shape of a peak and the forehead was decorated by a trident-shaped mark and a blob of red sandal paste. Both the eyes were wide and bright, but they looked brighter with the character's manly resolve. That was an unusual, supernatural performance.

Hemendra Prasad Ghosh wrote: 'While acting in the role of Raghupati in *Bisharjan*, he was so absorbed that, at the time of using a large falchion, he really had forgotten its sharpness. One of the actors realized his condition and took Dhruba (Aswani) away, otherwise an accident might have happened.'

The felicitation accorded to Maharaja Radha Kishore Manikya didn't boost only his pride; it made Tripura proud. His acquaintance with the qualified persons and intellectuals of Calcutta society had opened the gate of cultural exchange between Bengal and Tripura.

Shailesh Chandra Majumder requested Rabindranath to take charge of the editorship of *Bangadarshan* to reanimate it. The poet at first did not agree. At last, after much persuasion, he gave his consent. However, Radha Kishore's reply to Tagore's letter dated 21 April revealed that Rabindranath was already keen to accept the offer.

> The news of the reappearance of Bankim's *Bangadarshan* is very good. The enthusiasm of famous writers makes the news greater. In my opinion, without further delay and hesitation you should take charge of the editorship. You just tell me what I have to do. I'm ready to undertake its charge in all respects.

There was no doubt that the assurance had encouraged Rabindranath to accept the editorship of *Bangadarshan*. But news reached his ears that the courtiers were very critical about Maharaja's decision. As Tripura was below the poverty line, they wanted all charities to be stopped henceforth. An aggrieved Rabindranath wrote to Mahim Chandra: 'If you all have got the slightest doubt about *Bangadarshan*, don't hesitate to let me know it. I shall be in a happy state of mind to relieve you fully from your commitments. I don't want to put the Maharaja in any sort of trouble. I only want his kind friendship; other things are immaterial.'

In his next letter to Mahim Chandra, he expressed his grievances more clearly:

> When *Bangadarshan* came to my hand, I was eager to make it a first-class paper. Unfortunately, the expenditure and effort needed could by no means be met in my present condition. I sought the help of the Maharaja for this eagerness to lead *Bangadarshan*, without considering what was before or after. But you all imagined it as my selfish motive. I thought, you all are courtiers, you do not have faith in the honest intention of the people; you look at everybody with eyes of suspicion—you all have obscured the usual magnanimity of the Maharaja.

The matter did not end there. An aggrieved Rabindranath penned a letter straight to Maharaja Radha Kishore:

> I don't want my friendship with the Maharaja to be such that people label me as self-serving ... Thus, I've decided not to take any financial help from the Maharaja for the job I've undertaken. Noble deeds have no value without hardship or sacrifice. I would feel proud if I can cross the limit of my present capability in the running of *Bangadarshan* ... Jagadish Babu's talent and large-heartedness ... his opinion in all matters is supremely important to me.

It was evident from the letters written to Mahim Chandra and Maharaja that Rabindranath was struck very badly by the allegations of his being blinded with selfishness. He was so perturbed that he sought Jagadish Chandra's opinion in this matter. But Maharaja Radha Kishore did not pay any heed to it. He wrote to the poet: 'Agartala is a place of irresponsible rumourmongers. The only reason for this is that worthless people coming from outside have settled here. If you intend to accept the meaning of their abusive words, it will be an injustice done to me.'

In this letter he further added,

> The help I'm rendering to *Bangadarshan* is not out of my friendship with you—it's for Bengali language and culture. The same thing applies in the case of Ved Vidyalaya (Brahma Vidyalaya) at Bolpur. Just because I'm connected to these matters, you shouldn't feel any sort of hesitation. On the other hand, it may ascribe unnecessary weakness to both of us. Indulgence should not be granted by any means. (Undated letter, Brahma Vidyalaya was then established.)

This letter worked wonders. Rabindranath got rid of his hesitation and was ready to face any opposition. Antagonism, of course, could not be impeded, but even then, the relationship did not deteriorate. The Maharajas of Tripura, one after another, helped him throughout, and Rabindranath wholeheartedly maintained the relationship in all circumstances.

The simmering resentment of the courtiers soon appeared in the open. Radha Kishore had always known about it, of course, but Rabindranath had to face it for the first time. In the opinion of the critics, the first duty of the king was to develop an undeveloped Tripura. Tripura desperately needed help from outside. An advanced Bengali community and Bengal did not need charity at all from poor Tripura, backward in all respects. Apart from this, the appointment of high-ranking officials from outside the state and the respect shown to them, instead of the sons of the soil, wounded the pride of the critics.

Rabindranath was very sorry as the Maharajas of Tripura and Nator, and Jagadish Chandra could not attend the marriage ceremony of his daughter Bela; but the sorrow vanished with the news of Jagadish Chandra's victory. Jagadish Chandra, on 10 May, had delivered a lecture on the subject, 'The response of Inorganic matter to Mechanical and Electrical Stimulus', at the Royal Institute in London, for which there was tremendous excitement among the scientists. Rabindranath immediately kept the Maharaja informed by a telegram. At this time, he wrote an article on Hindutva. In that article, Rabindranath put forward the theoretical interpretation of Hindutva and wrote a letter advising Radha Kishore about its application:

> The *Manusamhita* outlines the ideal duty of a Hindu king. In our king's domain, the king has got the right to duty only and no right over riches ... in Europe, the kingdom means everything to a king. In ancient India, the realm of a king is seen as a social and personal duty and not as an embodiment of pleasure and power ... If the kings are wakeful and keep the qualified sagacious persons awakened, only then may Hindu society walk the path of prosperity. The kings should attract learned men in the royal court and for the welfare of mankind make all sorts of deliberations on religion ... and carefully introduce a welfare system to establish in his own kingdom a high all-round social ideal.

In order to establish Radha Kishore as an ideal king, Rabindranath could not resist the temptation to impart some knowledge to Radha Kishore. He wanted to remind Radha Kishore that he had only a right to duty and no right over wealth as a king. In other words, his charitable deeds were part of his duty. But Rabindranath himself admitted in no uncertain manner that: 'The lofty impression that arises in the mind after studying the Indian Puranas and poems about the ancient kings, I have noticed those qualities amongst the Maharajas of Tripura'.

What was the purpose of such an advice? Perhaps, Rabindranath wanted Radha Kishore not to be influenced by the criticisms and, therefore, imparted some knowledge to suggest the way of life the Maharaja should follow.

Radha Kishore resolved to appoint efficient teachers to improve the educational system of Tripura. He sought Rabindranath's help in the selection of teachers. Basanta Kumar Gupta was appointed at Rabindranath's recommendation. In this matter, he wrote to Mahim Chandra: 'Lawrence (who was the private tutor of Rabindranath's children) does not want to leave me. You might have read the writings of the modern litterateur and scientist Jagadananda Roy. This man is not only well-read but also gentle and virtuous. If you intend to get a good man and a good teacher, I can offer him.'

After the plan to establish a Brahmacharya Ashram at Shantiniketan, he recommended Lawrence and wrote a letter to Radha Kishore on 3 September. On that very day, he also informed Mahim Chandra: 'The Maharaja has done a noble job allowing wretched Hesh to stay at Ballygunge palace.'

Rabindranath sought the Maharaja's help for Sashi Kumar Hesh, apprising him about his (Hesh) miserable conditions. Sashi Kumar Hesh was a talented artist of that time. After his return from abroad, he was without shelter, being left off by his relatives and friends. Rabindranath sought the Maharaja's refuge to help Hesh in his personal difficulties. The Maharaja kept the poet's request and allowed Hesh and his wife to stay for a few months at Tripura Palace, Ballygunge, Calcutta. Aware of their financial distress, the Maharaja, in order to not hurt the couple's self-esteem with a donation, purchased one oil painting, *Boy with a Pitcher*, to give them temporary relief from adversity. This picture still adorns a wall at Ujjayanta Palace.

Jagadish Chandra's deputation period of fifteen months in England was about to end soon. The invention was as yet incomplete. He had to either comeback or seek employment abroad. The love of science and his patriotism deterred him from the temptation of doing a service. He knew very well about the indifference of his own people to help others. He started writing letters one after another to Rabindranath echoing his heartfelt lamentation. Rabindranath's only strength was Radha Kishore. In the meantime, Radha Kishore had sent another 5,000 rupees to Jagadish Chandra through Rabindranath. Before that, by slashing the expenditures on the ornaments of his would-be daughter-in-law at the time of prince Birendra's marriage, Radha Kishore had already paid ten thousand rupees by cash, another ten thousand rupees by money order, and fifteen thousand by cheque. Rabindranath knew all about it but was helpless. What else could he do but write a letter to Maharaja Radha Kishore, his last resort? He wrote:

> This is the time to do something for Jagadish Babu. A critical time of his research work has arrived ... Maharaja, let me tell you frankly—if unfortunately for the indiscretion of others I had not been entangled cap-a-pie in the net of debt, I would not have stood at the door of anyone for Jagadish Babu; I would have taken his full charge. My main grievance is that being in distress I can do nothing but excite others to act for the welfare of the country ... I am willing to canvas directly before the Maharaja for Jagadish Babu—for this I am ready to go to Agartala. I can't depend on Mahim, etc. I have gradually lost my faith in them ... They are not suitable assistants or subordinates of the Maharaja so far as noble resolve and lofty intentions are concerned. For

this, I am longing to enter the solitary private durbar of the Maharaja ... The courtiers of the Maharaja will say so many things; suspecting various kinds of motive, they will harass me, but I shall bear it on my head.

This letter was written on the date of the wedding of his middle daughter Renuka Devi. From this, it transpired how anxious the poet was for Jagadish Chandra. At one time Rabindranath wrote to Jagadish Chandra:

Well, if you want to do your job staying in this country, can't we all together make you independent? Fie on us, if we can't pay the scanty money that you get from service. But will you courageously accept this proposal? How can you do your job with feet fastened and being reprimanded at every step? We intend to make you free—I don't think it will be difficult for us to achieve.

Jagadish Chandra did not want to leave the certainty of his government job. Rabindranath was the only saviour. He had to carry the beggar's bowl for Jagadish Chandra, with a face hanging down in shame. Rabindranath had intimate relations with the affluent societies of Bengal. But none of the elite, not even the Maharajas of Nator, Cooch Behar and Dwarbhanga, Nawab of Murshidabad and Rai Bahadurs, nor the Tagore family offered to help Jagadish Chandra Bose in his crisis. It was a shame for the Bengali community that they revelled in reflected glory, but never shared his miseries when Jagadish Chandra was in dire financial crisis. This speaks volumes about the opposition of the courtiers to the charity given outside Tripura. In fact, Tripura had no minerals; its income depended solely on forestry and agriculture. It had no single industry. The total revenue of Tripura in 1901 was not more than 10 lakhs, maybe even less. The main source of revenue was from East Bengal's Chakla Roshanabad, the zamindari of the kings of Tripura. Tripura as such had no revenue potential for itself. If not for Chakla Roshanabad, Tripura would have starved. Considering various expenses relating to administration, roads and transport, welfare activities and payment of tax to the British Government, the remainder was minimal. In his autobiography, *Abarjanar Jhuri*, Nabadwip Chandra had detailed the king's financial plight thus: 'The other day, father (Maharaja Ishan Chandra Manikya) completed his daily worship and was explaining the need for some items of negligible expenditures to a court employee amounting to a few paisas; the man hesitated and submitted that even a few paisas were not available in the treasury.'

This indicates how hard it was for Maharaja Radha Kishore to finance the advancement of scientific endeavours in India. Being the king of a small state, he did not keep himself confined to the periphery of his sovereignty but was keen to prove himself as a true Indian by defying the dictum of the British Government. This again goes to show that Tripura, from its inception, was a part of Indian culture and civilization.

Rabindranath, for the second time, visited Tripura in November 1901, his purpose being to collect the necessary amount of money for Jagadish Chandra's stay in England. This time, the poet stayed in Jora (Joint) Bungalow. The two bungalows facing east were situated to the north of Jagannath temple. Satya Ranjan Basu gathered the accounts of the poet's stay at Agartala from the reminiscence of Maharaja Kumar Brajendra Kishore and Srijut Kalachand Deb Barma:

> On the north-west corner of the western large tank of the royal palace was the Jora Bungalow. Two bungalows stood side-by-

side facing east ... Every evening, as a rule, there was a party. Everybody was absorbed in listening to the poet's talk. The talk about how to build the country with the help of native kings had drawn a deep line in the mind of Brajendra Kishore. Sometimes the poet recited the poetical works of Shelley and Browning and would then enthusiastically translate them for the benefit of Maharaja Kumar. At times, the poet made them listen to his new writings. On certain days, Brajendra Kishore, coming alone, saw that in the early morning, he (Rabindranath) was singing a prayer song with great emotion while playing an organ. The poet, with his eyes closed, was passionately singing *'Bol Dao, More Bol Dao'* (Give Me Strength, Give Me Strength).

Every now and then, in the evening, the poet used to play some fun little mind games with us. For instance, the poet would tell someone in the gathering to keep in mind the name of a famous person. Mentioning various qualities, others would question whether that man had those qualities. In this process, gradually that person and his specialties would be exposed. This kind of Twenty Questions game helped people exercise their minds.

One evening, it was decided to honour the poet with music at his rest house. Two boys could sing very well in school. They were Kalachand Deb Barma and Prafulla Kumar Majumder. They had learnt two songs from Jati Babu (Jatindranath Basu) and rehearsed. They were the poet's compositions: 'King of kings laurel of victory on thy fate' and 'O captivating the minds of people of the world.' The principal of the college, Kunjalal Nag Mahashay, played pakhowaj and khol. After the songs of the boys were over, Ramkanai Shil of Maharaja Bir Chandra's royal court sang Bir Chandra's composition (also set to music by Bir Chandra) *Joy Jagat Bandini, Hari Hriday*

Rangini, Braja Ramani Mukutmani Radhike—Sri Radhike'— (Glory be, thou who hast imprisoned the world, delight of Hari's heart, Braja woman, gem of their crown, Radhike, Sri Radhike). Lastly, Prasanna Kumar Thakur eloquently played the sitar with alap in a long measure.

However, Rabindranath's visit to Agartala yielded fruit. He wrote a letter to Jagadish Chandra from Agartala:

I've come to Tripura to serve your purpose. I'm here for a few days as a guest of the Maharaja. You know very well how much he admires you; I therefore felt no hesitation putting up my prayer before him. Most probably, within one or two mails, he will send you 10,000 rupees. This money I will send to you in my name. He himself promised to send another 10,000 within this year. Recently the Maharaja is involved in various expensive works, like rebuilding the palace; otherwise, he on his own accord could have helped you up to half a lakh. His enthusiasm has drawn my heart towards him more firmly. I've never seen such a model of spontaneous generosity.

It is worth mentioning that Rabindranath, in his letter addressed to Jagadish Chandra, wrote: 'I will send this money to you in my name.' It is needless to say that the generous Radha Kishore detested propaganda and wanted to stay behind the curtain in complete silence and, therefore, had imposed a condition on Rabindranath to keep all his charitable deeds a secret. After the death of Radha Kishore, secrecy could not be maintained. The episodes of assistance and favour linked up with the royal magnanimity of Radha Kishore came to light by the grace of Rabindranath and a little bit by Jagadish Chandra.

One matter must be made categorically clear. The kings of Tripura did not have an absolute right to enjoy the money kept in the royal treasury. In the annual budget, based on revenue collection, a fund was kept separate for the personal use of the Maharaja, which included family expenditures. Of course, the king being a sovereign, had the right to violate the convention, but it could lead to revolt by the courtiers and the general public who would be the worst sufferers. There was no commotion whenever Radha Kishore paid donations out of his personal fund. The amount of 10,000 rupees paid for the first time to Jagadish Chandra via Rabindranath was out of his personal fund as is evident from his slashing the expenses for the ornaments of his would-be daughter-in-law. The money paid later on from time to time might have been partly from this personal fund. Rabindranath knew what sacrifices Radha Kishore had to undergo in the name of friendship.

Another controversial topic may be raised about Rabindranath's relationship with Jagadish Chandra: it at the most unidirectional. Rabindranath, no doubt, went all-out to help Jagadish Chandra in his scientific research. But did Jagadish Chandra pay any heed to the fact that Rabindranath could not always fulfil his lofty demands? Being a beneficiary, he did not keep any relation or write any letter; just one, directly to Maharaja Radha Kishore expressing his gratitude. That was why there was no direct communication between Jagadish Chandra and Radha Kishore. I would find no fault if the people of Tripura think (and they certainly do) that Maharaja Radha Kishore's sentiment was exploited by Rabindranath to achieve his goal.

What was that goal? Rabindranath had never in his dreams thought of winning the Nobel Prize. As a young writer and poet, he had to face unending criticism from famous writers like Dwijendralal Roy, Sajanikanta Das, etc. He was not given true recognition as a poet or writer till he received the Nobel Prize in the year 1913. Hurt as he was, he refused to accept any felicitation from the people of Bengal after winning the prize. Critics even cast aspersions on him, claiming that he got the Nobel Prize through his close acquaintance with Sturge Moore and W.B. Yeats. What I mean is that Rabindranath never thought that he would get worldwide recognition as a great poet; he might not have had faith in himself to become a Nobel laureate, but he had full faith in Jagadish Chandra that he would one day become a renowned scientist and that he, Rabindranath, would be remembered as the man behind Jagadish Chandra's success. Perhaps he'd wanted to bask in reflected glory. That was why he did not hesitate to play the role of a beggar and face all kinds of adversities. In fact, Radha Kishore told him categorically, 'I don't know specifically about Jagadish Chandra and his achievements. What I give, that will be given to you only; it's none of my business to know what you'll do with that.' These words of Maharaja Radha Kishore reflected his attitude towards Jagadish Chandra who had never cared to keep any contact with the Maharaja and always persuaded Rabindranath to speak on his behalf. This does not speak well of him. Radha Kishore in fact, contributed to a noble cause and not to Jagadish Chandra, whom he hardly knew. This is what is called royal greatness.

No one should make a mistake thinking that the above observations are intended to belittle Rabindranath Tagore's immortal talent. In poetic faculty and music (Rabindrasangeet) he is peerless in the world, not just in India. He is remembered worldwide even for his paintings. He had taken the Bengali language four hundred years ahead, otherwise we would have continued with Ishwar Chandra Vidyasagar's Bengali. No doubt, a talent as vast as he was deserved the Nobel Prize. He is adored as Gurudev, but to a devotee like me, he is everything. I only wanted to point out that in one's own country, when one does not get the due recognition for years, it almost becomes impossible to assess one's talent by oneself.

At the time of his stay in Agartala, Rabindranath expressed his desire to establish the Brahma Vidyalaya at Bolpur. There was a long discussion about it between the poet and the king. The Maharaja encouraged Rabindranath to establish the school and assured him of all kinds of financial help. The poet told the Maharaja categorically that he had no financial power to run the school; it could only be possible by the favour of the Maharaja. The Maharaja gave his word. As long as Tripura was a native state, until 1949, the next generations of Maharajas also did not break this promise. The promise instigated Maharishi Debendranath to convey his blessings to the Maharaja.

On 7 Poush 1308 Bengali Era (January 1901), Rabindranath established Brahmacharya Ashram and a school at Shantiniketan. After learning from Mahim Chandra's telegram that the Maharaja had come to Calcutta, Rabindranath reached Calcutta on 10 February and sought an interview with the Maharaja. Madhyam (middle) Rajkumar (Prince) Brajendra Kishore was not allowed to join Shantiniketan despite the Maharaja's wish because of the vicious circle of state politics. As no definite decision was taken for Brajendra Kishore's education, a temporary arrangement for this purpose was made at Comilla. The Maharaja did not send his sons to Ajmer as he firmly believed in Indian culture. It was believed that both of them discussed the future of Brajendra Kishore.

Rabindranath returned to Shantiniketan on 9 June 1902 and stayed there for a month. He had written a letter two days earlier, informing the Maharaja that from the beginning of the year his health was not good, and he had, above all, been stricken with mental anguish. 'I've written to Maharaja before that I was very tired and unwell for some time—as if one invisible evil was wrestling with me day in and day out...'

He wrote the same thing to Jagadish Chandra on 20 June and added further: 'Come back after hoisting your flag of victory in Germany and America. Don't be in a hurry. Probably within one or two months I will be of some help to you—I've made the arrangements.'

Within a short time, the arrangements had taken effect. Expressing his gratitude, the poet wrote a letter to Radha Kishore, dated 9 August: 'My heart is full of gratitude for the Maharaja sending 5,000 rupees to Jagadish. I will always remember the Maharaja's greatness; how can I express it in words?'

Even though after having faced the antagonism of the courtiers for the first time, Rabindranath had expressed his annoyance to Mahim Chandra and Maharaja and declared that he would not take any help for running *Bangadarshan*; but he ultimately changed his mind and solicited help. He informed Dinesh Chandra Sen via a letter dated 23 April 1904: 'The Maharaja has written today, "I've made arrangements to some extent to help *Bangadarshan* and Bolpur Vidyalaya. From the present month of April onwards, 50 rupees will be sent by money order in the name of your employee in the second week of every month. So, you should not worry.'

From the year 1903, Radha Kishore started sending students from Tripura with a stipend to Shantiniketan, making all arrangements for their boarding. Shantiniketan never had to bear any expense for the students of Tripura. The first student from Tripura to Shantiniketan was the respected Satya Ranjan Basu. Among those who joined later were Jogendra Ganguly, Upendra Bhattacharya, Jogesh Bandopadhyay, Somendra Dev Burman, two sons of Nabadwip Bahadur—Kumar Prafulla and Prasanta (brothers of S.D. Burman), and others—the foremost among the Shantiniketan alumni. The arrival of so many students from a border state like Tripura was rare in the history of Shantiniketan. Rabindranath in this context wrote to Mohit Chandra

Sen: 'Nabadwip Chandra Bahadur, an uncle of Tripura Maharaja had written that he would send two of his sons to school—some two to four boys are also coming—therefore, a new house is needed.'

In the meantime, Radha Kishore was in deep trouble with the free college established by him. The free college was set up in 1901 and, immediately thereafter, the British Government was adamant on dismantling it. As it was a free college, the students from nearby British India started enrolling en masse. Victoria College, especially, was the worst hit, as its number of students had reduced considerably. Calcutta University relented to the pressure of the British Government and refused to give a nomination to this college. The British Government in clear terms informed Radha Kishore that institutes of higher learning all around British India would be compromised if there happened to be a free college. Radha Kishore did not agree to introduce fees in his college. His words were firm: 'Hindu kings impart learning gratuitously, never sell it.'

Aggrieved, pained and angry, Radha Kishore was forced to close the college in 1904. The news was published in *Amrita Bazar Patrika* dated 20 August 1904: 'The Maharaja of Tripura was compelled by the Bengal Government against his wishes to abolish his highly flourishing Agartala College ... Great distress and consternation prevail ... The Maharaja is extremely sorry and has declined attending the birthday durbar on Wednesday.'

The Maharaja had donated all the instruments of the science lab and other goods and chattels from this free college to Rabindranath's Brahma Vidyalaya. The most astonishing fact was that Radha Kishore had given Victoria College a one-time donation of 15,000 rupees and a grant of 500 rupees a year—and the free college had been closed for the sake of this very Victoria College!

In his reminiscence, the famous painter Dhiren Krishna Deb Barman said how proud he felt seeing the scientific instruments at

Shantiniketan: One day, in the science room, our teacher Santosh Majumder was taking our class. Incidentally, during a conversation, he said to me, "In the adjacent room, all those glass cupboards and big telescopes you saw were donations made by the Maharaja of Tripura."

Rabindranath had always harboured a deep desire to host the Maharaja at Shantiniketan. At last, Rabindranath's wish was fulfilled. Radha Kishore accepted the hospitality of the poet at Shantiniketan on 23 Poush 1311 (1904). Apart from yearly help to Brahma Vidyalaya, he gave word to provide temporary monetary help as and when required. These regular and irregular donations in critical times had saved this institution from fading into oblivion. All these assistances continued for more than half a century. Prabhat Kumar Mukhopadhyay, in his book *Rabindra Jibani*, mentioned that 'no Maharajas of this lineage had come to this Ashram (residential institution)'. It was not correct; not only Radha Kishore Manikya, but others like Birendra Kishore and Bir Bikram Manikya had visited Shantiniketan. In response to the felicitation given by Sahitya Samaj at Agartala, the poet himself had raised this topic: 'Amongst the people of our country, I received regular financial assistance only from Radha Kishore Manikya. He himself accepted hospitality in our Ashram and made us joyous and honoured.'

The reign of Radha Kishore was not a happy one. After his ascension to the throne, a series of critical challenges impaired the state: the royal palace was destroyed by an earthquake; the treasury was draining, and economic revival seemed impossible; the struggle for the throne intensified; there was an acute lack of efficient officials to run the administration; etc. He was disturbed about the paucity of funds. Rebuilding the palace was the top priority but the royal treasury was almost empty and could provide no help. Above all, he was entangled in a huge debt taken from the government.

It was against such a background that Rabindranath entered the political stage. He knew very well that, to comply with the royal duties as a king's friend, he had to encounter antagonism and settle all disputes face to face. Rabindranath came to know from Jatindranath Basu about the pecuniary condition of the state and the Maharaja's intention of taking on a huge debt; he realized that only a proficient minister could save the state from such misery. He wrote a long letter on 14 June with plenty of advice and sent it by registered post. Radha Kishore did not destroy this letter despite Tagore's request to do so. Rabindranath wrote from his personal experience of taking debt and its subsequent repayment; each line of the letter reflects this experience and the poet's anxiety. The poet repeatedly warned his friend about the diplomacy of the Englishmen: '... the administration of zamindari, and to some extent control over income and expenditure, has to be handed over to a government-nominated English supervisor...' In the same letter, Tagore wrote: 'In order to help the Maharaja in the governance of the state, an efficient, farsighted and resolute economist needs to be appointed ... The heart of the Maharaja is quite soft and, therefore, to save himself from his own qualities of forgiveness and magnanimity, he is badly in need of able assistance from a proficient minister.'

In another undated letter, wherein he again wrote 'kindly destroy the letter' (it is fortunate for us today that the request was not kept), he elaborated on the same theme and recommended Ramani Mohan Chatterjee (Chattopadhyaya), the youngest son-in-law of Dwijendranath Tagore to be appointed as the required minister. Rabindranath initially hesitated to suggest Ramani Mohan's name for the role as he was a close relative of the poet, but at the end, he prioritized the welfare of Tripura and went ahead with his recommendation. Here lies the difference between Rabindranath and others. He did not feel embarrassed to don a beggar's garb for

Jagadish Chandra, and he was not afraid of dealing with a public scandal to save his royal friend Radha Kishore. He was firmly resolved to tolerate all kinds of insult for the sake of friendship. In a long letter, Rabindranath wrote:

> That the Maharaja should take a loan from the government has become a matter of special interest for some people here. The person whom the government will appoint for the recovery of the loan—I have heard that he belongs to the planter's class. It will not be difficult for a man like Shandiz to bring him under control.

Now, to introduce Shandiz, a quotation from another letter needs to be given. Shandiz was the personal secretary of the Maharaja. Rabindranath noted his impression about him in this letter: 'I don't believe Shandiz Saheb at all. I've heard from so many sources that Shandiz extorts the Maharaja's money by means of different tricks…'

Shandiz was pressing the Maharaja to accept the proposal of taking a loan from the government. Shandiz even met Rabindranath and requested him to bring the Maharaja to Calcutta on the pretext of medical care. Rabindranath divulged the bad intentions of Shandiz in the next part of his letter:

> Having the Maharaja in seclusion in Calcutta, he will put the Maharaja in a chokehold … Shandiz is not a man who comes to anyone out of mere courtesy … It is doubtful that a loan will not be available from the Bank of Bengal and therefore, a loan has to be taken from some other private banks. It is easy for such men to advance their own agenda with a private bank … If the Maharaja must be compelled, having no other alternative, to abide by

the government's conditions in order to take a loan and also to accept the person from the government for the administration of zamindari, then the Maharaja should appoint an efficient man of his choice as the minister—kindly do not mix up both.

In order to vindicate his recommendation of Ramani Mohan in the post of minister, Rabindranath, after stating his qualifications, wrote:

Truthfully speaking, the Maharaja needs such a person, one that selfish people, by fear or friendship, will not be able to convert to their own party. The person in all circumstances will be by the Maharaja's side ... This is the only way in this critical time to shield the Maharaja against conspiracies... I feel very hesitant to name Ramani. It is not because he is my relative, but because it is very delicate to shoulder the responsibility of nominating someone at this critical juncture. I have tried to overcome this hesitation thinking of only the duty of a friend. I surely know that if Ramani is appointed here, I would have to accept considerable disgrace.

If these letters would have been destroyed, as requested by Rabindranath himself, then the form in which Bengal had not seen him, that appeared only in the small state of Tripura—as the judicious, shrewd and pragmatic politician and economist—these unheard-of features of the poet would have been forever lost to the world. He wanted to see Tripura as an ideal native state, which was reflected in his countless letters.

In the meantime, Jagadish Chandra Bose returned from England with a laurel of victory. He had successfully proven that plants had life. When Rabindranath learned of this news, his emotional outburst revealed how elated he was by the achievement of his friend: 'My heart is dancing on hearing the news of your victory like a peacock delighted by the sound of thunder...'

After his return to the country, Jagadish Chandra invented an instrument for the measurement of the growth of plants and paid close attention to his research work. As suitable plants were not available in Calcutta, Rabindranath wrote to the Maharaja:

> The thin bamboos that grow in Tripura have very rapid growth in the infancy stage. The saplings of this tree are urgently necessary for his experiment. It will be very beneficial for him, if the Maharaja gives an order to immediately send just-sprouted saplings of thin bamboos to his address. So that the trees do not die on the way by getting the top of the saplings pressed, it will be necessary to put the trees with roots in soil in pack-boxes with a cage cover above. For the time being, he will require twenty to twenty-five trees... As the trees could not be located in nearby Calcutta, his experiment has remained incomplete. (June 1905)

Maharaja Radha Kishore Manikya's reaction to Jagadish Chandra Bose's victory was not known. But Jagadish Chandra had never requested the Maharaja for help, even though they had met once and had a cordial friendship. This sort of an unexpected behaviour from a person of Jagadish Chandra's stature might have hurt Radha Kishore very badly. He wondered why Jagadish Chandra did not speak or write to him for anything he wanted to be accomplished! Why did he want a medium when he knew the Maharaja so well? He could not get any answer from within. The beneficiary all along sat on a pinnacle without any sense of gratitude and the medium played the role on his behalf. It was hard to imagine that an intelligent man like Rabindranath was not aware of the fact. It had brought disgrace to royal decorum. However, the saplings were sent as directed by

Rabindranath. Radha Kishore was himself neck-deep in debt, yet he never disappointed his friend Rabindranath and kept his request for assistance every time.

This time, the poet himself wanted to go to Tripura. He wanted to find a solution for the monetary crisis by discussing it with Radha Kishore. It was not good for one to sit idle while a friend was in need. He set out on a journey to Tripura in July 1905 to be apprised of the real state of affairs right on the spot.

Rabindranath again stayed in Jora Bungalow. At the inauguration of the Tripura Sahitya Sammelani on 1 July, Rabindranath read out an article titled *'Deshiya Rajya'* in the meeting held at the Umakanta Academy. An eyewitness of the event, Mahim Chandra wrote:

> A meeting was held on 1 July 1905 in a large room of an English high school in Agartala to felicitate Rabindranath on the occasion of establishing Sahitya Sabha. In that meeting, on the dais, one seat was fixed for Maharaja Radha Kishore and the other for Rabindranath. At the start of the meeting, Maharaja Radha Kishore Manikya welcomed Rabi Babu as the president of the Sabha ... When Rabindranath requested the Maharaja to sit on the seat fixed for him on the dais, Maharaja said, "In the field of literature, your seat is the highest, you are the king of literature, I am your devotee and friend only, this high dais is not my place."

The audiences and the people were charmed by the great modesty exhibited by their Maharaja and felt proud of him. Rabindranath was overjoyed by this scene.

There is a saying in Sanskrit: 'The king is worshipped only in his own country, but the learned man is worshipped everywhere.' Radha Kishore was a shining example of high-mindedness, courtesy and respect for others. There was perhaps no king in the world who, with such humbleness, had received a poet. Nowhere in the history of the world do we find a king who shunned royal egotism before his own subjects. And remember, Rabindranath was not particularly famous at that point of time. Rabindranath earned this respect by his merit and this respect was only his due to Bir Chandra, who for the first time accorded recognition to the poet, and Radha Kishore just proved to be the worthy son of that great father.

Let us go back to that meeting. In his article *'Deshiya Rajya'*, Rabindranth explained that every country develops its own form of humanity. The Sanskrit words imprinted in the royal insignia of Tripura state, *'Kil Bidurbiratang Saramekang'* ('Valour is the sole object') should be followed religiously. The country declines for the lack of this valour and it can't be saved by mimicking foreign mores.

Rabindranath further said,

In spite of errors and omissions and the slow movement of the native states, it is a matter of satisfaction that whatever gain is there, it is absolutely ours ... For this very reason I cannot but cast an eager glance towards the small state of Tripura.' Hinting at the litigiousness, disturbance and conspiracy prevailing in this state, he added, 'For this, if I come to know that for trivial selfishness and to gain a tiny profit and small advantage for the present, there is no hesitation to loosen the foundation of the temple of the goddess safeguarding the kingdom and looking after its welfare, I cannot then remain unworried taking this guilt as a small matter of a small state.

Simply on this basis, Rabindranath entered the vicious circle of state politics and recommended Ramani Mohan as a minister with the intention to run the administration free from any kind of self-serving agenda.

Keenly aware that under British rule, it was impossible to realize India's true potential, Rabindranath reposed his hopes on the native states. As the flag of British art and culture fluttered in every direction, he believed Tripura represented an alternative and had an intense desire to see it blossom into an ideal state.

He had great respect for the cultural heritage of Tripura. That was why he pronounced:

> Remember, valour is the sole object. These words are absolute truth. Parliament is not the sole object ... valour is the sole object. At a particular place and time, and in different people, valour shows itself in various forms—someone is valorous in scriptures, someone is valorous in sacrifice, someone is valorous in the enjoyment of earthly pleasure, someone is valorous in religion, someone is valorous in work.

The next day, he inspected Thakur Boarding. In the book of inspection, he wrote: 'This afternoon I am satisfied after having inspected Thakur Boarding. 2 July 1905. Sri Rabindranath Tagore.'

The main purpose of Tagore's address was to improve the internal rules and regulations and arrangements of Tripura. During this period, he placed a draft titled 'Bharat Rajanya Sabha' before Radha Kishore. Rabindranath also created the zonal divisions. The target of his plan was to improve the affairs of the native states.

This time, Rabindranath came to Tripura to play the role of a saviour. He was determined to save the king from political intrigue and economic difficulties. During his stay in Agartala, he had a long discussion with the Maharaja. He was restless to find a way to solve the problems. So that time should not stand as a bar, he wrote a long letter dated 4 July about the royal service holders, sitting on a steamer at Goalnand on his way to Calcutta: 'All the persons through whom the Maharaja is talking to the government are proving to be entirely futile due to the Maharaja's difference of intention. Not only that—they are trying to project a negative image of the Maharaja to the British.'

Thereafter, an anxious Rabindranath appeared as a counselor and demonstrated his realistic approach:

> It is not necessary to mortgage the whole of Chakla Roshanabad in the hands of a new man for the loan repayment. It was decided to make the magistrate understand that the Maharaja wants to keep only one part ... An effort is going on to dislodge the Maharaja from the control of his zamindari. I am indeed thinking how the Maharaja will continue discussing with the government before the appointment of a faithful and efficient person. Those in charge are against it.

Chakla Roshanabad deserves some clarifications. A large part of East Bengal, though under the domination of the British Government was acknowledged as a zamindari of Tripura. This large region of plain land was known as Chakla Roshanabad, which contributed ninety percent of the revenue of Tripura state. In fact, the economic stability of Tripura was fully dependent on the revenue earned from Chakla Roshanabad. Had this zamindari gone, Tripura would have faced disaster. Rabindranath knew that very well and, therefore, cautioned the Maharaja again and again.

This zamindari covered a total land area of 395,631 acres, divided into four parts—southern division (79,502 acres with its headquarters at Feni), Central Division (146,186 acres with its headquarters at Comilla), northern division (140,943 acres with its headquarters at

Mogra) and Sylhet Division (29,000 acres with its headquarters at Laharpur). From the records, it transpires that though the British Government did not acknowledge the sovereignty of the Maharajas of Tripura over Chakla Roshanabad, they accepted their rights over the estate because Chakla Roshanabad was under the occupation of Tripura from time immemorial.

The aforesaid letter was sent in an envelope to the address of Jatindranath Basu to avert antagonism. Even before, the letters which the poet requested to be destroyed were sent to the Maharaja by registered posts. This shows that he was suspicious about the activities of the courtiers. He did not have faith in anyone. From his fear, one can understand how far the intrigue of the royal durbar had expanded. It further brought to light that Rabindranath was a true well-wisher of the Maharaja.

After his return to Calcutta on 5 July, Rabindranath sat with Ramani Mohan and discussed the problems of Tripura at considerable length. He advised Ramani Mohan how to get rid of the problems and what solutions to put in place. On 12 July, he wrote a letter to Radha Kishore from Patisar informing him that Ramani Mohan had agreed to join as minister, but Rabindranath had a request before the Maharaja: 'Hand over the job in such an unhindered manner to Ramani Mohan, so that he does not fail in any part and finds a place to apply his full expertise.'

The last part of the letter showed how anxious Rabindranath was to do something good for the welfare of Tripura at this critical stage. The strong friendship with Tripura's royal family, that had developed steadily from 1882, made Rabindranath feel like their sorrows and happiness were his own. He could not remain stoic in the face of their calamities. He considered it his solemn duty to serve Tripura for its welfare by his strength of character and merits. The concluding part of the letter was a revelation in this regard:

I feel that God has made me vow to fix the system in the kingdom of the Maharaja. My heart is eager to take leave from service, but I have clearly understood that this work has to be accomplished by me. I am religiously bound to it—even the Maharaja will not be able to set me free from this. Amid my present problems relating to property, the thought of the Maharaja's kingdom is by no means leaving me. It is not for the Maharaja only; I shall have to apply my mind to the Maharaja's work so as to be released from my own anxiety.

It seemed Rabindranath was in favour of transferring absolute power to the minister. No doubt valuable time is lost if, for every matter, there needs to be a consensus. The work that needs to be done gets delayed and hampered. The ultimate authority to take decisions lay in the hands of the minister, and the officers under him would have to give effect to it. In fact, Rabindranath had no faith in the merits of the royal courtiers. He had held them responsible for the miseries of the Maharaja; otherwise, Rabindranath, a spokesman of individualism, had no faith in absolute power. He only wanted to bestow absolute power to his recommended man for the good of the state and to save the Maharaja from the present crisis. Radha Kishore kept Tagore's request and gave absolute power to Ramani Mohan, antagonism against which had spread like wildfire. It was heard that the Maharaja was secretly derided as a puppet in the hands of the minister; Rabindranath was labeled the ringleader.

In such an atmosphere of suspicion and disbelief, the manner of writing letters had also undergone a change. Radha Kishore also started sending his letters through Jatindranath. Rabindranath wrote: 'I have received your letter via the hands of Jati. These few days, I have discussed everyday with Ramani, an elaborate account of which you will get from Jati.'

After laying the conditions to confer absolute power to Ramani as minister, Rabindranath wrote: 'I am informing the Maharaja again that if Ramani is appointed in royal service, the Maharaja will be satisfied and unperturbed by his faithfulness, efficiency, farsightedness and magnanimity. I shall be gratified if I can totally rescue Maharaja from the great danger of all his disguised enemies.'

Rabindranath marked Mahim Chandra as one of the disguised enemies. It seems the Maharaja had a different idea about Mahim Chandra. The Maharaja never had any doubt about his loyalty. Mahim Chandra might have taken wrong decisions for his lack of intelligence but the Maharaja never dreamed that he meant any harm. Though Rabindranath changed his opinion later, he suspected Mahim Chandra during this period and wrote: 'Whenever I discussed with Mahim about the advancement of Tripura, Mahim would start lamenting after mentioning all kinds of insurmountable obstacles. I do not know whether he was aware that one of the obstacles against advancement was his own weakness.'

Rabindranath had also pointed his finger at Mahim Chandra, blaming him as a confidant of Shandiz Sahib's malicious loan idea. Mahim Chandra was a close friend of Rabindranath even before Radha Kishore had come into the picture. Indeed, Rabindranath would send most of his messages to the Maharaja via Mahim Chandra. The letters for assistance were also written to Mahim Chandra so that he could take up the matter with the Maharaja to do the necessary. Mahim Chandra was very respectful towards Rabindranath throughout his life and tried to help him whenever he could. From the days of Maharaja Bir Chandra, the talented Mahim Chandra devoted himself faithfully to the welfare of the state. The faith of Maharaja Radha Kishore in Mahim Chandra influenced Rabindranath to some extent. The Maharaja also wanted to put an end to this misunderstanding between the two. Let me repeat what Rabindranath once categorically admitted: 'He (Radha Kishore) had an extraordinary ability to understand a person. I am astonished at seeing it.' Now it was the time of repentance. To get rid of unbearable anguish, Rabindranath wrote a letter dated 1 August 1905 to Radha Kishore:

> Although doubt had crept into my mind again and again about the mean-mindedness and the weakness of Mahim Chandra, I didn't leave him as a friend... As it was an extreme act of breach of trust on my part, I am suffering punishment for that from the Almighty. Hence, I would request Maharaja to kindly show this letter to Mahim. Had I had respite, I would have someday or other clearly expressed my apprehensions before Mahim, but I didn't get such an opportunity.

The Maharaja's wisdom ultimately settled the relationship between Rabindranath and Mahim Chandra. In the later stage, the bond of friendship was doubled as would be evident from the letter dated 10 February 1906; but before that, it is necessary to bring to light the background of it. After the death of his wife and daughter, Rabindranath wanted to renounce the world. The poems of *Kheya* written in this period echo a profoundly spiritual feeling. His turn toward spirituality is quite clearly reflected in the letter he wrote to Mahim Chandra:

> I did apply my mind very specifically to Tripura. It became more and more a matter of my desire to improve the administrative system of Tripura. For this, I dealt with a lot of needless anxiety and pain. But I have understood that this sort of attachment is not worth paying for. God did not give me alone the responsibility

to purify everything—he will do his job ... there is no point scourging myself with thoughts about the result... I should only keep my mind wide open. The Maharaja had done too much good to me, I love him from the bottom of my heart—I have tried for his well-being all that was within my ability. Maybe I was wrong. Maybe my attempt to do good resulted in greater harm ... I am earnestly praying to God to release me from all my self-created burdens; whatever burden he places on me, I shall bear it without any trouble of mind—I shall not go beyond my right to be caught in a net.

In this letter, Rabindranath expressed his grief in a spiritual tone. He wanted to strike back against those who accused him of selfishness in the political arena of Tripura; he was eager to make it clear that the welfare of Tripura was his sole object and that he was not motivated by self-interest. Saying that he would engage himself only with a God-given task and not like to be a target of criticism, he reminded everyone that he was committed to his mission. In this instance, Rabindranath revealed the strength of his character by highlighting the importance of his duty.

In the meantime, the Maharaja again invited the poet to Agartala. The Maharaja desired Rabindranath to be present at a durbar on the occasion of Ramani Mohan assuming his ministerial post. Rabindranath started his journey to Agartala on 6 November 1905. Four days later, Ramani Mohan was installed as minister by a proclamation announced at the royal durbar. This time, Rabindranath was not alone; he had Jagadindranath, the Maharaja of Nator with him. Rabindranath, for the first time in his life had to wear the dress of the durbar. While setting the turban, Maharaja Kumar Brajendra Kishore made a small mistake. In this context, Brajendra Kishore said in his reminiscence:

After he wore churidar pyjama (salwar for men plaited at the fringes) and achkan (a kind of long coat of Persian origin), I could not touch his head to tie the turban. Being amused, he sat on a chair with a sweet smile. I then tied the turban with pleasure. How funny! The way I used to fasten the turban on my head didn't work—what happened was just the reverse. Where the left ear goes below the turban, the right ear had gone in its place. This was called the left turban.

Rabindranath did not allow any further opportunity to Brajendra Kishore to rectify the mistake. In the dress of a king with turban, achkan, churidar pyjama, nagra shoes and sword in a waistband, Rabindranath sat on a special chair, lighting up the whole durbar with his charismatic glow. Unfortunately, no photograph of his in this royal dress could be found.

What did the poet see after coming to Tripura? 'I have seen that partisanship has become very acute there—in this condition, it is not possible for any party to stand for Maharaja ... Each party's top priority is to foil the other party and gain strength for one's own party; as such, it is inevitable that the Maharaja will come to harm.'

Having firsthand experience of the chaotic conditions of Tripura, the poet did not hesitate to give advice: 'At present, it is absolutely necessary for the Maharaja to have a self-sacrificing, educated and efficient person as his minister—someone who has no connection with local factionalism.'

Even after the appointment of Ramani Mohan as minister, Rabindranath remained anxious. He was writing letters one after another to keep himself abreast of the latest affairs in Tripura. Though he was deeply involved in his writings and charitable works, he didn't ever forget Tripura. For the problems that arose after the appointment of Ramani Mohan, Radha Kishore again invited Rabindranath to

Agartala to work out solutions for the same. Despite the antagonism of the courtiers and the anguish they caused him, Rabindranath did not shirk from his duties. Thinking about the political turmoil in Tripura, he was in two minds whether to go or not. After careful consideration, he wrote a letter to Mahim Chandra:

> In the newspaper *Arun*, grave discussions have been reported about the present royal administration. Meanwhile, if I put my hand to any kind of affair relating to Tripura, I would no doubt become a subject of discussion. I don't care if something good or bad is written about me in the newspapers and so I have nothing to be worried about myself. I would request you all to consider whether any harm will be caused if my association with the royal duties in person is specifically discussed in the papers. You will be disliked by many people in the process of the reformation of the work culture. At convenient times, all these people may use my name in such a manner that you all will become suspects before the new authority. You are aware of the temper of your government and, therefore, after discussing my letter with the Maharaja, if you write to me with instructions, I shall be ready to execute them accordingly. If my going to Agartala is considered appropriate, I will be able to start after the departure of Rathi and others to America. They are leaving very soon.

From this letter, it appeared that Rabindranath was conflicted with himself. He was caught in two minds. Having involved himself in state politics, he did not think of its consequences; he was much more worried about the welfare of the Maharaja and his state. He then wrote asking him whether it would be proper for him to go to Agartala at this time because his presence there might complicate things further. He would be the last person to embarrass the

Maharaja at any point of time. He even cautioned Mahim Chandra to be on guard and to not allow opportunists to take advantage of the situation and cast him as a suspect in the eyes of the Maharaja.

In April 1905, Rabindranath was supposed to go to Barisal to preside over a literary function to be conducted by the Bangiya Pradeshik Sammelan. He came to Agartala for a couple of days on his way to Barisal.

After arriving in Agartala, he was entangled in so many problems that he wrote an exasperated letter on 8 April to Monoranjan Chattopadhyay: 'I've been recently detained at Agartala. I shall have to go to Barisal. After that, I'm supposed to go to Chatgaon, but my mind is revolting. I feel like going to Bolpur and diving deep into complete effortlessness. Saturn is causing my turnabout; the sun cannot vie with it.'

During this visit, there was no chance for a respite. The newly posted minister had submitted the annual budget of revenue and expenditure to the Maharaja for his consideration. The Maharaja informed Ramani Mohan that he would offer his comments after discussing the matter with Rabindranath. Rabindranath did not agree with a few of the basic principles in forming the budget. So, he submitted a 'humble petition to the Maharaja about certain principles before an elaborate discussion on the budget.' The opinion that he had given in favour of unitary administration in his recent writings, 'Swadeshi Samaj', and later in 'Deshnayak', was echoed eloquently in this document as well. Keeping in view the criticism of the weekly newspaper *Arun*, he advised to keep the personal and state division separate so that they could operate independently of each other. He wrote:

> There are two natural divisions in the state. One is the Maharaja's personal domain and the other is for the state. If they are not

separate, they may start striking against each other; great harm will be caused on this pretext, and there is every possibility of the growth of malicious conspiracies at the juncture of these two divisions ... Ministers or others should not be given the right to set their hands on the Maharaja's personal field, which includes the domestic affairs division, his own funds, travelling expenses, etc. The personal division should, therefore, be independent of the minister's right; the minister should be in charge of the state division.

Ramani Mohan, being a leader of the freedom movement, prevented the ladies of the inner mahal from accompanying the Maharaja at the time of the prince of England's tour to Calcutta. It created terrible agitation amongst the royal service holders and was covered by *Arun*, which vehemently lodged its protest against the minister's actions in its editorial column. Ramani Mohan was unmoved; he coolly informed the Maharaja the reasons for this kind of an act:

> The reason for my prohibition is that I'm a leader of the freedom movement. I'm against the purdah (curtain) party, which was held at Belvedere. If zenana mahal (ladies of the inner court) came to Calcutta and Maharani Ishwari Mata glorified the party by her presence, it would have led to dishonour, I have, with this intention, therefore, forbidden the Maharaja to bring the zenana mahal along with him.

Rabindranath soon came to know about this incident. He did not approve Ramani Mohan's interference, and so he opined that the minister should not have any right over the Maharaja's personal matters. Applying the theory of economics, he justified why divisions were necessary to run the state administration:

If the boundaries of the Maharaja's personal and state division are fixed, then the minister, being aware of the extent of revenue and strength of his departments, will do the necessary, and those who are sheltered by the Maharaja will turn their greedy eyes away, knowing the fact that state division is not a place for the realization of one's own interest. If the quantity of expenditures of the Maharaja's personal division is fully determined, then, with the balance of the revenue, the minister will repay the debt and carry on the expenses for state administration.

In the other part of the budget note, the poet dedicated his eternal message to the Maharaja for the welfare of Tripura: 'Being self-restrained by one's own rule, and keeping a watch on the welfare of the state befits a king; indeed, it is the duty of a king.'

Ramani Mohan could not guess Radha Kishore's great love for the Bengali language. Bengali had been used in royal administration in Tripura for the last thirteen centuries. The change for the first time from Bengali to English perturbed Radha Kishore so much that he ordered Ramani Mohan:

From time immemorial, Bengali has been used here and different types of initiatives have been taken for the advancement of this language, which I think is especially creditable for a Hindu king of Bengal. I love the Bengali language as my life, and I consider it my only duty to try to uplift the language day by day. Keep a sharp lookout on this matter—so that the purpose and system of this state cannot be foiled by the English educated officials.

Even before that, Radha Kishore, by an order dated 1.9.18 (year not confirmed) to the then minister Ananda Charan Gupta, stated:

Bengali is the royal language of this state. Government texts are desirable only in Bengali. I've come to know that in some places at this time the English language is being used. Take measures so that such things do not happen. Of course, where use of English is inevitable, it is to be used, such as the "political department". It will not be proper to use English except in this sort of instance, disregarding the language in vogue.

These proclamations substantiated that Bengali was more loved and respected in Tripura than in Bengal. At that time, in British-ruled Bengal, there used to be debates over who was more proficient in English than others. Bengalis would be proud of themselves if they spoke English well. Now consider a non-Bengali king of a native state proudly proclaiming, 'I love the Bengali language as my life.' Even after that, if the Bengali community do not salute Tripura for the advancement of the Bengali language, it will be a clear instance of ingratitude.

After the Poush ceremony at Shantiniketan, Rabindranath had to rush to Calcutta on 23 December 1906 as Radha Kishore was eagerly waiting to meet him there. The Maharaja's crisis had gradually become unmanageable. A loan of 15 lakh rupees to be paid by installments was taken from the Bank of Bengal. It had become extremely difficult to repay the loan after meeting the expenses of the state administration. The total revenue of Tripura and Chakla Roshanabad was only ten to twelve lakh rupees. Rabindranath perceived self-repugnance in the administrative system itself. Sometimes he thought that Radha Kishore's excess of goodness was responsible for their failure to overcome the crisis. Even a long discussion with the Maharaja at the Park Street house could not satisfy him. Rabindranath, who was in favour of a unitary system of government, wanted to give absolute power and full freedom to

Ramani Mohan to run the administration, but now he was struck with wonder hearing that the root cause of the agitation was due to this handover of absolute power. The agitators gave a proposal for the government to be run by a council. The grudge that was created in the state could be measured from the discussion in *Banga Bhasha* magazine, edited by Maharaja Kumar Surendra Chandra Deb Barma:

> The worst result of running the state's administration by others (and not by the sons of the soil) is that we become downright ignorant about what relation we have with our own country and what relation we should establish in the future ... Due to the lack of opportunities, we are unable to work compassionately for our own country. Even we are afraid of and hesitant to say something about our country lest we are to become rebels or laughing stocks.

Hearing all these news, an infuriated Rabindranath wrote a long letter to the Maharaja before his departure to Shantiniketan:

> The Maharaja has by his constant indulgence increased their strength ... whereas slowly and steadily he should've reduced that strength and liberated himself from the network of these selfish characters; should he put the responsibility of running the state administration in their hands and further strengthen their powers of destruction?

There was another proposal to appoint C.W. McMinn, the retired commissioner of Chattogram division, as the manager of Chakla Roshanabad. Rabindranath vehemently objected to this proposal.

Knowing that the Maharaja was considering the appointment of a legislative council, Rabindranath expressed his disapproval in the same letter:

Nowhere is work said to be done by the council. Keeping the council as an advisory body, one leader does all the work. In that case, the members of the council are bound to obey the leader. Otherwise, there would be no end of shrewd conspiracy, mutual antagonism and disorderliness. Does the Maharaja have real respect for the present courtiers? Do they have the capacity to shoulder such an enormous responsibility? Would the Maharaja surrender his well-being in their hands?

An anxious poet concluded his letter thus: '... I'm praying to God; may He rescue us—He happened to make my relationship with the Maharaja; I have no excuse if I fail in my ability to do good for this relationship ...'

In the conclusion, he wrote: 'God's will shall prevail; I'm indebted to the Maharaja's love and affection. May God bless the Maharaja.'

In fact, one has to judge both the poet and the king in their proper perspective, putting them in their respective position and looking at them as an unprejudiced witness. The poet, being overly enthusiastic, thought that those who were creating disturbances in the state should be sacked from service. Moreover, the poet held the Maharaja responsible for the disorderliness as, in his opinion, the Maharaja's indulgence led to this chaos, which could have been avoided if he had been strict in his dealings. Obliquely, then, the poet had marked the Maharaja as a weak man. As the poet wanted to see Tripura become an ideal state, he was intolerant towards anything that would hinder its progress. On the other hand, think of the miserable plight of Maharaja Radha Kishore Manikya! None but the sufferer knows his trouble. After all, he had to carry on with his own countrymen, live with them, share with them every bit of his life. If their emotion was not given due importance or respect, the country would end up in the doldrums. It was not possible for him to do something that might hurt their sentiments and lead to an insurgency. In such a precarious situation, where the state was being run by the outsiders and the sons of the soil had no say in governance, no one could be blamed if they felt their self-esteem was being compromised. There was nothing wrong in their expectation that they would run their own government, and none from outside Tripura should be allowed to hold absolute power to rule over them. They raised certain questions, such as: who would demand and pursue the welfare of Tripura—Tripuris or outsiders? The people of Tripura did not at all like the idea of converting their Maharaja as a 'magnificent cipher.' They wanted to revere the Maharaja as an all-powerful sovereign head having everything under his command and control. A minister, an outsider enjoying absolute power that was the king's own, was not tolerated by the people as they deemed it a great insult to the Maharaja. Radha Kishore had no answers to their queries. If it was said that the sons of the soil were incapable of running the administration, it might have created a turmoil. To minimize all these factors, Radha Kishore kept everyone in good humour. In their own way, both the poet and the king were right, but the sufferer and the witness was Maharaja Radha Kishore, and not Rabindranath, as the former remained in the thick of the action.

Ramani Mohan went back to Calcutta on six months leave before the completion of his tenure of two years. On 19 March 1907, the following piece of news was published in the *Bengali* newspaper: 'We understand that Mr Ramani Mohan Chatterjee, MA, is to be joint secretary of the Bengal Technical Institute with Dr Nilratan Sircar and B.L. Chowdhury.' In place of Ramani Mohan, Rai Bahadur Umakanta Das was appointed. Rabindranath had no hand in Umakanta's appointment. It was not known whether he tried to persuade Ramani Mohan to return to Tripura, but his intention not to desist from doing good for Tripura was reflected in his letter dated 20.03.1907, written to Mahim Chandra:

> My relationship with this state is religiously fixed. As much as I wish, I can't make my mind indifferent towards it. Sometimes, I feel like going away for good from all of your company, the reason being that the climatic surroundings of every Maharaja are such that the king is always surrounded by conspiracy. But I don't know why God has brought me here; I have a bond with the Maharaja. At present, I don't see any possibility of my doing something good for the Maharaja—I've got no ability, time and opportunity. My earnest request to all of you is that for your certain weakness, don't be weak in doing good for your country.

Somendra Chandra (he had an M.A. degree from Harvard University), son of Mahim Chandra, was one of the students who came from Tripura to study at Shantiniketan. He was a true disciple of Gurudev Rabindranath till his death. A day before his death, he was at Shantiniketan along with Rabindranath and Maharaja Bir Bikram Manikya. He earned distinction as a high official in Tripura. He died prematurely in a railway accident. The merit of Somendra Chandra attracted the poet's attention. Rabindranath marked him as a pioneer for the welfare of Tripura. He wrote to Mahim Chandra:

> I want to set your son fully free from the nagpash (refers to a mythical missile that could produce snakes that bound the victim) of pomp and grandeur and adorn with human qualities, so that after becoming an adult, he does not get himself bound by prejudices that hinder his duties. I hope, when he will become an adult, that he'll be an asset to your state.

Another prince of Tripura, who was very near and dear to Rabindranath, was Maharaja Kumar Brajendra Kishore. Both Somendra Chandra and Brajendra Kishore held a special place in the poet's heart. They were blessed by him. We will talk about them later.

At that time, Rabindranath was distraught by a lack of funds to run Shantiniketan. He could find no way out. Whatever he might have got, even some paisas, he accepted it as God's gift. The financial condition had become severe even after the annual grant received from the Maharaja. Nobody offered any help. On 16 April 1907, Rabindranath wrote a desperate letter to Jatindranath Basu:

> The first issue (*Bichitra Prabandha*) of my prose book has already been printed. I've given the copyright of this book especially to Bolpur. If some books are sold, it will lessen a bit of my burden. It will be a help to me if you can persuade the Maharaja to buy some portions of this book. Whatever number of books you think is possible for him (Maharaja) to purchase, take them from Jadunath Chattopadhyay or Shailen (Shaliesh) at a time and give one hardcover book to the Maharaja as my gift. Try to sell the books to someone known to you. At present, running the school has become very difficult.

Jatindranath Basu could not take the books along with him while returning to Tripura but, immediately after he reached, the books were sent to him, and it was found that the Maharaja had paid 125 rupees as the price for a hundred copies of this book. From this, it is once again proven that whenever Rabindranath was in difficulty, his last resort was always Maharaja Radha Kishore. Radha Kishore, without fail, continuously provided financial help to Rabindranath either directly or indirectly.

Rabindranath's eagerness though was dampened a bit by the antagonism of the courtiers and the Maharaja's inability to strictly deal with the issues of governance, Rabindranath always sought shelter with Maharaja Radha Kishore in times of necessity. And despite having a burden of debt to the extent of 15 lakh rupees, the Maharaja's assistance to Rabindranath continued without cease.

Rabindranath had a very affectionate relationship with prince Brajendra Kishore. Brajendra Kishore was then appointed as a personal secretary to the Maharaja. However, Rabindranath at that time was not showing any active interest in the internal matters of Tripura, but he used to get all his information through his correspondences with Brajendra Kishore. He did not at all hesitate to write a letter dated 14 April 1908 to Brajendra Kishore, recommending the name of Anukul Chandra Roy for the post of justice in Tripura. After the recommendation, he wrote: 'Today is New Year's Day. God has widened your field of activities. I bless you; He will awaken your strength and make you overcome all opposition.'

It did not escape notice that so many people were appointed in service of Tripura on Rabindranath's recommendation. But in Bengal, his recommendations never had the same effect. He recommended the name of Professor Bogdanov for the post of the Persian-language professor in Calcutta University to the then vice chancellor Jadunath Sarkar. The poet used to send people to Calcutta University with his recommendations. Likewise, he sent Syed Mujtaba Ali to Shyama Prasad Mukherjee. Neither Bogdanov nor Syed Mujtaba Ali got a position. But in Tripura, the poet's desire was never dashed; it was always fulfilled. It showed how much respect he used to command in Tripura.

The burden of the kingdom had become too heavy for him to carry. Radha Kishore wanted desperately to get rid of this burden.

Therefore, he appointed his sons as probationers to learn how to run the administration. He employed prince Birendra Kishore in the charge of the revenue and political departments, and prince Brajendra Kishore was given the charge of the police, military, personal funds and the administrative functions of private secretaries. A devoted Vaishnavite, Radha Kishore set out on a pilgrimage to set himself free from the mundane problems of the kingdom. Who knew it would be his last journey! While going to Sarnath from Kashi, he met with a car accident on his way and was seriously injured; he passed away on 12 March 1909.

How distressed Rabindranath was by the pangs of separation from his bosom friend was not known, but there was no doubt that he was indeed grief-stricken. In the later period, Rabindranath, on many occasions offered his respect to Radha Kishore, remembering his friendship and magnanimity; but, for the present, he looked at this death in a philosophical way. In his speech on '*Mrityo O Amrita*' ('death and nectar') at Shantiniketan on 17 March 1909, he spoke thus: 'Very recently, and suddenly, my friend passed away ... I've been reintroduced to death again...'

I have already mentioned earlier that the Maharajas and the royal family of Tripura were not only patrons but also players in the field of art and literature. Maharaja Radha Kishore's love for the Bengali language has also been discussed at length. His contribution to the advancement of Bengali was unparallel. His reign saw the beginning of the spiritual relationship between Bengal and Tripura. The acquaintance of the Maharaja with the intelligentsia of Bengal, by the grace of Rabindranath, had added a new dimension in the arena of art and culture. Most of the impeccable writings and paintings of the Maharajas, queens, princes and princesses had already been lost due to neglect. Others were in the queue on their way to oblivion. In the art of writing letters, Bir Chandra and Radha Kishore's artistic language and exchange of ideas had earned Rabindranath's adulation. He said, 'The letters of Maharaja Bir Chandra and Radha Kishore, which I have with me, are invaluable assets par excellence. As I go through these letters, one can deduce what kind of high culture they had.'

Right from his childhood, Radha Kishore had nurtured a deep love for Bengali. A magazine named *Barshiki* was published under his editorship in the year 1876 when he was only twenty-one. Radha Kishore was also thoroughly proficient in composing poems. He used to sign them off under the pseudonym of Brindaban Das. He was always found absorbed in discussions on literature with his queen Tulshibati, who was also a great poet. They used to judge each other's poems and compare the artistry of their compositions. Maharani Tulshibati was a learned woman. As far as literary activities were concerned, the king and the queen were made for each other. We may have a glimpse of the sensitivity of Radha Kishore's heart from one of his unique poems—

> Behold the swinging sidelong glance infinite lust falls in drops
> The laughter sprinkles nectar
> The lustre of pearl bursts forth on the teeth
> A mind-blowing flute on the lips as red as bimba fruit.
> Young lad Shyam (Lord Krishna) standing bent
> Captivates the world
> Kalia (Lord Krishna) is the simile of beauty Kalia is beauty's limit
> Brindaban Das narrates.

Maharani Tulshibati was also equal to the task. Her poems written in Brajabuli continue to enchant many readers even today. Here is one of her poems:

All these confidantes dance in delight
Spray coloured powder, red paste and musk over Shyam's body
The body becomes red; Rai-Kanu are perplexed
The crown bends; he plays an enchanting flute
Beholding the amazing incomparable beauty of Rai-Kanu
Tulshibati kisses their crimson feet.

In the reign of Radha Kishore, the collection of rock inscriptions and translations of *Brihannaradiya Purana* in Bengali had started. The re-editing of *Rajmala* had also begun during his reign. Radha Kishore was in favour of freedom of the press. He did not interfere with the independence of the newspapers, despite the fact that newspapers like *Arun*, *Bangabhasha* and *Panchapandi* were often severe in their criticism against his state administrative policies. All the members of the royal family came forward to support India's freedom struggle. Prince Mahendra Kumar Deb Barma was not afraid of singing nationalistic songs in the open. The British government did not take Radha Kishore's patriotism kindly and, therefore, severing 'Maha' from 'Maharaja', they used to address him as 'Raja' in their correspondences.

Radha Kishore issued a proclamation for the advancement of education in every stratum of the state. He gave a grant of 5 rupees per head for each student of the hill areas, but there were still no students available. He even declared an additional reward on and above the pay of the teachers to arouse eagerness for education amongst the hill boys and girls. He had shown special interest in the development of the road and transport infrastructure. In his reign, ten post offices and two telegram offices were established.

As the poetic talent of Rabindranath was not receiving adequate attention and recognition, Maharaja Bir Chandra wanted to publish elegant editions of the poet's compositions by spending more than a lakh of rupees, a plan aborted by his untimely death. For this, Rabindranath was endlessly regretful. Radha Kishore didn't merely help him in poetic works; he helped him in all spheres of life. Let us have a look at how, despite his severe economic distress, Radha Kishore helped Tagore in various ways:

1. Lifetime grants of 25 rupees and 30 rupees for Dinesh Chandra Sen and Hemchandra respectively.
2. Grant of 50 rupees per month for Jyotirindranath's *Sangeet Prabeshika*.
3. Assistance of 50 rupees per month for *Bangadarshan*.
4. Assistance of 60,000 rupees paid in instalments to Jagadish Chandra Bose for his travelling expenses and stay in England.
5. Lifetime grant of 1,000 rupees per year for Brahma Vidyalaya alias Shantiniketan (paid from 1901-1947).
6. Donation of scientific instruments to Brahma Vidayalaya.
7. Donation of scientific instruments for the laboratory of Bengal Technical Institute.
8. Financial help for the construction of a ward in Calcutta's R.G. Kar Medical College.
9. Shelter to painter Sashi Kumar Hesh for several months and financial help at the request of Rabindranath Tagore.
10. Donation of 15,000 rupees to Victoria College, Comilla, and a grant of 500 rupees per year.

If the comparative value of money is calculated based on that period (1901-1902) and the present, one will be stupefied to find that the value of 60,000 rupees paid to Jagadish Chandra comes to more than 6 crores pounds. Along with this, consider the condition of the royal treasury. It was not only empty but also burdened with a huge debt of 15 lakh rupees. Even then, Radha Kishore never disappointed Rabindranath whenever he asked for any financial help. Who knew more than Rabindranath about the pecuniary crisis of Radha Kishore? Still Rabindranath did not hesitate to reach out to his friend for any sort of financial help as and when required, and Radha Kishore always obliged him. This shows Radha Kishore's infinite humane qualities. Bhupendranath Chakraborty, writer of *Rajmala* for children, had rightly evaluated the human qualities of Radha Kishore:

> Sitting in his native state, his mind could have been confined to the enclosure of the series of hills, and the world outside could not have come to know him; but by his own extraordinary talent, he has weaved in one string the thought of the welfare of his native state with that of the welfare of the whole of Bengal … seeing this, one cannot but be amazed.

3

Rabindranath and Maharaja Birendra Kishore Manikya

Birendra Kishore's period of reign: 1909-1923

A devoted soul in music, literature and painting, Birendra Kishore loved solitude right from his childhood. Introspection was his distinguishing attribute. His love for the fine arts created a different world for him. He had no interest or curiosity about the world outside. Birendra Kishore was distinctly different from his brothers and used to spend his time fully absorbed in art and literature. It remains a wonder why, with his artistic interests and practice, he didn't have much connection with Rabindranath! The answer remains elusive. Birendra Kishore never wanted to publicize his art. He loved to stay behind the curtains. Neither was he interested in presenting his paintings to the public. His natural habit of keeping himself aloof did not allow even Rabindranath to come to know about his profound artistic self.

On the other hand, his younger brother Brajendra Kishore was a sociable man, an extrovert. Each member of the royal family harboured a deep passion toward art, literature and culture. Music flowed through their veins—and just a scratch of their pens or brushes birthed poetry and paintings. Brajendra Kishore was a true connoisseur of art and had a deep love for music and literature. His attachment to literature attracted him towards Rabindranath. Whenever Rabindranath came to Tripura, Brajendra Kishore was always found by his side on all occasions. Another matter to be pointed out was that prince Birendra Kishore, in his boyhood, had to abide by certain protocols. He was not supposed to move out anywhere he liked. His movements were restricted by decree. Brajendra Kishore, however, had the opportunity to associate more frequently with Rabindranath. For him, there were no restrictions; eventually, the poet treated Brajendra Kishore like his own son.

It was noticed that from the days of Maharaja Bir Chandra Rabindranath used to express his submissions to the Maharaja through other persons. For this purpose, he would select a faithful spokesman. During the reign of Maharaja Bir Chandra and Radha Kishore Manikya, the spokesman was Mahim Chandra Deb Barma. Later, when Mahim Chandra became a suspect in his eyes, he gave the charge to Jatindranath Basu. And when Birendra Kishore Manikya was on the throne, Brajendra Kishore became his worthy spokesman. Rabindranath wrote a few letters to Maharaja Birendra Kishore but, unfortunately, those have been lost; only two letters are available at present.

As a prince and son of Radha Kishore, he was aware of his father's bonhomie with Rabindranath. He met the poet several times in Calcutta and at Agartala. He was well aware that the poet had helped to mitigate the opposition against his nomination as a prince. It did not even escape his notice that, at the fag-end of Radha Kishore's regime, the courtiers and the people of Tripura harboured a grudge against Rabindranath. He gave full credit to Rabindranath for his education. Teachers like Mokshada Kumar Basu and T.R. Williams were appointed at the recommendation of Rabindranath, men who, like torchbearers, had shown him the illuminated path of knowledge. And it was impossible to get a private secretary like Jatindranath Basu. And Maharaja Birendra Kishore remembered all this with a deep gratitude.

Rabindranath mentioned in his letter dated 8 April 1909, written to Brajendra Kishore, that after the sudden untimely death of Radha Kishore, he wrote a letter of advice to prince Birendra. This letter could not be traced. On 23 April, he advised Brajendra Kishore to maintain good relations with his elder brother and to work together for the welfare of the state:

> In your hardest times, your virtue itself will protect you. *"Shukhang Ba Jadi Ba Dookhang/Priyang Ba Jadi Ba Apriyang/ Praptang Praptamupasita Hridayena Parajita"* (that is, whether in happiness or sorrow, circumstances favourable or unpleasant—always move ahead with an indomitable will in your heart) … you must stand with your heart and soul in favour of the person on whom the burden of governing the state has been bestowed. The welfare of the state means the welfare of all of you. There are many enemies on all sides of the royal throne. At this time, you must protect your new king from all false friendships. At present, you are his closest relative, closer than all the others—the good relationship between you two should never break; if it does, the enemies will avail of this opportunity. They will, no doubt, try in many ways to create dissension between you two. I pray to God that these wicked conspiracies should fail in the days to come; nobody should at any time be able to create suspicion in the king's mind about your loyalty. You should win over all sorts of intrigues by your truthfulness and honesty and apply your strength to the welfare of your state.

The aforementioned shloka was very dear to Rabindranath. He quoted it in many letters. The poet used to gain strength from this *shloka* and from the song *'Bol Dao'* ('Give strength'). Whenever he was stricken with grief, he felt the strength embedded in this *shloka* and dived deep into the sea that lies beyond happiness and sorrow. He applied this *shloka* as a mantra to gain strength and even to relieve others from the pang of sorrows. It was no exception in the case of Brajendra Kishore.

Birendra Kishore was a peace-loving person. He loved to paint in his studio in seclusion, whenever he could save a fraction of time from his royal duties. While engaged in painting, he used to forget his daily routine. Engaging in quarrels meant disturbing his own sense of tranquility. So, he thought it proper to win over his so-called enemies as a part of his duty.

Radha Kishore, in the wheel of events, created many enemies amongst his close relatives. To name a few: Bod Thakur Samarendra Chandra, Nabadwip Chandra, Uncles Chakradhwaj and Nil Krishna, prince Surendra Chandra, along with some of the courtiers. The editor of *Bengali* magazine, Surendranath Bandopadhyay, was also not friendly towards him. Even the grievous untimely death of Radha Kishore failed to draw the sympathy of his magazine. Birendra Kishore, therefore, desiring to end the dispute, had sent Brajendra Kishore as an emissary to Bod Thakur Samarendra Chandra. Touching his feet, Birendra Kishore requested Samarendra Chandra to forget their past disagreements. He asked for his forgiveness. In his attempt to end the family feud, Brajendra Kishore prayed for the blessings of the poet. In reply, the poet wrote a letter dated 26 Chaitra 1315 (1909):

> I earnestly wish that the vow with which you've come to Calcutta should be fulfilled. It's good that you've taken Ashu (Barrister Ashutosh Choudhuri) as a mediator. If this crisis of yours is over,

you'll be able to work emphatically. There will be no hindrance in cleaning the dirt. By any means, even by sustaining a loss, this work should be done.

Rabindranath in his letter wished Brajendra Kishore success. From this letter, it transpires that Rabindranath understood Samarendra Chandra's position, but for the poet, loyalty to the king remained the topmost priority; in the dispute over the succession to the throne, he firmly stood by the side of Radha Kishore.

The most deprived man of them all was Nabadwip Chandra Bahadur, son of the late Ishan Chandra Manikya and father of great musician S.D. Burman. His uncle Maharaja Bir Chandra defrauded him from his legitimate right over the royal throne. Nabadwip Chandra was banished to Comilla, one of the headquarters of Chakla Roshanabad. He never set foot even for a day on the soil of Tripura during the regimes of Maharaja Bir Chandra and Radha Kishore Manikya. This time Birendra Kishore called him with due respect. He prayed humbly to Uncle Nabadwip Chandra to take over the charge of royal minister. The sincerity of the invitation touched Nabadwip's heart. Putting an end to the anger and vanity of all those days, Nabadwip Bahadur returned to Agartala after forty years of banishment.

In case of Samarendra Chandra, the uncle of Maharaja Birendra Kishore, a similar resolution had been reached. With the poet's blessings, Brajendra Kishore went to Samarendra Chandra's house in Calcutta with trepidation. At that time, Rabindranath's brother Jyotirindranath too was there. Seeing Brajendra Kishore, he exclaimed in joy, 'What a joyous day it is—I've witnessed the reconciliation of uncle and nephew.' This had indeed taken place. Birendra Kishore's sincerity was the root cause for this happy situation. Everyone was relieved after the end of the continuous family feud.

Rabindranath intended to be present to settle the dispute with Samarendra Chandra, but wisdom prohibited him from doing so as there might have been criticism of interference in royal duties. Showing immense affection towards Brajendra Kishore, he wrote: 'I will never forget the friendship of your father and grandfather ... After that, from the day I have come to know you, my affection towards you has gradually deepened.'

In the last part of the letter, he wrote: 'I have written a letter to your elder brother giving some advice. Has he received it?' (8 April 1909)

Peace had returned to the family front. Now it was time to solve problems that had arisen in the closing years of Radha Kishore's regime. Constant deliberations with well-wishers of the kingdom were held. Birendra Kishore made it known that he would not like to do anything that might provoke agitation. If difficult conditions prevailed again, they would seek Rabindranath's help. The poet was at that time determined not to interfere in the administration of the state. In fact, at the end of Radha Kishore's reign, the poet was trying to slowly distance himself from state politics. He perceived shadows of conspiracy all around Tripura, about which he wrote in his letters. He did not like being criticized for his willingness to do good for Tripura. His wish was to see Tripura emerge as an ideal state, but he only could find conspiracies all over. He was annoyed at Radha Kishore for not acting against the conspirators, and he termed it as the king's weakness. Over time, he felt that he had made a grave mistake by interfering in the administrative system of Tripura. For that, he did not want to entangle himself with the problems of Tripura any further, though he was certainly an enterprising man. He knew very well that severing the relationship with Tripura for good would be disastrous for Shantiniketan.

When crisis was imminent, sitting idle was not an option the poet chose. Thus, he hinted to Brajendra Kishore that the grant for Brahma Vidyalaya had not yet been received, but there was no result. The pecuniary condition of Shantiniketan was getting graver day by day. The poet therefore took out his pen and wrote a letter directly to Radha Kishore's successor, Birendra Kishore, on 26 August, reminding him that:

> It is not beyond your knowledge that Bolpur Vidyalaya has been receiving annual grants from the late Maharaja. That generosity has saved this school at the time of adversity; my relationship with the late noble person will at no time break away and I shall remember throughout my life his affection towards me. I am writing this letter to know whether we can hope to get that grant of the late Maharaja from your Majesty. We cherish this hope in our hearts that our relationship with Tripura state will not sever.

In the concluding part, he wrote to assure the Maharaja: 'In our school, there is no hint of any political discussion ... The students here never participate in any political meeting or movement.'

The reason for this clarification was obvious: Rabindranath was in real distress at that time. The intelligentsia of Bengal was against the establishment of Shantiniketan and criticized it as being driven by malintent. On the other hand, the British Government was after it to prove that the institution was manufacturing patriots and revolutionaries. The angry look of the government frightened the guardians of the students of Shantiniketan. As a result, most of the students left Shantiniketan, leaving it in dire financial straits. The Directorate of Public Instruction of East Bengal and Assam issued a secret circular in early 1912: 'Shantiniketan, or Brahmacharya Ashram at Bolpur, is a place altogether unsuitable for educating the sons of Government servants. Any connection with the institution in question is likely to prejudice the future of the boys who remain pupils of it after the issue of the present warning.'

It is to be noted that Maharaja Birendra Kishore did not pay any heed to the British Government's attitude and, in 1912, sent the maximum number of students (forty-three) to Shantiniketan with scholarships in order to help Rabindranath overcome the difficult pecuniary situation.

Even this letter did not hasten the grant. In fact, at that time, the preparation for the coronation ceremony of Birendra Kishore was in progress. The renewal of any grant could be made effective only by the stamped impression of the new king. Rabindra nath waited with dwindling patience for two weeks, then wrote a letter on 12 September to Brajendra Kishore: 'Don't bother at all for the grant of the school. Consider it whenever it is convenient for you—don't be in haste. I'll be unperturbed if I get the news that discipline and peace have been established in the royal administration.'

A reading of this letter reveals that Rabindranath wanted to know from Brajendra Kishore the reason for the delay in getting the grant for Shantiniketan. Most likely, in his reply, Brajendra Kishore enlightened him about the royal rules and regulations.

The language of these two letters was so well phrased that an endeavour to create pressure could only be implicity apprehended. It was like his poems that often create the possibilities of multiple meanings, such as *'Dekhilam, Nahi Dekhilam Ki Tahatey Achhe Lekha'* ('I saw, yet I didn't see what was written on it'). Rabindranath's artful use of language created among his readers a sense of awe and bewilderment.

Rabindranath had a few landed estates in the district of Rajshahi. After his son Rathindranath returned from abroad, he had to undertake a very long journey by river to acquaint the future zamindar with his subjects. At Patisar, he got the invitation letter for Birendra Kishore's coronation. Radha Kishore, as mentioned earlier, had passed away on 12 March 1909. The coronation ceremony of Birendra Kishore was held on 25 November. Both Birendra Kishore and Brajendra Kishore invited Rabindranath separately to attend the ceremony. In reply, Rabindranath wrote to Birendra Kishore on 22 November: 'As I've been out at sea for a while, the cordial invitation of the Maharaja reached me rather late. Recently, I've been engaged in such property matters that it'll be impossible for me to attend the Maharaja's coronation ceremony. I'm a friend of the Maharaja's father and I earnestly pray for the welfare of Tripura.'

Now let us go back to the past. Most probably, Birendra Kishore was acquainted with Rabindranath in the year 1904. The play *Bisharjan* was staged at the felicitation ceremony of Maharaja Radha Kishore, organized by Bharat Sangeet Samaj. Birendra Kishore was awestruck at witnessing the performance of Rabindranath in the role of Raghupati. He was dumfounded by the poet's many talents. From that day, Birendra Kishore became an utter devotee of Rabindranath. He was so inspired by the poet that, after coming back to Agartala, he expressed his desire to have this play staged in the royal palace. The first dramatic performance was held in the royal palace's Bir Chandra Library. Some changes were made in the library house to make it suitable for a dramatic performance. The outfits and ornaments for the female characters were supplied by the inner mahal. The bodies of the female characters were sparkling with real gold, jewels, diamonds and pearls. After that, *Bisharjan* was staged several times in Ujjayanta Rajprasad. Rabindranath's place was installed permanently in the devoted soul of Birendra Kishore.

In the history of Bengali poetics, the name of Ananga Mohini Devi is written in golden letters as one of the first female poets. The daughter of Maharaja Bir Chandra and the aunt of Birendra Kishore, she gifted Rabindranath her two books of verses, *Shokagatha* and *Kanika*. Her third book, *Priti*, was not published then. Among the female poets of Bengal, she occupied a special place for her poetical compositions.

In the poem '*Chirasmriti*' of *Shokagatha*, Anangamohini Devi's doleful grief for the imminent death-agony of her husband had been depicted in right earnest:

> Day and night, ever in this heart strikes
> Only that sorrowful last memory.
> The sad farewell kiss once and for all
> Weary of pain in that pale face.
> Nonplussed with grief, we hold hand in hand
> The tearful glow-less eyes look here and there.
> In the whole of my life, from morn to eve
> Only that streak of last memory shines in this heart.

After receiving the two books, Rabindranath wrote a letter dated 17 Shaon 1318 (1911) to Anangamohini Devi:

> I am glad to have been gifted your compositions, *Shokagatha* and *Kanika*. In your poems, I perceive a sort of natural poetic imagination. Their beauty is candid and graceful—nonetheless, the artistic skill is natural to you. This skill has blossomed in your last book of verses ... I pray, in your poetic genius, all your sorrows and grief has become especially poignant and significant.

In this letter, the poet mentioned Bir Chandra's affection and his own friendship with Radha Kishore. In just a few words, he had beautifully analyzed the poetic genius of Ananga Mohini Devi. When female education all over the country was rather primitive, at that very time, Ananga Mohini Devi, though not conventionally educated, served as a shining example of female artistry.

Birendra Kishore was an artist. As he was perennially engaged in royal duties, his artistic practice was obstructed. He wanted a good man as a minister so he could devote time for his creative pursuits. The installments for the repayment of the 15-lakh-rupee loan taken from the Bank of Bengal were being paid regularly. There was no perceptible discontent among the courtiers. At this time, he would be relieved if an efficient minister took over the charge of the state. Uncle Nabadwip Chandra was neck-deep in managing the personal and state divisions. He was all set to retire because of his old age. Brajendra Kishore was told to write a letter to Rabindranath praying for his help in the appointment of a minister. Brajendra Kishore went to Calcutta to meet Rabindranath. After coming to Calcutta forthwith, the poet came to know that Brajendra Kishore had an interview with Ramani Mohan Chattopadhyaya in the meantime and requested him to take over the ministerial role. Ramani Mohan modestly informed him that it would not be possible to leave the job of Deputy Chairman of the Calcutta Municipality and accept the post in Tripura. The poet took Brajendra Kishore along with him to meet Sri K.G. Gupta, who had retired from the state of Baroda. K.G. Gupta also declared his incapacity for the role and asked to be excused. Nobody could be appointed as minister. Rabindranath told Brajendra Kishore with a gentle smile, 'Your father had dragged me from poetics into politics; I therefore can't ignore your call.'

In the year 1912, Rabindranath went to America. A proficient student at Shantiniketan, Somendra Chandra (son of Mahim Chandra Deb Barma) was getting ready for higher education. Rabindranath requested the Maharaja to send Somendra Chandra for higher education to America with a grant. He also assured the Maharaja that he himself would make all the arrangements. The

Maharaja gave due importance to the poet's eagerness and agreed to bear all the expenses relating to Somendra Chandra's education in America. Somendra Chandra passed his MA creditably from Harvard University and was appointed as a high official in Tripura.

At the time of going to America, Somendra Chandra suffered from seasickness due to the turbulent ocean. From the ship named *City of Glasgow*, Rabindranath wrote a letter to his daughter Meera Devi delineating Somendra Chandra's condition in a humorous way: 'Saying off and on that he is feeling dizzy, Somendra has been flat on his back in his cabin, asleep for twenty-four hours ... He's eating in the royal style, lying on the bed ... I've never even seen the Maharaja of Tripura himself resting like this.'

During this journey, Rabindranath was engaged in discussions with renowned geniuses like William Rothenstein, Stopford Brooke, H.G. Wells, Yeats, Russell, Fox Strangways, Ernest Rhys, Upton Sinclair, Sturge Moore, Ezra Pound, C.P. Andrews and A.C. Bradley, among others. Somendra was fortunate enough to be acquainted with those great personalities as he was there with Rabindranath. Somendra Chandra was a constant companion of Rabindranath and a witness of all that was happening in Europe at the time. His unique reminiscence of this 'nobel' journey was published in the *Bichitra* magazine with the title *Rabindra Sangamey Europe Prabahser Smritikatha*. He stated that, while in Paris for a few days, Rabindranath met the intelligentsia of France, and the Swedish orientalist Professor Esaias Henrik Wilhelm Tagner, who knew Bengali and played a vital role in his getting the Nobel Prize.

The famous artist William Rothenstein was at Shantiniketan in 1910-11. The prose translation of *Gitanjali* (Song Offerings) was started in 1909. The encouragement and inspiration of Rothenstein had motivated an otherwise hesitant Rabindranath to translate the songs into English. After his arrival in London, Rabindranath made it a point to meet Rothenstein immediately, who had urged him to visit England with the English version of *Gitanjali*. Rothenstein wrote about this meeting in his autobiography:

> At last, he (Rabindranath) arrived, accompanied by two friends (Kedarnath and Somendra) and his son. As he entered the room, he handed me a notebook in which, since I wished to know more of his poetry, he made some translations during his passage from India ... That evening, I read the poems. Here was poetry of a new order, which seemed to me on a level with that of the great mystics.

Rabindranath was quite hesitant to translate his poems from Bengali to English. He was not that confident and, therefore, got his poems translated by Ajit Chakraborty, Kumar Swamy, Rabi Dutta and Loken Palit. From Somendra Chandra's reminiscence, we learn that the poet was thoroughly busy on his way to London, absorbed in translating the poems of *Gitanjali* into English in a small notebook that he carried in his pocket right from the start of the journey in India. The poet also had in his hand some of the translations of Ajit Chakraborty and Kumar Swamy. Somendra Chandra wrote:

> All these translations were not to his liking and, therefore, the poet himself had started translating some of the poems of *Gitanjali*. I saw Rabindranath totally absorbed in translating *Gitanjali* while on road, rail or ship. The way a mother adorns a child in different ornaments and attains an ecstatic state in her own joy, so was he wholly absorbed in his own happiness after decking his own poems with alien dresses. He was hesitant to show or read them out to anyone ... During our conversation, he used to say, "I am floating as if in the great flourish of a new

creation, but I know not whether these kinds of writings will be after one's own heart. It is especially doubtful whether this trend of thought will create any waves in European literature. Rather, it is better to end this futile effort." But the writings went on increasing in volume. Off and on he used to read out the translations at noon or after dinner.

This time, Rabindranath came prepared with the intention to showcase his poetic talents before the intellectuals of Europe. Rothenstein gave the typed copies of *Gitanjali* to W.B. Yeats, Stopford Brooke and Andrew Cecil Bradley. A second meeting was held at Rothenstein's house on 7 July 1912. It was attended by May Sinclair, Ernest Rhys, Fox Strangways, Charles Trevelyan, Ezra Pound, Alice Maynell, Henry Nevinson and C.P. Andrews, to name a few. Yeats recited the poems with great emotion. Rathindranath wrote about the ambience as an 'almost painful silence that followed the recitation ...' C.P. Andrews, full of wonder, spent the whole night roaming around under the open sky. He wrote: 'I remember how immeasurably happy I was that night as I went away. The new wine of Rabindranath's poetry had intoxicated me. The recital that I heard that evening was the full measure, pure and undiluted.' Not only Andrews: others were also wonderstruck by the genius of Rabindranath. This meeting had put a permanent seal of recognition on Rabindranath's divine talent. Let me quote the impressions of some of the great personalities who attended the session that evening:

> I know of no man in my time that has done anything in the English language to equal these lyrics. Even as I read them, in these literal prose translations, they are as exquisite in style as in thought. I have carried the manuscript of these translations about with me for days, reading it in railway trains or on the top

of the omnibuses and in restaurants, and I have often had to close it lest some stranger would see how much it moved me. —W. B. Yeats

[...] I have read them with more than admiration, with great gratitude, for their spiritual help and for the joy they bring and confirm, and for the love of beauty which they deepen far more than I can tell. I wish I were worthy of them. —Stopford Brooke

It looks as though we have at last a great poet amongst us again. —A. C. Bradley

In this context, it was anticipated that something extraordinary was going to happen in the life of Rabindranath. And it did. Fellows of the Royal Society of Literature of the United Kingdom had already recommended the name of Thomas Hardy for the Nobel Prize. But a Fellow of the same Society, Mr. Sturge Moore, who was captivated by the talents of Rabindranath, sent a separate proposal recommending his name for the Nobel Prize. The letter was very simple, but it evoked tremendous interest amongst the members of the Nobel Committee.

NO. 17 Rabindra Nath Tagore

To
The Secretary of Nobel Committee of the Swedish Academy, Stockholm

Sir,
As a Fellow of the Royal Society of Literature of the United Kingdom, I have the honour to propose the name of Rabindra

Nath Tagore as a person qualified, in my opinion, to be awarded the Nobel Prize in Literature.

T. Sturge Moore

The Nobel Committee, under the chairmanship of Herald Hjarne, did not recommend the name of Rabindranath Tagore. Twenty-eight names in total were proposed for the Nobel Prize from various countries. Noteworthy among them were Benito Perez Galdos (Spain), Carl Spitteler (Switzerland), Grazia Deledda (Italy), Ernest Lavisse, Anatole France and Pierre Loti ((France). A Fellow of the Nobel Committee, Mr P. Hallstrom, was given the charge to report on the viability of the proposal for the Nobel Prize to be awarded to Rabindranath. He submitted a long report quoting several of Tagore's poems and concluded as under: 'It is certain, however, that no poet in Europe since the death of Goethe in 1832 can rival Tagore in noble humanity, in unaffected greatness, in classical tranquility.'

The next chairman of the Nobel Committee, Per Hallstrom, also submitted a report that made no impact on Herald Hjarne, who was unwilling to commit and expressed the opinion, 'It must be difficult to decide how much in Tagore's enchanting poetry was his own personal creation and how much must be attributed to the classical traditions of Indian literature.' Even the opinion of orientalist philosopher Esaias Henrik Wilhelm Tagner (Fellow of the Swedish Academy) could not sway him. When the decision of the Nobel Committee was placed before the Swedish Academy for consideration, the great poet of Sweden, Carl Gustaf Verner von Heidenstan, who had become a Fellow of Swedish Academy only a year earlier, came out in open support of Rabindranath. However, as luck would have it, the writing of Heidenstam and the report of Hallstrom worked in favour of Rabindranath despite Chairman Hjarne's opposition. The Fellows of the Swedish Academy were greatly influenced by them and voted in favour of Tagore. Gunnar Ahlstrom wrote in this context: 'More and more of the Academicians began to read *Gitanjali* and gradually succumbed to the charm of these rhythmic ideas. Then the unexpected happened. The committee's recommendation on behalf of Emile Faguet was rejected by a decision of the Academy in pleno. Of the thirteen who voted on November 13, twelve were in favour of Rabindranath Tagore.'

All's well that ends well. But that was not the fate of Rabindranath. As much as he received a glorious tribute worldwide, there was also criticism. Of all people, W.B. Yeats, who greatly helped Rabindranath's recognition across Europe, stood against him after the announcement, claiming that he had 'left out sentence after sentence' of Tagore's prose translation of *Gitanjali*. While reciting the poems of *Gitanjali* in front of intellectuals in Europe, Yeats was effusive in his praise, saying that, 'Even as I read them, in these literal prose translations, they are as exquisite in style as in thought.' Why, then, did he do a 180? In a letter to Kshitimohan Sen, Rabindranath wrote: 'Last night I had dinner with the poet Yeats. He read some of the prose translation of my poems ... I had no faith at all in my own English. He said, "Whoever thinks that the prose translation (of *Gitanjali*) can be further improved, does not know anything of literature."'

The allegation of W.B. Yeats after Tagore's receipt of the Nobel Prize was very dangerous. It challenged the very existence of *Gitanjali* as Tagore's own. But it was proved totally wrong and frivolous and therefore, nullified by one and all. Rabindranath, in his letter dated 4 April 1915, written to Rothenstein, talked about his method of translation and also about Yeats's claim that *Gitanjali* was rewritten by him:

> My translations are frankly prose—my aim is to make them simple with just a suggestion of rhythm to give them a touch of

the lyric, avoiding all archaisms and poetic conventions... I think Yeats was sparing in his suggestions—moreover, I was with him during the revisions ... Though you have the first draft of my translations with you, I have unfortunately allowed the revised typed pages to get lost, in which Yeats penciled his corrections.

Now let me quote the comments of none other than Ernest Rhys, who was greatly involved in this matter:

It has been rumoured by skeptical critics in India that *Gitanjali* was in the process indebted to an English ghost; and the name of Mr. W. B. Yeats has been particularly associated with his mysterious office, thanks, it may be, to his known uncanny powers. It may be as well to say, then, that the small manuscript book, in which the author made these new English versions when he was on his way here in 1912, is still in the possession of Mr. William Rothenstein; and anyone who takes the trouble to compare the pocket book with printed text will find that the variations are slight, while in certain instances the printed reading may be criticized as not an improvement on those in the manuscript.

The handwritten manuscript of *Gitanjali*, which Rabindranath had handed over to Rothenstein, is kept preserved in Harvard University's Houghton Library. Professor Sourindra Mitra in his book *Khyati Akhyatir Nepathye* has shown with mathematical precision the changes made in the original manuscript. It is found that out of the 83 poems containing 10,000 words, changes have been made in 45 words only and out of 500 sentences, a slight touch of change has been observed in 43 sentences (partly and not wholly). It is, therefore, proved beyond doubt that the allegation levelled by

Yeats was baseless and thrown into the open out of sheer jealousy. Ernest Rhys had rightly pointed out the falsity of Yeats' allegation. We Indians are proud that Rabindranath emerged spotless from this intellectual brawl.

Ezra Pound wrote a beautiful analytical review of *Gitanjali* on March 1913 stating: 'The poems do not seem to have been produced by storm or by ignition but seem to show the normal habit of his mind. He is at one with nature and finds no contradictions. And this is in sharp contrast with the Western mode.' He further added, 'So many people say that *Gitanjali* is based on the subjects taken from the ancient books of India' noting how the common cultural heritage of India had inspired Tagore and his creative pursuits.

Rabindranath also had to face criticism from his fellow writers. Rothenstein's stay at Shantiniketan gave him an edge to judge the character of Bengalis. He observed how the Bengali community is mortified by another's good fortune or wealth. He wrote: 'I wonder whether Bengal will realize what your simple visit has done for its history.' Rothenstein was right. The way Dwijendralal Roy vented his fury after Rabindranath was awarded the Nobel Prize was not only shameful but also a blot on the history of Bengali literature. He wrote a satire (drama) named *Ananda Biday* to ridicule Rabindranath. People like Sajanikanta Das, Suresh Samajpati, Bhuban Vidyarnava and Panchkari Bandopadhyay also joined the band of Dwijendralal Roy.

After spending many days in foreign lands, Rabindranath came back to India well aware of Sturge Moore's move to raise a proposal to award him the Nobel Prize. In England this time he was honoured in many respects. Indians are always hesitant to honour their fellow countrymen if he is not honored by the West. This is an absolute truth about the Indian character. A great hubbub, therefore, surrounded Rabindranath after he returned. To flee from the noxious fumes of fame, the poet domiciled himself at Shantiniketan and wrote a letter on 12 October 1913 to Somendra Chandra, who was staying in America:

> After my spell abroad, I have come back again to the Ashram. What a relief! I have received a series of felicitations and honours in my country and abroad, but they are nothing like the peace and light of the open sky here. Holidays are underway now in school. All the boys have gone home; only the boys of the entrance class and some of the old students are staying here. I have taken shelter here in seclusion ... But I have heard that, after the vacation, in the month of November, that they are planning to make a splendid arrangement for felicitations in the Town Hall, where I would be dressed up as a clown. Therefore, I must leave Bangladesh and go somewhere else for a few days before November.

But no such felicitation was given to Rabindranath by his countrymen after he returned from abroad.

Is it possible to flee from the light that fame brings? Had the poet previously ever thought of the peak of fame he would ascend in the year 1913? In a meeting of the syndicate of Calcutta University, it was decided that Rabindranath would be given an honourary Doctorate in Literature. Fortunately, this decision was taken a fortnight before Tagore's receiving the Nobel Prize; otherwise, it would not have been laudable for him to obtain the honour from his country after getting the Nobel Prize from Europe. Rabindranath's reaction to it, after reading the news in the papers, was reflected in a letter dated 2 November written to Surendranath Dasgupta: 'A fear like this, that this title would sit on my head, never occurred to me even in my dreams. And it has happened at an age when one should leave his home and hearth and go to the forest to pass the remaining days of life in meditation.'

On 13 November, Thursday, in Stockholm, the news was announced: 'The Nobel Prize for literature for 1913 has been awarded to the Indian poet Rabindranath Tagore.' Preparations had been made for a series of felicitations and meetings. After the news was published, 500 people reached Shantiniketan by train to felicitate Rabindranath Tagore. In his speech on that day, his hatred of hypocrisy and the wound of rejection by his fellow citizens were expressed unknowingly:

> All of you have assembled here today to confer honour on me in the name of the country but to accept it entirely and unhesitatingly is beyond the range of my ability. I did not know that the worship I offered to the deity sitting on the eastern bank of the sea would accept my offerings by extending her right hand on the western bank of the sea. I have been blessed with her favour—this is my true gain. Whatever may be the reasons, however, Europe today has granted me the garland of the highest honour. If it has got any value, then that's only a reflection of the taste of learned people there; it has no genuine relation with our country. The Nobel Prize cannot increase the quality or flavour of any writing. I, therefore, stand before you all with folded hands and say—whatever is truth, even if it is hard, I will accept with my head bowed, but whatever is the illusion of momentary excitement, I will never accept that.

Although Rabindranath turned his face from his own country, he had no aversion for Tripura. The book of poems, *Bhagna Hriday* had compelled Tripura to confer on him the title of a 'Great Poet' years ago. The recognition that the poet did not receive from Bengal, he got in plenty right from the beginning of his career as a poet from Tripura. The poet remembered this throughout his life.

The news of the Nobel Prize awarded to Rabindranath Tagore made the general mood in Tripura festive. Brajendra Kishore convened a huge meeting to felicitate Rabindranath and spearheaded the initiative. Maharaja Birendra Kishore was the patron. In that meeting, so many people talked about the close relationship of Rabindranath with Tripura. Brajendra Kishore praised Tripura for having maintained a close, deep relationship with Rabindranath Tagore. A political agent, Captain Williams, was present at that meeting. What Captain Williams said, let us hear through the words of Brajendra Kishore:

> Consider the painting of some artist. The artist is talented. With the fusion of perfect colour combinations and solemn themes, the painting enchants every onlooker. The artist achieves his desired effect. But where is the beauty of art in photographs? Likewise, even the English translation of Rabindranath's poetry has bewitched the learned society of the West—it is analogous to a photograph. But if the learned society (of the West) had the ability to enjoy the elegance of the poetry in his own language, then they would have been overwhelmed.

Brajendra Kishore wrote a long letter to Rabindranath giving an elaborate and vivid description of the meeting, mentioning that the people of Tripura were joyous and proud of his having received the Nobel Prize. Rabindranath in reply wrote to Brajendra Kishore on 2 December 1913, thanking Tripura profusely: 'This is my real award, that you all feel genuine joy for the honour I have received.'

The utterance of the poet proved that he looked at Tripura with different eyes. Whenever Tripura conferred honours on the poet from time to time, even in the last days of his life, he accepted them with grace.

As the appointment of a minister was not possible from outside Tripura, Birendra Kishore nominated his younger brother Brajendra Kishore as the minister and informed the government accordingly. Brajendra Kishore had some reservations holding this post as it might again give rise to dissension and family feuds. Hearing this news, a joyous Rabindranath wrote a letter congratulating Brajendra Kishore, saying, 'there cannot be anything more beneficial for Tripura than this'.

At this time, he was reminded of Mahim Chandra's son Somendra. It would be a happy match if Somendra also took the leadership. The poet had made all the arrangements for Somendra's higher education in America. Thinking of Tripura's bright future, he wrote to Somendra: 'Come back after finishing your studies as a man of high status, come thoroughly filled, come with the blessings of the universe.'

He cherished the prospect that Brajendra and Somendra would steer Tripura towards a bright future. Meanwhile, knowing that Brajendra Kishore had already joined as the minister, his joy knew no bounds. With blessings and advice, he wrote a long letter to Brajendra Kishore:

> Your state administration should be nourished as your practice of virtue; don't allow slackness anywhere. No important work can be done only by merit; it requires a good conscience … In whose hands the power lies, it is his responsibility to restrain that power with rules and regulations … Arouse the deity of fortune: spread education and healthcare all over the country. The duty that you have done towards your subjects for a long time, do that with all your effort; you will become successful in that way.

However, Rabindranath's joy was short-lived as Brajendra Kishore resigned from the post of minister before the completion of the second year. In the article '*Tripuray Rabindra Smriti*', Satya Ranjan Basu mentioned that Brajendra Kishore, by the order of the Maharaja, was prohibited from taking legal action against one 'special' person, after which he submitted his resignation. Who was that special person? Referred to with the adjective 'special', it transpires that the writer knew the person well but intentionally withheld the name. There were not one but two persons against whom legal action was contemplated. They were Mahim Chandra Deb Barma and his brother Jadav Chandra Deb Barma.

In this context, some parts of the diary of Daroga Babu (the officer in charge of a police station), who was an eyewitness, was published in a daily newspaper, *Dainik Sangbad* (on 1 July 2007), with the title, '*Dekha Shonar Ateet: Tripurar Katha*'. The writer of the diary had died long ago. The name of the officer (writer) was kept a secret as requested by his son. He had copied the petition against Mahim Chandra filed before the court. He described every step of the conspiracy very minutely. Let us look at it in brief.

Mahim Chandra's younger brother Jadav Chandra started the Tripura Sundari Lottery. He was the chief manager. The value of each ticket was only a rupee. The first prize was 10,000 rupees and, serially, the second, third and other prizes. Thousands of tickets were sold in Tripura and British India. But complaints started coming to minister Brajendra Kishore and to the police department to the effect that the money collected was not deposited in the lottery fund, as it should have been in keeping with the custom.

Before we proceed further, it is necessary to acquaint ourselves with the background of this incident. ADC Mahim Chandra Deb Barma did not allow the superintendent of police, Ananda Mohan

Guha, to enter the royal durbar as he was not properly dressed. Ananda Mohan felt greatly insulted. Meanwhile, to run the Tripura Sundari Lottery, an advisory committee was formed. State advocate Sri Binodlal Bandopadhyay, advocate Sri Nishikanta Gangopadhyay and some others were members of this committee. The committee met on and off. Once, when the meeting was going on, Mahim Chandra, in the course of altercations, scolded Binod Babu, saying that 'you are not a public prosecutor, you are a public prostitute'; he also abused Nishikanta Gangopadhyay of being shameless. It is better to say here that the previously mentioned diary writer was staying at the house of Ananda Mohan Guha at the time. All the conspiracies took place in front of his eyes. Binod Babu, Nishi Babu and auditor Jatindranath Moulik used to attend the secret meetings regularly held at Ananda Mohan's house. A petition of complaint against Mahim Chandra was drafted. At midnight, the diary writer was asked to copy it. As magistrate of the Sadar (head quarter), Sri Mahim Chandra Dutta refused to accept the petition without the signature of the petitioner; Ananda Mohan forced the sub-inspector of Sadar Court, Sri Nagesh Kar, to sign on it. That very day, Mahim Chandra was removed from the post of ADC. by an order of the royal palace. The police went to Mahim Chandra's house with a search-and-arrest-warrant issued by the court. However, on that very night Mahim Chandra and Jadav Chandra, after being arrested, were released on bail. Mahim Chandra had many enemies. Even the members of the royal family were jealous of him because of his proximity to Radha Kishore Manikya as a royal courtier. Maharaja Kumar Sri Mahendra Chandra Deb Barma raised the issue of Mahim being a real 'Thakur' in the open court and insulted him no end. Mahim and Jadav Chandra were disgraced, defamed, sentenced to three months of un-rigorous incarceration and fined 1,000 rupees. The jail sentence was revoked after an appeal. There were commotions and differences of opinion when they prayed to the Maharaja to forgive the penalty. Maharaja Birendra Kishore sent all the records and papers to Sri Dwarkanath Chakraborty Mahashay, the justice of the Calcutta High Court, and after apprising him of the facts of the case asked for his valuable opinion. Accepting the verdict of Justice Chakraborty, Birendra Kishore had them acquitted.

This was the real incident. This incident confirmed that, in the administrative system of Tripura, state factionalism, brawls, killing of enemies and politics of retaliation were in full swing. The main manager of the lottery was Jadav Chandra, but Mahim Chandra was the most harassed. Mahim Chandra had to pay a heavy price for the use of abusive words. The verdict of the court was not in their hands and therefore, it was impossible to ascertain who was guilty or innocent. Brajendra Kishore was also not above partisanship. The comments of the diarist, an ordinary employee, are worthy of mention in this regard:

> Just after I joined the service, Nabadwip Bahadur resigned from the post of the minister because of old age. In his place, the younger brother of the Maharaja Sri Brajendra Kishore Deb Barman (Lalu Karta) was appointed as minister. He was no doubt educated, intelligent and clever, but not experienced enough to handle the complicated politics of the native state. He was, therefore, not able to do his job impartially. It did not take much time for an ordinary employee like me to understand this fact.

Brajendra Kishore resigned from royal service as he could not tolerate the intervention of the Maharaja in the matter of Mahim Chandra. Did he know who was guilty and who was not? He believed the versions of Ananda Mohan and Binod lal Bandopadhyay. When the news of the resignation reached Rabindranath, he was very upset, and he expressed his concern and anxiety thus:

> Is this news true? Have you left your position? You will surely attain your peace of mind. But I earnestly hope that this matter will not seriously harm your domestic affairs. I am anxious to know what sort of conversation you had with the government and what arrangement was made with the Maharaja.

Rabindranath expressed his paternal concern for Brajendra Kishore in this letter. He was concerned that Brajendra Kishore might land up in financial crisis after having left the ministerial job. There was a system of monthly grants for the members of the royal family even if they were not employed in a royal post. The grant to a royal employee was sufficient to meet the family expenditures. The monthly salary was used to be paid over and above the grant. This letter was a proof of Rabindranath's affection towards Brajendra Kishore.

The first MA (from Harvard) amongst the people of Tripura, Somendra Chandra, after completing his studies in America, returned to the state and was appointed as a high official in a royal post. Maharaja Birendra Kishore appointed him as the secretary of the education department and made him responsible for widening the educational system in all spheres of society. The poet wanted Brajendra Kishore and Somendra Chandra to work together as a team for the welfare of Tripura. He still had respect for the ideals of Brajendra Kishore but didn't agree with the reasons for which Brajendra Kishore left his job. The poet understood that sacrificing petty egotism would prove to be beneficial for Tripura's wellbeing. Maharaja Birendra Kishore requested Brajendra Kishore to withdraw his resignation and join as a minister, but he persevered. In the meantime, when Somendra Chandra also informed Rabindranath about obstructions, the poet in his letter replied: 'Fighting with hindrances is a matter of pride.' After that, he wrote to Somendra Chandra to inspire Brajendra Kishore to take up the ministerial role again:

> Take Lalu (Brajendra Kishore) out of his corner. He should not run away, fearing defeat. The responsibility to restore the reputation of Agartala lies with him. He has got that strength. He must occupy his place by force—
> Beholding a closed door
> Will thou come back like that?
> Push the door again and again
> The door may not tumble—
> But for that, don't worry.

Rabindranath learned from his experiences that the hills of opposition had to be crossed over—otherwise, nobody could achieve success in life. Despite the volley of criticisms that he had faced throughout his life, he remained undeterred in his work and had unending faith in his talent. And thus, those who criticized his world-famous talent were burnt to ashes by the heat of 'Rabi' (sun) and lost in oblivion. History had forgotten them. In the concluding part of the letter, he cautioned Somendra Chandra not to be slack in the performance of his duties: 'That is your own country—and the responsibility for your life is only your own.'

Sri Bikach Chowdhury, the writer of *Rabindra Sannidhey Tripura*, retrieved some of the unpublished letters stored in the record room of the Tripura government, in which the enmity of the brothers at that time are vividly reflected. If we scrutinize Rabindranath's letter, written to Brajendra Kishore, where he anxiously asked whether

Brajendra Kishore's resignation would create serious economic problems at his domestic front, we see that it reveals his paternal concern. But the main point was: if Brajendra Kishore was interested in ending the family feud by mutual deliberation, why did he then beg at the gate of the British Government to increase his family grant? Was Rabindranath's anxiety responsible for it? But apparently, he was in favour of mitigating the family feud and wanted Brajendra Kishore to take up the ministerial post again and had asked Somendra Chandra to persuade Brajendra Kishore for the same. Brajendra Kishore was getting an allocated grant of 4,000 rupees over and above his salary in 1905. Despite doubling his family grant to 8,000 after his resignation, what was it that prompted him to file a complaint to the British Government for increasing this grant?

Let me quote Bikach Chowdhury on this issue:

Rabindranath's worries were already there, but the British Government also played a significant role. It was heard that the decision of his resignation from the ministerial post perturbed the British Government. There was pressure on the Maharaja from the Governor of Bengal to not take a hasty decision. In this matter, we have some hints from the letter of Birendra Kishore dated 16 July 1915, written to the Governor of Bengal, where it was noted that Brajendra Kishore in the meantime had already received a letter dated 6 July from Mr Gourlay. In that letter, Mr Gourlay had assured Brajendra Kishore that the British Government would try its best to restore him to the post. But with that, he also expressed his apprehension that it would be difficult for the Maharaja to change his decision.

That the Governor of Bengal had put pressure on Birendra Kishore in that matter was evident from his letter:

> This and the state of things indicated in my previous letters led me to take immediate action as I believed and still believe that any delay would have added to the embarrassment, and I had not the remotest idea that I was acting against Your Excellency's advice, which I would be ungrateful on my part to forget or in any way disregard.

Birendra Kishore had already taken a firm decision, but for the sake of courtesy he gave a lame excuse to the Governor. In the concluding part of the letter, he emphasized his firmness:

> If in any way I misconstrued Your Excellency's wishes, I am extremely sorry, and as you have been pleased to remark, it is not possible to undo it. I may be permitted to state that the unfortunate estrangement was already too well known to the public, and I venture to think that further delay would have given rise to a good deal of idle speculation and possibly to intrigue.

Though there were misunderstandings on the administrative front, Birendra Kishore had no shortage of love and affection for his younger brother. Brajendra Kishore wanted to quit Tripura and sought the help of the British Government. Birendra Kishore was deeply offended by this move. In the above letter, it was mentioned thus:

> I am sorry to find from Mr Gourlay's letter that it would be better for my brother to leave this territory and to stay outside for the present. I venture to hope that this is not due to any view that I might have expressed to Your Excellency as to his future conduct or treatment of my brother, who, I assured Your

Excellency, would receive the same kind of treatment as before ... I have personally told him not to think of leaving this place.

Brajendra Kishore stuck to his decision and set out on a journey to Calcutta on his way to Shimla. The Governor of Bengal, Mr Carmichael, called on him there and expressed his desire to appoint him as a high official under the British Government. Brajendra Kishore politely refused to accept the proposal. After a few days, the political agent of Tripura, Mr J. Bartley, ICS, requested the Maharaja to increase Brajendra Kishore's family allowance. Maharaja Birendra Kishore was aggrieved by this unauthorized intervention. He informed Mr Bartley by a letter dated 31 October 1915 that:

1. There is no justification for the increase proposed. If Lalu resides away from Agartala he ought to choose a cheaper place, if he can't manage in Calcutta with the liberal allowance he is getting at present.
2. Lalu's personal allowance has been more than doubled since 1905 when he was in receipt of over 4,000 rupees.
3. Lalu did no doubt enjoy special advantages and favours while here, and I have been too indulgent a brother to him in times past. But favours cannot be extorted or continued or repeated at the pleasure of the recipient.

From these exchanges of letters, the actual reason for Brajendra Kishore leaving the ministerial post cannot be ascertained. It is hard to believe that he requested the British Government to increase his family allowances. Somebody might have pulled the strings secretly, otherwise the whole matter did not befit his character. This incident highlighted the special traits of Birendra Kishore's character. He had plenty of love and affection for his younger brother as is evident from his admission that 'I have been too indulgent a brother to him.' The extra family allowance that Brajendra Kishore could not manage to get from the British Government, he could have perhaps easily got it—if he had requested the Maharaja to do so on the virtue of his right to love and affection.

During the reign of Maharaja Birendra Kishore, Brajendra Kishore remained at the centre of Rabindranath's relationship with Tripura simply because, as a person, Birendra Kishore was very shy and never wanted to be exposed to the limelight. He used to adore Rabindranath as a fascinated disciple. While Brajendra Kishore was especially close to Rabindranath, who loved him as his son, and the exchange of ideas took place majorly through him. After his resignation from the royal service, Brajendra Kishore was thinking of severing relations with Tripura and he also started staying away from Agartala for most of the time; this was thus a ripe moment for Birendra Kishore to come out into the open and reclaim his space in relationship between Rabindranath and Tripura. Therefore, he cordially invited the poet to come to Tripura.

Rabindranath came to Tripura on 9 November 1919 after visiting Guwahati and Sylhet. It was his sixth visit to Tripura. After the demise of Maharaja Radha Kishore, he found himself in Tripura again, fourteen years after his last visit. This time, he stayed in the Kunjaban Bungalow, which was in the eastern part of the garden house, Malanchabas, situated at the bottom of the Kunjaban hillock. The bungalow is surrounded by smoky, verdant hills which compelled the poetic imagination. The twinkling of sun rays through the opening in between the leaves of trees and the chirping of unnamed birds delighted the poet no end. In his reminiscence, the poet talked about his stay at the Kunjaban bungalow: 'I have seen many beautiful places in the world, but that white house on the hillock of Kunjaban in Tripura can never be erased from my memory.'

The next day, 10 November, the poet went to Umakanta Academy for an inspection. Pandit Krishna Kumar Kabyatirtha read out a short laudatory hymn in Sanskrit in the western veranda of the school hall. Headmaster Shital Chandra Chakraborty, felicitating the poet for the Nobel Prize, said, 'We are accustomed to see the setting of the sun in the western sky but now by the pompous colour of the rise of *Rabi* (sun) on the horizon of the West, the whole world is elated.'

The poet spent a long time with the students and teachers. He gave plenty of advice to the students. While leaving, he wrote in the inspection register: 'I am grateful for the reception given to me by the students and teachers at this school, and I'm greatly pleased with what I saw.'

After his return to Kunjaban bungalow from the school, there was a wonderful surprise awaiting him. The blind singer, Dwijadas Roy, from the village of Kalikachchha, was waiting to sing a song before Rabindranath. He sang some songs of *dehatatya* (the doctrine that holds the body as the seat of all truths). Rabindranath listened to the songs with full attention, amazed. The poet arranged for the singer's medical treatment after returning to Calcutta, but his blindness couldn't be cured.

This time, Rabindranath and Maharaja Birendra Kishore had a long heart-to-heart conversation about music, art and literature. Knowing that the Maharaja was an adept musician, poet and litterateur, and above all a great painter, Rabindranath inspired him to carry on with his pursuits. It was not known whether the poet saw the famous paintings of Maharaja Birendra Kishore, namely, *Jhulan* and *Sanyasi*. Had he seen them, he would have been astonished. In their discussion, the poet mentioned building a hospital at Shantiniketan. He also informed the Maharaja with regret that, due to the pecuniary situation, the hospital project could not come to fruition. On hearing this, the Maharaja immediately put 5,000 rupees in the poet's hands and promised to pay a further 5,000 rupees soon. However, a record of this assistance has been intentionally omitted from the annual report of Shantiniketan for the year 1919 as Birendra Kishore insisted on not being named since he was wary of facing antagonism from the courtiers. Principal Kshitimohan Sen said: 'There is the possibility of improving the hospital in the coming year. For this, 5,000 rupees has been received from outside. We earnestly thank the donor for this act of kindness.'

In other parts of the report, of course, the name of Maharaja Birendra Kishore was mentioned and gratitude conveyed:

> The school has been receiving donation and assistance only from the Tripura Durbar in Bangladesh; for that, we are particularly grateful to the said royal family. The late Maharaja Radha Kishore Dev Manikya was a great friend of this school and the present Maharaja Birendra Kishore Dev Manikya has also shown his great kindness ...

It is worth mentioning that Rabindranath had come to Tripura for the sixth time, and as always, he never returned from there empty-handed. The poet was at Agartala, but Brajendra Kishore was not in station. There was no dearth of respect for Brajendra Kishore in Tripura. He was also not banished like Nabadwip Bahadur. This absence thus was not worthy of his royal stature as a prince of Tripura. Meanwhile, Birendra Kishore sacrificed his family's pleasure and paid the money from his personal fund to Rabindranath. The courtiers and the people of Tripura were dead set against any charity being given outside Tripura and, therefore, Birendra Kishore did not put his hands in the funds of the state division.

Brajendra Kishore was missing from Agartala. He was probably in Calcutta on vacation. The poet surely was aware of his whereabouts for Brajendra Kishore always kept the poet well informed about his travels and deeds. Rabindranath, as a venerable person, should have acted as an intermediary to settle issues between the two brothers to make their union possible. He had previously actively participated in all the affairs of Tripura even in the face of antagonism. Why, then, did he now show this sort of partisanship? The only answer was the blind love between a 'father' and his 'son'. It was Brajendra Kishore's closeness with Rabindranath that created distance between the Maharaja and the poet. However, though Brajendra Kishore was absent, his whole family was very much at Agartala. The poet went to meet them. The sudden appearance of the poet elated them all. Mata Maharani, Brajendra Kishore's mother, his wife and grandchildren welcomed him cordially. Generally, the queens and princesses never used to appear before a man other than their close relatives, and observed strict rules of purdah, but in the case of Rabindranath, the custom of the inner mahal was not followed. This fact itself proved beyond doubt that the royal family of Tripura accepted the poet as an intimate friend of the family; in other words, as one of them and not as an outsider. As Rabindranath was fully aware of the purdah system in the royal family, he did not appoint a Brahmo lady as a confidante of the princess, and later Ramani Mohan prevented Maharaja Radha Kishore from taking the zenana mahal along with him to attend the Governor's party in Calcutta. With what reverence the royal family adored him could be made clear by a simple instance: after the introduction, Mata Maharani asked Rabindranath whether she would be permitted to call her husband's friend as a friend. Rabindranath lovingly replied. 'You may surely call me your friend'. In this unexpected get-together, the songs sung by Brajendra Kishore's youngest daughter, Navina Devi, enchanted Rabindranath. Rabindranath remembered throughout his life this kind-hearted reception by the members of the royal family.

The Manipuri prince of Tripura, Buddhimanta Singh, for the first time, laid down the foundation of Rabindranritya in this year. Agartala was the main centre of Manipuri dance. The poet was enchanted by the performance of a Manipuri Rash dance.

Rabindranath loved the Manipuri dance so much that he expressed his desire before the Maharaja to introduce Manipuri dance, as an element of Rabindra dance, at Shantiniketan. The Maharaja was requested to send one Manipuri dancer to Shantiniketan. Within a few days, Buddhimanta Singh was sent at Rabindranath's request. In the initial stage, the girls were reluctant to perform the steps and movements of the body as directed by Buddhimanta; the poet, therefore, even at his old age, started dancing at Buddhimanta's instructions, to ease the girls into it. Seeing this, the bashfulness of the girls gradually faded away.

After a few days, Rabindranath wrote a letter to Maharaja Birendra Kishore, requesting him to visit Shantiniketan. In another letter dated 2 February, he wrote:

> We are glad and grateful to the Maharaja for sending Buddhimanta Singh to the Ashram. The boys, with all their enthusiasm, are learning this dance form from him. Our girls are also eager to learn this dance and also Manipuri art. If the Maharaja gives an order to send Buddhimanta Singh's wife here, our purpose will be served. It is our wish that the girls from good families practice works like weaving cloth; one teacher from Assam has been appointed for this purpose. But the art of the Manipuri women I have seen in Sylhet is much better than this. I have made my proposal to Buddhimanta. He has said that if he gets the consent of the Maharaja to bring his wife, he will arrange to teach Manipuri art and dance to the women here. About this matter and for this purpose, I am waiting for the consent and order of the Maharaja.

Rabindranath returned to Calcutta from Tripura on 12 November 1919. This journey had given him immense satisfaction. After the warm felicitations received and the elaborate lectures given in Guwahati and Sylhet, the calm environment of Tripura consoled his heart. About this journey, he wrote in a letter dated 3 December to Kalidas Nag, an inhabitant of Sri Lanka, which proves how this visit to Guwahati, Sylhet and Tripura made him joyous:

> While returning from the mountains, I visited Guwahati, Sylhet and Tripura. It goes without saying that there was no dearth of lectures. Often in a day, I had to give four long lectures. I agreed to this sort of intemperance of tongue because I was amazed to see the people there still treating me with excessive indulgence ... They did not know me as well as the people of Calcutta ... Getting the opportunity, therefore, I opened my heart before them ...

Birendra Kishore was famed as a painter. Whoever saw his paintings, *Jhulan* and *Sanyasi*, appreciated his rare talent. In the typical tradition of the great artist Ravi Verma, the paintings of Birendra Kishore were vibrantly alive. His paintings were a fusion of Western and Indian styles. Rabindranath had come to know that the Maharaja wanted to collect the paintings of Ajanta, but getting no direct confirmation from the Maharaja, the poet wrote to Somendra Chandra: 'I would come to understand his intentions better if he does not respond about the matter of his attachment towards the useless copies of Griffith's Ajanta.'

Birendra Kishore had a God-gifted natural talent. He did not learn the art of painting in a conventional way; he learned only by observing the paintings of others—yet in portrait-painting his talent was impeccable.

Birendra Kishore and his queen, Maharani Prabhavati Devi, were connoisseurs of art like Radha Kishore and his queen, Maharani Tulshibati Devi. Their poems might not be considered excellent today, but back then they were worth praising. Here's a roughly translated Rash festival song composed by Birendra Kishore:

> Beautiful sweet heart Radha is an elegant dancer with a pig tail like snake
> Mind-stealer of Shyam, necklace on breasts swings nicely.
> Charming in smile, amorous, delicately adorns with jewels and
> Pearls shed from the elephant's head,
> Graceful lady love Radha Kishori.
> Son of Tripura King Birendradas narrates the beauty
> Of beloved of Shyam, spark off by the rays of nine gems.

Here's a song on the same theme composed by Prabhavati Devi, the chief queen of Birendra Kishore, in the *kirtan* style:

> The eyes are drowned with the savour of fascinating image
> With beautiful dress and smile Rai graces beside Shyam
> Leaves with golden lustre as if bloom near the blue mountain,
> Seeing the endless beauty, the soul dances with an urge of love.
> Prabhabati is desirous to behold those heaps of beauty.
> Let the people of Tripura come to view the beauty unblemished.

Maharaja Birendra Kishore was extremely shy of publicity and loved to stay behind the curtains, hiding his talent from the world. The comments of Dr Ramani Mohan Sharma about the multifarious talents of Maharaja Birendra Kishore are worthy of mention:

| Maharaj Birchandra Manikya | Maharaj Radhakishore Manikya | Kobiguru Rabindranath Thakur | Maharaj Birendrakishore Manikya | Maharaj Birbikram Manikya |

Four generations of Tripura Maharajas and Rabindranath Tagore

Ujjyanta Place, Tripura

Picture of the throne of Tripura

Maharaja Bir Chandra Manikya

Maharaja Bir Chandra Manikya

Maharani Bhanumati Devi

Maharani Manmohini

Maharaja Bir Chandra Manikya and Maharani Manmohini

Rabindranath at Kurseong (1896); photographed by Maharaja Bir Chandra Manikya

Another photograph of Rabindranath taken by Bir Chandra Manikya at Kurseong in 1896

Maharaja Radha Kishore Manikya

Maharaja Radha Kishore Manikya

Rabindranath and Radha Kishore Manikya

(Standing, from left) Rathindranath, Col. Mahim Thakur, Surendra Thakur, (sitting, from left) Lokendra Palit, Jagadish Chandra Bose and Rabidranath at Agartala

Maharani Tulsibati Devi

Bodthakur Samarendrachandra Debsharma

Minister Umakanta Das

Minister Ramanimohan Chattopadhaya

Colonel Thakur Mahimchandra debbarma

Archival photographs of Bodthakur Samarendrachandra Debsharma, Minister Umakanta Das, Minister Ramoni Mohan Chattopadhaya, Colonel Thakur Mahim Chandra Deb Barma

Jatindranath Basu, Kumar Nabin Kishore and Brajendra Kishore

First Manipuri Dance Guru—Buddhamanta Singh

Maharaja Birendra Kishore Manikya with Maharani Arundhati Mahadevi

Maharaja Birendra Kishore Manikya

Birendra Kishore painting in his studio

Sanyasi—a painting by Birendra Kishore Manikya

Jhulan—a painting by Birendra Kishore Manikya

Maharaja Bir Bikram Kishore Manikya

Maharaja Bir Bikram Kishore Manikya

Maharaja Bir Bikram Kishore and Maharani Kanchanprava

HH Maharaja Bir Bikram Kishore Dev Burman with Rabindranath Tagore

Felicitation Ceremony of Rabindranath by Kishore Sahitya Samaj at Agartala in 1926

Inauguration of 'Rabindra Mela' by Maharaja Bir Bikram in Calcutta Town Hall in 1931

Maharaja Bir Bikram at Shantiniketan (Shyamali) with courtiers in 1939

Maharaja Bir Bikram and Rabindranath at Shantiniketan in 1939

Last visit of Rabindranath at Agartala in 1926

Photograph of Rabindranath in the Abyss of Oblivion

Prince Brajendra Kishore

Prince Brajendra Kishore at a young age

Prince Brajendra Kishore in his old age

'Bharat Bhaskar'—a title of honour received by Rabindranath Tagore at Shantiniketan in 1941

Bhubaneswari Temple, Rajnagar, Udaipur, Tripura

Kunjaban Palace, Tripura

Rabindranath's favourite gol verandah at Kunjaban Palace

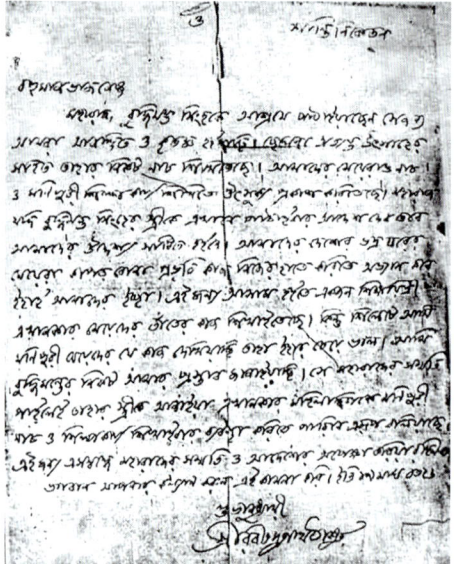

Lion motif, Ratna Manikya   Lion motif, Nasiruddin Mahmud   Chaturdasadevata, Ratna Manikya

Taghra-type, Barbak Shah   Ardhanarisvara, Vijaya Manikya   Krishna with tow Gpis, Ananta Manikya

Vishnu Garuda motif, Ananta Manikya   Krishna one Gopi, Yashodar Manikya

Handwriting of Gurudev Rabindranath   Tripura Coinage

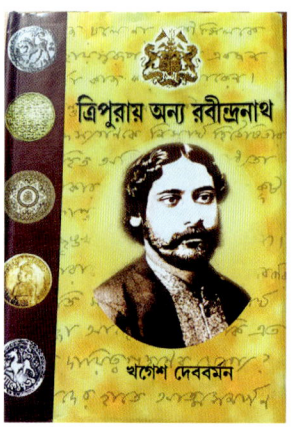

Cover of the Bengali book *Taripuray Annya Rabindranath*. The picture of Rabindranath was taken by Maharaja Bir Chandra Manikya

Birendra Kishore Manikya was a philosopher and a poet of merit. He had a great flavour in the cultivation and culture of fine arts. A distinguished artist and painter, he delved deep into the beauties of nature, which found eloquent expressions through his brush. He also took an active interest in clay sculptures. He had an appreciable sense of decoration—this was reflected in his paintings and the adornments he designed for the family deities. His intelligence, refinement and talents in music, art and science placed him far above the average ruling chiefs of his time.

Birendra Kishore was also adept at playing the sitar, esraj, Manipuri khol and the flute. He recorded raga Todi in sitar and Malkosh in flute. He did not allow the record company to release the record despite repeated requests. In those days, people who embraced music as a livelihood were considered outcastes in society. Gentlemen and ladies belonging to the middle and upper classes, who recorded music with record companies, used to write 'amateur' within brackets beside their names, suggesting that no money had been exchanged in the deal. It was thought that the crescendo of music must reverberate within the confinements of the inner mahal and should not be sold to the public. The Maharajas of Bengal, like those of Cooch Behar, Nator and Burdwan, used to practice music and literary activities, but their creations remained inaccessible to the general public. Bengali culture had been enriched by the contributions of the Tripura Maharajas and also by the Maharajas of Bengal in the field of music, art and literature. I hope a detailed history of this era of art will be written in the future.

Maharaja Birendra Kishore was not as generous as Karna, the epic character from the Mahabharata known for his benevolence, yet he continued the Tripuri Maharajas' tradition of generosity toward Rabindranath. Whatever assurances were given to Rabindranath during the regimes of Maharaja Bir Chandra and Radha Kishore were sustained as royal duties till the reign of the last king of Tripura, Maharaja Bir Bikram Manikya. Apart from that, Birendra Kishore donated 1 lakh rupees to the war fund at the time of the First World War. He paid 1,40,000 rupees for the relief of the distressed and homeless. He also donated 5,000 rupees to Sarala Devi's Shakhi Samiti. While Lady Chelmsford created an all-India fund to render service to women and children, Birendra Kishore on his own donated 25,000 rupees.

The British Government used to address Maharaja Radha Kishore as 'Raja', omitting the word 'Maha'. During the regime of Birendra Kishore, they wanted to go one step further and snatch the title of 'Manikya Bahadur'. A person of self-respect, Birendra Kishore protested this move vehemently. The British Government accepted defeat in the face of his adamant opposition and returned not only the title 'Manikya Bahadur' but also 'Maharaja' at the same time with due respect.

Birendra Kishore's regime continued for only fourteen years. Suffering from a long illness, he breathed his last on 13 August 1923 at the relatively young age of forty. After the death of three generations of Maharajas, Rabindranath was now introduced to the Maharaja of Tripura of the fourth generation.

4

Rabindranath and Maharaja Bir Bikram Manikya

Bir Bikram's period of reign: 1923-1947

Bir Bikram was only fifteen years old when Maharaja Birendra Kishore Manikya passed away. An administrative council was formed to run the government on behalf of the minor king. This time, Brajendra Kishore returned to royal service. He was the member and head of the administrative council.

In the year 1925, Rabindranath had written a letter to Brajendra Kishore requesting him to send a Manipuri dance teacher to Shantiniketan. The trend in the art of Rabindranritya which was set by Buddhimanta Singh, was developed into its full-fledged form by his follower Navakumar Singh. Buddhimanta Singh had to face considerable hurdles while trying to train the girl students at Shantiniketan. In Agartala, Rabindranath was so enthralled by the beauty of the dance in the festivals of Rash Leela and Basanta Utsav that he resolved to introduce the dance forms at Shantiniketan. He wanted dancers from Tripura and not from Manipur since the latter were less likely to speak Bengali. Rabindranritya not only involves parts of Manipuri dance but is also inspired by other dance forms from around the world. In his reminiscence, Navakumar mentions: 'From time to time, the poet talked to me about his experience of the dance forms he'd witnessed in different places. The dances of South India, the folk-dance of Sylhet and even his experience of the art of dance in the island of Java were not excluded from the discussion.'

Rabindranath tried to assimilate and synthesize all the dance forms he had witnessed all over the world. He went to Colombo, taking Navakumar Singh along with him for the purpose of staging the dance drama, *Shapmochan*. He wanted Navakumar Singh to add new elements in Rabindranritya after seeing the Ceylonese dance. Navakumar Singh did not disappoint him. Buddhimanta Singh and Navakumar Singh were the foremost exponents of Rabindranritya.

Lord and Lady Lytton visited Shantiniketan a while after Navakumar Singh and his younger brother Baikunthanath Singh had reached. About that day, Navakumar Singh wrote:

> The then Lieutenant Governor of Bengal, Lord Lytton, came to Shantiniketan on a private visit … The poet had arranged a hospitable reception for the guests. A music and dance performance were scheduled for the occasion. I remember I had rehearsed a Manipuri dance piece with the help of a few girls. In the song that accompanied the dance, the last stanza was *'Govindadas Tai Jai Balihari'* (Govindadas remains dumbfounded). In the concluding lines of the poem, I had replaced 'Govindadas' with Rabindranath's name without taking his permission … I was afraid of how the poet would react. But he praised me for the gesture with a bright smile, and all my apprehensions immediately vanished.

There was no denying the fact that, under Rabindranath's umbrella, the dance of Navakumar developed enormously. Navakumar, no

Rabindranath and Maharaja Bir Bikram Manikya 151

doubt, learnt from Rabindranath how to express one's delicate feelings through facial expressions and eye movements, how to occupy and cover the stage with easy rhythms and how to demonstrate the inner meaning of the performance with graceful movements. Navakumar, therefore, had no hesitation in gratefully admitting his debt to Rabindranath:

> In the long spell of staying abroad, the poet's friendly attitude, his bright smile and, above all, his expertise in music, dance and stagecraft always inspired me. I could not forget him even for a day. I had once been proud of my dancing ability, and that pride remains even now. But after reaching this last phase of life, I can unequivocally declare that, without the constant company of Kabiguru, I would never have known how to harmonize dance and poetry while maintaining emotional intensity. In this matter, my apprenticeship had begun at his feet.

About Navakumar Singh's brilliance, Shantidev Ghosh, a distinguished maestro of dance, said:

> He was a true dancer before he came to Shantiniketan. He used to repeat what he had learnt. He never thought of innovating. After coming here, for the first time, he had to think of it, and with the counselling of everyone he was able to show the path toward new possibilities. Srijukta Navakumar Singh would be remembered forever in the history of the Manipuri dance movement of this age.

In the year 1926, Rabindranath was on a journey to East Bengal (now Bangladesh). After coming to Comilla from Dhaka, he requested Brajendra Kishore to meet him there. Seeing the opportunity,

Brajendra Kishore invited the poet to come to Agartala. The poet hesitated to go to the minor king's state at the invitation of the minister; he was also worried whether his presence in the capital would provoke resentment. At last, he responded to Brajendra Kishore's cordial invitation, yet with great hesitation. This time, the poet was not alone; he came along with friends, relatives and followers. His companions were Pratima Devi, Rathindranath, Dinendranath, Professor Hirji Bhai Pestanji Morris and many others. On 22 February, at ten at night, the poet set foot in Kunjaban Palace.

Haridas Bhattacharya was responsible for looking after the poet. An ex-student of Shantiniketan, Haridas Bhattacharya later wrote in the magazine Ravi, about the poet's seventh visit to Tripura. In the form of a diary entry, Bhattacharya reminiscences about the poet's daily activities and gist of his conversations. On this trip, the poet discussed a great deal about Maharaja Bir Chandra and Radha Kishore.

Kunjaban Palace was in the lap of nature. A meandering road from Ujjayanta Rajprasad, after reaching Kunjaban Palace on a hillock, rotated like a wheel around it. The flower trees, such as Kamini, Madhabi, Mallika, Golap, Beli, etc., bending their heads in the wild winds invited the bumblebees to come. There were plenty of birds, and getting up early in the morning, the poet stood or sat in the 'gol (round) veranda like a sage absorbed in meditation' listening to the birds chirping all around him. Let us see what Haridas Bhattacharya said:

> The next day (23 February), early in the morning, I saw the poet observing the beauty of the rising sun with a steadfast gaze from his drawing room. The eastern side was illumined with a reddish flash—it seemed as if the multicoloured birds in diverse tunes were cordially felicitating the poet.

Another direct witness was Dwijendranath Dutta, whose description of the incidents is reproduced below in my own words: On the afternoon of 23 February, the poet, sitting in the gol-veranda on the eastern side of the palace, was engaged in an informal and friendly talk with others. In the rendezvous, there were Dinendranath, Mr Morris, Maharaja Kumar Ranbir and Narendra Kishore, headmaster Shital Chandra Chakraborty and many others. The poet fondly recollected his old memories of Tripura. Regarding Bhubaneshwari Mandir, he once said:

> The steps went up from the heart of Gomati (a river) to Bhubaneshwari Mandir—nearby was the palace of Govinda Manikya. Yes, Maharaja Bir Chandra helped me a lot at the time of writing *Bisharjan*, providing me the history, legends, rhymes of the hill, fairy tales of Tripura and various photographs. But I have drawn the entourage in my own imagination in *Rajarshi*. You say you will show me ancient Udaypur and the palace of Govinda Manikya—I don't want to see them. *Rajarshi* is a product of my imagination and should stay in that way forever.

In reply to someone saying that going to Udaypur (now Udaipur) would not be troublesome, the poet said with his usual smile, 'My body and mind are tired. My bodyguards will not give me permission to go to Udaypur by boat, moving upstream for three days in the river Gomati.' Saying this, he smirked with a look at Dinendranath.

Night was imminent, the air was full of the noise of crickets. The wind rustled the grove of tamarisk trees. The stars appeared gradually, a throng of dots twinkling overhead. It was the tenth day of the bright fortnight. The moonlight hadn't pierced the darkness yet. The poet started humming:

> What I see today—the darkness of black hair cascading down
> In layers, the evening stars light up like jewels…

Dinendranath joined in:

> The sky today is filled with the melody of songs,
> The shimmer of crickets tremble near her feet.
> Your prayer is in the fragrant incense of the flower garden
> Today you appear in the enchanting form that captivates the world.

It seemed as if the tune of the song was eternal. At that enchanting moment, Brajendra Kishore's sudden appearance interrupted the whole show. He wanted to take the poet and his companions out for a car ride to see Agartala.

On 26 February, Kishore Sahitya Samaj gave a cordial reception to the poet at Umakanta Academy. Brajendra Kishore presided over this meeting. The welcome address of Kishore Sahitya Samaj said:

> You are the poet of Bengal—the poet of India—the poet of the world … We feel elated at having you in this capital of Tripur kingdom … you have given immortality to ancient Tripura and its royal family in your poetic writings… your love and affection overjoyed Bir Chandra, Radha Kishore and Birendra Kishore. Where the Bengali language was given honourable eminence as the royal language, where Bengali was the life of the royal history *Rajmala* … Today, in that place, this newly established Kishore Sahitya Samaj prays for your blessings … Your message will inspire all of us.

In reply, the poet recounted how he owed a great deal to Bir Chandra and Radha Kishore. He also said:

By the grace of God, many honours, even from the royal hands of Europe, were received by the dint of my good fortune. But the honour I received from the kings of my home and homeland, the value of that in my personal life remains much higher. Just for that, my connection with Tripura was not that of a transitory guest. This connection was entwined with the memories of the king's father and his forefathers. I earnestly pray for the welfare of this state... Now, in spring ... I have not come here as a famous poet to receive any honour; the love and respect that I got here from the late Maharjas in my youth, I want to reciprocate that feeling, and thus I say that, *"Sarba Starato Durgani Sarbo Bhadran Pashyatu"* (May you all be blessed with prosperity and welfare).

Most of his long speech was taken up by his reminiscences of the time spent in Tripura. I have restrained myself from quoting the whole speech to avoid repetition. He recalled again and again, with gratitude, the bounties he received from Tripura. An act of charity cannot be bound within the limit of a particular place and time. The critics were all out to unearth Rabindranath's selfish motives in receiving charity funds from the Maharajas. But I would like to state that the donations reached their intended destination and were used for the benefit of the people. If he himself had enjoyed those charities for selfish interests, he could not have raised his voice in public and expressed his profound gratitude. He established Shantiniketan not for himself but for the well-being of the country. He did not hesitate to wear the garb of a beggar to show proper respect to Jagadish Chandra's talent and to brighten the face of Mother India in the field of science. The ideal that urged him to establish Brahma Vidyalaya, he explained that to Brajendra Kishore in a letter dated 24 Chaitra 1308 (1901), where for the first time he declared the mission of the proposed Vidyalaya:

Following the ancient ideal of brahmacharya (a mode of life marked by the devoted study of sacred texts and abstinence from worldly pleasures) in India, I want my students to be in seclusion without worries and to become proper human beings, pure and clean—I intend to initiate them into India's grace and holiness, guarding them from the lure of British luxuries.

The night before, after dinner, the poet's room was found to have its lights on. The following day, at noon, the poet started writing with rapt attention. As evening came on, the diwan Bijay Babu, Narendra Kishore, Ranbir Kishore, Dwijendra Chandra Dutta, Dinendranath Tagore, Mr Morris and a few others assembled in the big hall waiting for the poet to emerge. When it was almost dark, the poet came and sat in the gol veranda. He was in a light mood:

Spring, in the true sense of the term, I have enjoyed only at your place ... Spring has arrived. Bhairavi, the raga of the bliss of incessant longing for the blossoms in the forests and gardens, has started ringing. Are we only human beings, and not an integral part of nature? ... The diversity of the world compels the human mind to reflect, and herein lies the difference between animal and man. All the doors of the royal palace of nature are open for you all.

Everybody listened attentively. The poet, absorbed in his reverie, continued: 'Love nature, have faith and send letters to her. Wait for the postman to arrive with her sweet note; only then will the invocation of the forest deity yield fruit.'

After a short silence, the poet changed the subject of the conversation which continued till the time for dinner drew near.

The next afternoon, 25 February, Rabindranath went to see the agricultural fields at Pratapgarh. The poet was greatly impressed by the beautiful gardens. He took an active interest in the process of tilling the lands. He talked about his own experiences of preserving the liquid in soil:

> After digging the whole ground about one hand deep, the soil that comes out has to be deposited in one place separately, so that the whole ground can be drubbed. Thereafter, you are to mix the deposited soil with manure and spread it all over the ground. Then there will be no dearth of liquid in summer or winter and for that matter in all seasons. At the end of each monsoon, you are to make the soil loose.

While he was talking, a dark cover of clouds covered the entire sky. The clouds were flying towards the horizon with the gusting wind. This marvelous scene overwhelmed the sensitive poet and he exclaimed: 'Build a cottage for me here. I shall spend the last days of my life witnessing this celestial beauty of nature.'

He reached Kunjaban in the evening. Rash Leela was going to be staged that night at Brajendra Kishore's house. He called everyone and said:

> We are going to Lalu's place to enjoy a Manipuri dance performance. They will likely be coming right now. All of you get ready. The southerly winds have spread the myrtle's charming mantra (sacred hymns) to every corner. At the advent of spring, the formless apothegm of expectation must be given its form ...

Brajendra Kishore came right on time. Then, everyone started their journey towards Brajendra Kishore's house together. When the poet arrived and sat at 'Rash' pavilion, the dance began. The girls of the royal palace had trained vigorously for days together to show Rabindranath the 'Rash Leela' dance. The dance of the girls, adorned with unusual floral ornaments, enchanted the poet no end. The mridanga and mandira players also danced in a circle. The poet was beside himself with joy. Emotionally overpowered, he said, 'My coming to Tripura has become meaningful. I'll never forget this evening.' And he really did not forget. In his reminiscences, this evening was mentioned repeatedly.

After witnessing Rash Leela, the poet was so overcome with emotion that he composed a dance drama, *Natir Puja*, within the framework of the Manipuri dance.

In *Rabindra Jibani*, Prabhat Kumar Mukhopadhyay wrote that 'the poet was so enchanted by this dance that he appointed a dance teacher, Navakumar Singh, to teach at Shantiniketan'. However, this information is wrong. In his reminiscence, Navakumar categorically mentioned that he joined Shantiniketan as a dance teacher towards the end of the year 1925. The salary register of Shantiniketan also shows that Navakumar Singh and his brother Baikuntha Singh took over the charge as dance teachers on 5 November 1925.

When Rabindranath came to Agartala, Bir Bikram was out of town for some urgent work. It was during this Rash dance–event that Rabindranath was introduced to Maharaja Bir Bikram Manikya, then only eighteen years old. The poet requested the young Maharaja to preserve the ancient deeds of Tripura. He also referred to his close relationship with the three generations of Maharajas. The young Maharaja was overwhelmed by the charm of the poet and became his disciple.

Although the poet returned to Kunjaban Palace almost at midnight, he sat up and worked late at night. He wrote a letter dated 24 February 1926 to the poet Amiya Chakaraborty: 'I am extremely tired. After coming here, I've managed to get some rest. The beauty of the forest is pronounced here; I am looking at it through the window of my room.'

Rabindranath arrived at Agartala on 22 February and left for Calcutta on the 26. On 23 February, the poet found the pre-spring landscape so pleasing to his eyes that he was inspired to write several songs that celebrated the beauty of Tripura. The song, *'Doley Premer Dolan Champa Hriday Akashey'* ('The Dolan Champas [a kind of flower] of love swings in the expanse of my heart') was written on that day. The other songs were: *'Phaguner Nabin Anandey/Gaanguli Ganthilum Chhandey'* (In spring's novel joy/ I weaved my songs in rhythm), *'Esho Amaar Ghorey Esho'* (Come, come to my home), *'Boney Jadi Phutloo Kusum'* (If flower blooms in the forest) and *'Apanhara Matowara'* (Free from this self, I am lost in delight).

Now it was time to leave. Rabindranath had come to Tripura a total of seven times over the course of his life, and this was going to be his last visit. After that, he lived for another fifteen years, but on account of his ill health and busy schedule, he could not visit Tripura again. The relationship never ceased. It continued till his death. On 26 February, the poet reached Calcutta via Chandpur.

It has been noted earlier that a council ran the administration of the state on behalf of the minor king. Bir Bikram's coronation ceremony was held on 29 January 1928. Rabindranath was also cordially invited along with all the important and respectable dignitaries, but as he was unwell, he could not attend the ceremony. It was a wonder of wonders that, of all people, Acharya Jagadish Chandra Bose had graced this occasion. Perhaps Jagadish Chandra wanted to show his gratitude to the royal family, which had financed his travel and stay in England. He sat with the artist Dhiren Krishna Deb Barman on the coronation platform. He deeply regretted for his not coming to Tripura while Maharaja Radha Kishore had been alive. After the coronation ceremony, he stood up and said to the assembled audiences in a voice heavy with emotion: 'I could not acknowledge my indebtedness to Maharaja Radha Kishore during his lifetime. Today, I am glad to be able to tell everyone about that noble king's exceptional generosity. I intend to vehemently express my gratitude before one and all.'

This acknowledgement of indebtedness to Radha Kishore came after the lapse of nineteen years of Radha Kishore's death. Before that, Jagadish Chandra, in his inaugural speech at Bigyan Mandir, gratefully remembered the days when his frustrations had been allayed by Maharaja Radha Kishore's assistance, without which his dream would have been shattered. *The Englishman*, dated 12 March 1918, reported:

> When his first experiments brought vividly before him the universal sensitiveness of matter and the outcome of this generalization in different realms of thought, he had a visit from the late Maharaja of Tipperah, Radha Kishore Manikya. The Maharaja was a great scholar in the vernacular, though he was totally unacquainted with the English language. According to the prevailing standard, the cultural value of his acquirements would be questioned. But the Maharaja's ignorance of English did not stand in the way of his instantly realizing the significance of the lecture's experiments. Indeed, his own mind was put to its fullest activities in answering the Maharaja's most intelligent questions as regards the trend of his work in clearing up many difficult problems. The reference to this subject may be opportune in view of the controversy whether the great Akbar was literate or illiterate and whether the University Commission should recommend the vernacular language as a suitable vehicle for scientific instruction. The Government of India sent him on his second scientific deputation to the West to announce his discovery and he experimentally demonstrated before the meeting of the Royal Society the sensitiveness of ordinary plants. The discovery was refused publication to reach the scientific

world. The period of his deputation was then nearing its end, and he had to make his choice of returning to India discredited or overstaying in England, risking his appointment or the chance of convincing some unbiased scientific men. While in this dilemma, he received a communication from the Maharaja assuring him of his firm belief and a large remittance towards the possibility of the continuation of his research. He was thus enabled to prolong his stay and thus secure many true friends among scientific men in England who stood for fair play, resulting finally in the acceptance of his work. It was a special request of the late Maharaja that he wished to remain unknown in this connection. He has now passed away and it is permissible to speak now of one who stood by him at a time when such friendship was most needed.

You might recall, while discussing the relationship of Maharaja Radha Kishore with Jagadish Chandra, I had mentioned Jagadish Chandra's apparent lack of gratitude to Radha Kishore. He was very much in India at the time of Birendra Kishore's marriage (10,000 rupees was given to Jagadish Chandra, slashing Birendra Kishore's marriage expenditure) and also at the time of his coronation as prince and as king; but he did not consider it necessary to send letters apologizing for his absence in all those ceremonies, in spite of personal invitations from Radha Kishore and Birendra Kishore. As Jagadish Chandra did not attend any of the earlier ceremonies, none could have blamed Tripura if he was not invited to the coronation ceremony of Radha Kishore's grandson, Bir Bikram Kishore, nineteen years after Radha Kishore's death. But Tripura was always gracious and grateful to the talented persons who had brought laurels to India and with whom Tripura had an intimate relationship. It was not at all a fact that due to the prohibition imposed by Radha Kishore to keep the financial assistance a secret, Jagadish Chandra could not express his gratitude in public. But all said and done, was there any prohibition to express his gratitude personally to Radha Kishore? He owed his indebtedness not to the public but only to Radha Kishore. Moreover, the assistance given to Jagadish Chandra was very much known to the people by the grace of Rabindranath Tagore even in Radha Kishore's lifetime. Now, after a lapse of nineteen years, Jagadish Chandra suddenly came out with a confession before the public. There is a saying: 'better late than never.' And in Bose's case, good sense had finally prevailed.

Surely, Radha Kishore's donations were not granted to undeserving persons. Talents like Rabindranath and Jagadish Chandra are sparse in the world. As the assistance was given to them at inopportune moments, Tripura's name was glorified. People all around the world would certainly remember Tripura for this act of kindness. There are no two opinions about it.

Now, let us acquaint ourselves with Rabindranath, the painter. In the year 1929, four painters from India went to London with a grant from the Government of India to paint the walls of India House. Artist Dhiren Krishna Deb Barman was one of them. While he was in London, Rabindranath, along with his son Rathindranath and daughter-in-law Pratima Devi came to London from Paris and stayed at Razina Hotel. An exhibition of Rabindranath's paintings was held in Paris, which earned vast critical acclaim. The then Principal of the Royal College of Art in London, William Rothenstein, was an old friend of the poet. He requested Rabindranath to have an exhibition of his paintings there. The exhibition was held at Birmingham. Several paintings were sold. The poet gave the charge of the selection of paintings to Dhiren Krishna prior to the beginning of the exhibition. In one room of Razina Hotel, Dhiren Krishna was selecting the paintings. At that time, the poet stood beside him and said with a smile: 'You are wondering what sort of paintings Gurudev has drawn! ... But you will be surprised to know that my paintings have captivated art critics of Europe; they are all enthralled by my work.'

Regarding that little exchange, Dhiren Krishna remarked: 'His statement of that day has become a truth. Now, the paintings of Rabindranath have reached an elevated place in the world of art. From London, Gurudev went to countries like Germany and Denmark, and his paintings were exhibited all over Europe.'

I do not know whether he was conventionally educated in the art of painting, but one cannot deny his expertise in the arrangement of colors. His eyes saw everything and were always on the move. He was a marvellous creator—lost in ecstasy, he wrote poems, lyrical self-composed songs (Rabindrasangeet), short stories, essays, dramas, novels and of course produced paintings. You might have noticed, in his paintings, that human bodies were never portrayed with all its limbs; they were always covered with a veil. He did not flawlessly depict all the limbs of the body, such as hands, feet and fingers, in different postures. The formless form of art was the main feature of Rabindranath's paintings, his canvas presents art in its most abstract form.

The seventieth birth anniversary of Gurudev Rabindranath was celebrated in Calcutta. On this occasion, young Maharaja Bir Bikram Manikya inaugurated Rabindra Shilpa Pradarshani and Mela, that was held on 25 December 1931, in Calcutta Town Hall. To honour Rabindranath's close relationship with Tripura, he was proclaimed as the 'Poet of Tripura'. Maharaja Bir Bikram, in his inaugural speech, said:

> You all have fastened me with the string of gratitude by appointing me as a conductor of this great ceremony ... By the grace of God,

the royal family of Tripura, from time immemorial, have been devotees of art and culture. That was why my great grandfather, most reverend late Bir Chandra Manikya, was attracted to the resplendent rays of the rising *Rabi* (sun). From then onwards, we have had a special relationship with the great poet that continues to foster under my father Birendra Kishore Manikya.

The poet's influence on the royal family of Tripura is not trivial. On the other hand, Tripura, adorned with mountains and waterfalls, the natural beauty of its green hills and the achievements of our forefathers like Govinda Manikya, and its various art forms attracted the great poet as well, a fact that makes the state as a whole very proud.

Forgive me please, for being so selfish as to mention my personal relationship with the poet. But Rabindranath, who is the poet of Bengal, of India, of the world—I pay him my tribute as a poet of Tripura.

For him even the daily life of an ordinary person is not a matter of neglect and he should not be deprived of the chance to peacefully integrate himself with the world at large. That is the ideal that he always propagates before everyone through his advice, works and lifelong activities. Thus, he never thought of art and culture as something to be enjoyed solely by the elites. We have learnt from him how to integrate the art and culture of our own country with a true spirit of truth and goodwill.

In contrast, the present generation of critics argues that Rabindranath was in fact the 'poet of the Maharajas' and not the 'Poet of Tripura'. They raise various questions such as: Why did Rabindranath not do anything to save the state's popular practices and customs, or take any steps for the advancement of the Tripuri dialect Kokborok? Why did he want to impose on Tripura the rule of outsiders, bestowing on them absolute power? Why did he not work to raise the level of education in Tripura so that the sons of the soil could have participated in the governance of their own state?

The simple answer to all these questions is that a bad workman quarrels with his tools. Why should Tripura depend on someone to do good for them? Why should Rabindranath be blamed for certain policies that weren't put in place? It was the duty of the king and the people of Tripura to save the ancient achievements and popular practices. Rabindranath could only suggest but not act upon it as he was not empowered to do so and, in fact, he did suggest to Maharaja Bir Bikram to preserve the glorious deeds of ancient and modern Tripura in his first meeting with him at Brajendra Kishore's house. Regarding the advancement of the Kokborok dialect, I would like to point out that the poet heard not a single word of it during his stay at Agartala. At that point of time, the hilly people rarely came down to the plains; they never settled there. If a person from the hills took up a government job, he was ostracized and barred from marrying any hill girl. They used to come down once in a blue moon, usually to purchase salt and dried fish and returned to their hilly homes as usual. The Bengali majority and a few thousand members of the royal family inhabited the plains of Tripura. In that case, who would develop Kokborok into a fully-fledged language? The hill tribes were entirely illiterate and ignorant of philology. Maharaja Radha Kishore's endeavour to educate them failed miserably. The hill tribes had no interest in education. Even the grant of five rupees per month for each student and free food and lodging did little to motivate them. Radha Kishore impressed upon the teachers the need to go to the hills to find students, and he also announced special awards and salary bonuses for them; but all his efforts were in vain. Those in the royal family who could have developed Kokborok to a certain extent were ignorant of that dialect; yet Radharamon

Thakur wrote a grammar of Kokborok in the Bengali alphabet, and even that aroused no interest among the gentry. Further, Bengali was the royal language of Tripura for thirteen centuries, and the hill tribes gradually picked up some broken Bengali. The perspective changed in the 1990s when educated hill folk started settling in the plains. Had this process begun during the reign of the kings, the dialect would have acquired the respect it deserved by this time. Unfortunately, since that didn't happen, blaming Rabindranath for its stagnation was meaningless. It would be a travesty of justice if Rabindranath is not considered from the perspective of what he himself saw in Tripura and realized. He saw Bengali culture as the supreme model in Tripura; on top of that, the honour and respect given to the Bengali language as the royal lingo in a non-Bengali state was a rather a novel phenomenon. Therefore, it was reasonably expected that if any language or dialect should be advanced, the royal language should be prioritized over the rest.

So far as rule by the outsiders and absolute power are concerned, I would simply like to say that a person should be judged by his intentions. Being a stern individualist, Rabindranath recommended absolute power in the hands of a minister only to strengthen the administration and nothing else. He had no motive behind it. Whenever his help was sought, he always extended his hand even in the face of opposition. His intention was crystal clear: he wanted to see Tripura as an ideal state. All his letters written to the four Maharajas vividly reflect this intention. He did not even hesitate to enlighten Maharaja Radha Kishore about the image of an ideal king quoting from *Manusamhita*. From the list of ministers, it was evident that most of the ministers were imported from outside. It was not a new incident in the history of Tripura. The point to be considered was of efficiency in running the government, which Tripura sorely lacked during that period. Therefore, what Rabindranath did was all for the welfare of Tripura. About the advancement of education in Tripura, I have already discussed the efforts made by Maharaja Radha Kishore. Nothing more needs to be added.

Outside the purview of the dominant Bengali culture, whatever he saw as the indigenous popular practices of Tripura, he accepted them with great love and affection. The beginning of the relationship of Tripura with the poet started on the solid ground of cultural affinity—a point that Rabindranath himself emphasized on different occasions. I request readers to recall Rabindranath's speech at the felicitation function accorded to Maharaja Bir Bikram in the mango grove at Shantiniketan. All the letters written from time to time were the witnesses of his earnest desire to see Tripura as an ideal state. He faced terrible opposition when he tried to improve the immobile administration and resolve the pecuniary crisis of the state, but he was undeterred in his resolution and alerted the Maharajas with his advice against the criticism of the courtiers. Behind his all actions was the sole thought of Tripura's welfare. For all that he had done, Bir Bikram Manikya rightly bestowed the title of the 'Poet of Tripura' on Rabindranath. He was in no way merely the 'poet of the Maharajas'.

Dependence on others is inherent in human character. S.D. Burman also had to face severe criticism on the grounds that he made no contribution to Tripura since he did not help local artists get a foothold in Bombay. But no nation in this world had reached the peak of development by depending on others. One must stand on one's own might; success, if it ever occurs otherwise through dependence on others, is usually short-lived.

It is time for us to go back to our original subject. After the aforesaid speech of Maharaja Bir Bikram, the poet recalled with gratitude his long relationship with Tripura. The speech is not quoted in order to avoid repetition. His statements were published in all newspapers and magazines. The poet took a round of the compound of the art fair with the Maharaja. At that fair, though there were plenty of things written by Rabindranath on display besides his paintings, it was the crafted bamboos and other works of Tripuri art that attracted the attention of the visitors. The poet invited the Maharaja to visit Shantiniketan.

Now, I think, we should say something about Maharaja Bir Bikram Manikya to bring to light his humane spirit. After the coronation, he was active in developing the state. He was essentially a modern and socially conscious person, and he aspired to get rid of racial discrimination and communal conflicts. Within a year of his coronation, the Anjuman-e-Islamia of Comilla felicitated Maharaja Bir Bikram in August 1928. The speech he gave on that occasion is relevant even today. The picture of an intellectual, thoughtful and benevolent Maharaja was unveiled in that speech:

> Today, I am telling you plainly that my highest and only desire is to create a harmonius environment in my state wholly different from the rest of the country right now. The fate of those people, which is strung in the same string with my own fate, whether Hindus or Muslims, I intend to make them understand that, in reality, there is no space for casteism or racism in Tripura. Each community is well regulated by the rules of the same general ideal. I want everybody to realize that religion is just a way of life, following which only we can reach the feet of the Almighty, the ultimate destination. My earnest request is that those who wear a fez and those who wear a turban should of course remain attached to the fez and turban. But I desire that the soul of each human being should throb for one another for the visible difference is insignificant, and the human soul demands—and wants to give—respect and love. I am in a position now to pass on to a

Hindu devotee of the king the responsibility of maintaining the welfare of all castes and races in our state ... On the destined day, I will be happy to handover in the same way the responsibility of taking charge of my Hindu subjects of the state to a humble Muslim who has faith in my ideal.

We hardly hear this kind of speech on tolerance from the present politicians. They occasionally ramble about secularism, but in practice only attempt to win over their vote banks. It is not known whether any young Maharaja in any part of India gave this sort of a message. Secularism, which is the main foundation of the Indian constitution, was laid for the first time by a small state called Tripura. It is a matter of great pride.

Bir Bikram was not at peace from the very day that he ascended the throne. Among the kings of Tripura, he was the first to deal with various political movements. The waves of revolutionary movements around the country had also reached Tripura by then. The students from Tripura who were studying in the colleges of Comilla or elsewhere had much contact with the revolutionaries and, therefore, after their return to Tripura, they began forming secret organizations. In the year 1927, the members of Anushilan Samiti and supporters of Jugantar had built organizations in the names of Chhatra Sangha and Bhratree Sangha respectively. Bir Bikram was a source of inspiration for the young society and for that matter he even awarded the young people who did physical exercises and social work. But on 26 January 1930, the administration became alert when, on the initiative of Bhatree Sangha, Independence Day was observed in different schools of Tripura. One after another, organizations like Matree Sangha and Milan Sangha were established.

During his tour to Europe and America from the year 1931 to 1936, Bir Bikram had the chance to be directly acquainted with several world leaders. He understood that the age of monarchy was going to end. He, therefore, took initiative to develop the state in the light of modern education and culture. He took special interest in the advancement of agriculture. He had inspired the hilly tribes to adopt more efficient methods of plough cultivation instead of their habitual *jum* cultivation. Some land was reserved for that purpose. The purchase and sale of land of the original inhabitants were prohibited. In each subdivision, a Town Committee of Development and a Public Works Development Committee were established. He had taken up a plan to convert Agartala to a planned city. In 1935, the State Bank of Tripura was established. An airport at Singerbhil was built during his reign. He had a plan, named 'Vidyapattan' through which he wanted to establish a village university where there would be a medical, agricultural, engineering, as well as an arts degree college.

In the year 1937, the people's revolutionary movement in Tripura was in full force. Politics plunged the state into turmoil. The Janmangal Samiti of Tripura started a people's movement with the demand for a responsible government under the control of the king. The political movements of Tripura on the one side, and the allegation of the British Government on the other that the Tripura regime sympathized with the revolutionaries made Bir Bikram falter. The British Government further alleged that Tripura was harboring armed revolutionaries, and the Maharaja was turning a blind eye. No doubt, Maharaja Bir Bikram had a soft corner for the revolutionaries. On the day Khudiram was to be hanged, a kirtan (religious song) was sung throughout the day for his rescue in the inner mahal of the palace. In response to Rabindranath's call, the ceremony of tying rakhi round the wrists of everyone was also performed in the royal family. The people of Tripura welcomed Maharaja Bir Bikram's desire for administrative reforms and the introduction of a welfare system. That was why, the newspaper *Dhaka Prakash* published from

Dhaka wrote in its editorial as under: 'We think it expedient to say some words to the people of Tripura. The all-round welfare of the state does not depend on the king alone. It depends mostly on the noble intention of the subjects. For this purpose, the king and his subjects need to cooperate in all matters.'

The news in *Dhaka Prakash* itself proved that Maharaja Bir Bikram wanted the state to be governed in a democratic manner, keeping pace with the times. He issued a proclamation on 1 November 1938 for the welfare of the people:

> By whatever system of government, a state may be administered, it is not possible to have good administration in a state without having dutiful employees. The all-round welfare of the state and its subjects depends solely on government employees. Amongst the employees, those who try to run the government effectively do proper justice forthwith without discrimination of race and religion, consider themselves as guardians, counselors and servants of the people, and devote themselves constantly to the state and its well-being; only those employees will be considered as faithful and will be appreciated by all as dutiful, honest government employees ... But at present, in view of the change of condition among the native states of British India, the method of running the government by the employees of this state is showing signs of instability ... Now, in British India the demand for self-governance is growing. I believe, by keeping with this trend, the bad reputation about the administration of Tripura can be corrected.

This proclamation once again proved that Bir Bikram was a farsighted person. His wisdom could read the writing on the wall. He knew he was the last king of the Tripura dynasty and declared it openly in royal court. However, he could not help responding to the poet's invitation to visit Shantiniketan even when the Congress-led other people's movements all over the state were well underway. On 7 January 1939, Bir Bikaram arrived at noon at Shantiniketan, along with his courtiers. Somendra Chandra, meanwhile, had reached four days before the Maharaja's arrival, to get everything ready for the Maharaja's stay. On 5 January, the rehearsal of the play *Tasher Desh* was going on in the western veranda of Uttarayan. Somendra Chandra was viewing the rehearsal seated beside Gurudev. The rehearsal was so extraordinary that Somendra Chandra said to the poet in an exultant voice: 'It would be better to show this dramatic performance to the Maharaja.' Hearing this, Rabindranath said with a smile, 'No, Somendra, this drama I will not show to your Maharaja. He may be unhappy to see it. I will show him *Chandalika* instead.'

The next day, the rehearsal of *Chandalika* was conducted. Seeing this, Somendra Chandra requested Gurudev to show both the dramas to the Maharaja. The poet said: 'Listen, Somendra, a lot of chaos happens in the administrative realm of the king in *Tasher Desh*. I don't want to offend him. I've decided to show him *Chandalika*. It'll be graceful.'

The ceremonial felicitation of Maharaja Bir Bikram Manikya was arranged at the mango grove on the evening of 7 January 1939. The ceremonial compound under the canopy was adorned with flowers and leaves, paintings on the floor, the scent of incense and the glow of lamps. The seats of the poet and the Maharaja were imprinted with graceful designs. Rabindranath himself, along with the directors of Visva Bharati, the principal, professors, all the students and other important and respectable men and women were waiting to welcome the Maharaja. When the Maharaja came to the meeting, the poet stood up to greet him and made him sit beside him. The moment the women blew the conch shell, a small girl received the

Maharaja and the poet with garlands and a dot of sandal paste on each of their foreheads. After the welcome song, Shastri Mahashay in Sanskrit and Kshitimohan Sen in Bengali read out the welcome address. Then it was time for the poet to deliver his speech:

> My heart, like the setting sun, disperses its blessings to you from the western horizon of my life. The light of another day's auspicious union enkindles my union today with you; I am happy to inform you of that incident. At that time, you were not born, and I was a boy. Once, your late great grandfather Bir Chandra Manikya sent his minister to Jorasanko only to convey that he wanted to honour me as a "Great Poet". This was the first time I received a felicitation from the country ... My relationship with your forefathers was ... a true relationship. Today, your arrival has brought the southerly wind of the happy memories of the past.

During his stay at Shantiniketan, the Maharaja was shown various departments of Shantiniketan and Sriniketan. The Maharaja was very pleased to see Patha Bhavana, Vidya Bhavana, Sri Bhavana, China Library and heaps of mementos received by the poet from the country and abroad as a token of respect. The exhibition of paintings at Kala Bhavana also enchanted him. The following day, *Chandalika* was staged at Singha Sadan. The poet sat between Mr Leonard Elmhirst and the Maharaja. He was explaining the main theme of the play to both. He tried to express by the gestures of his fingers the meaning of the music and the dance. This dramatic performance made a deep impression on Bir Bikram. During his reign, several plays were staged in the inner mahal, the inspiration for which he owed to Kabiguru Rabindranath.

After the play was over, the poet sat with the Maharaja in seclusion at Uttarayan. The poet informed the Maharaja that the plan to expand Sangeet Bhavana was hindered by tight finances. A bigger stage was urgently required. Maharaja Bir Bikram then and there promised to pay 20,000 rupees for this purpose. The money would be given in installments.

On 9 January, the Maharaja set out for Calcutta with his companions. That very day, an accident took place. A few days earlier, after receiving an urgent letter from his wife, Somendra Chandra had been forced to leave Shantiniketan for Lucknow via the Dehradun Express. Shailesh Chandra Deb Barma, the grandson of Mahim Chandra and nephew of Somendra Chandra, was then a student at Shantiniketan. A telegram soon reached him: 'Dehradoon Express disaster Renu (nickname of Somendra) going Lucknow no information.' Somendra Chandra had died in that accident. With tears rolling down his cheeks, the poet said, 'Somendra has paid his last fee to me as a Guru, bringing his Maharaja here.'

After coming back to Tripura, the Maharaja kept his promise. A sum of 5,000 rupees was allotted for Sangeet Bhavana and the poet was informed accordingly. Rabindranath's personal secretary, Sri Sudhakanta Roy Chowdhury, wrote a letter from Mangpu: 'I have informed the poet about the allotment of 5,000 rupees this year out of 20,000 rupees ... Hope that the balance amount will be received soon next year.'

The instalments were accordingly sent to Shantiniketan. Somebody might wonder whether there might have been occasional lapses in sending the promised sums. In response, one example would be sufficient to clarify such doubts. In 1901, when Brahma Vidyalaya was inaugurated at Shantiniketan, the late Maharaja Radha Kishore Manikya allotted a grant of 1,000 rupees per year to the school. However, the full grant could not be paid during the reign of Bir Bikram because of the onset of the Second World War. But Maharaja Bir Bikram paid all the arrears in the year 1941 along with the grant of 1,000 rupees. On 25 February 1941, Rathindranath Tagore, the working secretary, wrote a letter of gratitude to Dwijendra Chandra Dutta, the Maharaja's personal secretary:

> Allow me to thank you for your letter no. D.O3569/E dated 3 Poush 1350 (1941), conveying the order of His Highness the Maharaja Manikya Bahadur for the restoration of the grant having been paid at the reduced rate during the last few years. I am pleased that His Highness has given his usual sympathetic consideration to the cause of Visva-Bharati and I request you to kindly convey my gratitude to him.

After his return from Shantiniketan, Maharaja Bir Bikram, along with a few courtiers, set out on a journey to tour the world. While crossing the Atlantic and Pacific Ocean by ship on their way to Europe, America and Australia, the discussion with co-passengers frequently came around to the subject of Rabindranath Tagore. Bir Bikram was amazed by the kind of respect the foreigners had for the poet.

Bir Bikram returned to Tripura after seven months of his long world tour. Against the background of the Second World War, Tripura was in a rather chaotic condition. A companion of the Maharaja during his world tour, Dwijendra Chandra Dutta, informed the poet about the happy memories of this tour. Rabindranath replied to him in a letter dated 12 February 1940: 'I am happy to learn that you have been introduced to a few of my friends, who became my devotees during my spell abroad. Most of them are now scattered or dead. I do not know whether you have met Einstein ... Indeed, I have had the privilege of receiving true respect from far-off foreigners.'

On 14 February, Rabindranth's personal secretary, Sri Sudhakanta Roy Chowdhury, wrote: 'Without going abroad, no Indian will understand how Rabindranath has been received in foreign countries and how much respect he gets in Europe.'

In one of the many battles of the Second World War, the Tripura Rifles were skirmishing against the Japanese in the forested provinces of Rangoon. In the meantime, Rajmata Maharani Arundhuti Mahadevi passed away. At the shraddha ceremony, the Maharaja was absorbed in reminiscence. At that time, Mr Tailor, the station master of Akhaura Railway Station, came to the royal court and reported the urgent news about the dangerous situation on the border.

The year was 1941. A notorious riot at Raipura in the Dhaka district affected thousands of people from the Hindu minority forcing them to assemble at Akhaura Station to seek shelter. The Provincial Government of Bengal did not do anything to keep law and order under control to stop the infamous riot and was totally uninterested in giving shelter to the displaced. The District Authority of Comilla was a silent spectator. The news of the misery of the refugees moved Bir Bikram so deeply that he at once ordered Tripura's borders and facilities to be opened for them. The magnanimous Maharaja Bir Bikram Manikya not only opened the border but also released funds from the royal treasury for the service of imperilled human beings.

Against the backdrop of refugees coming to Tripura, the Maharaja circulated his New Year message in a proclamation dated 1 Baishak 1351 (1941):

> Those displaced men, women, children and old people who have been given shelter now in this state ... I hope that they will soon be restored to their normal lives. Tripura has always given shelter to people of various castes and creeds throughout its glorious history. It is a universally acknowledged fact that my forefather, the great king Govinda Manikya, gave shelter to Shah Shuja, who was being hounded by the wrathful Mughal emperor Aurangzeb

... I am firmly resolved by all means and at all times to continue this noble tradition of hospitality ... All the distressed who seek shelter in this large human society are equal in my eyes. My government and I strive to remain equitable in this regard. I plead with everyone this New Year to remember our history and to not impair unity, love and affection. 'I am proud to see my Hindu and Muslim subjects extending their hands in service to these beleaguered people. Let the Almighty bless all my subjects and the displaced people who now seek refuge in our land.

Those days were awful for Tripura. All work stopped. Offices, schools, business places and courts were closed. Tripura, in fact, had no capacity to bear the burden of thousands of refugees. Still, Tripura resolved to do it because it did not forget its own culture. Almost all the newspapers of India covered the tales of the Maharaja's glory. The director and the editor of United Press, Sri Bidhubhusan Sengupta had depicted a clear picture of that time in his letter dated 17 April 1941, written to Dwijendra Chandra Dutta:

> All roads lead to Tripura now and all eyes are directed at its wonderful Ruler with reverence and love. Tripura has done a miracle and has aroused the admiration of the whole country. May the flag of Tripura fly high for all time to come ... I am afraid you are all extremely busy with His Highness, who is personally succouring the Daridranarayan. I do not, therefore, propose to prolong my letter but shall be delighted to have a line in reply.

Perhaps, in all of world history, it has never been heard that a king's royal court, used for administrative purposes, was used as a place to celebrate the birthday of a poet. On account of Rabindranath's old age and illness, Maharaja Bir Bikram desired to celebrate the poet's eightieth birthday in a way that was never done before. His great grandfather Maharaja Bir Chandra had felicitated the poet for the first time with the royal honour of the 'Great Poet'. Bir Bikram, also following Bir Chandra, cherished the idea of conferring a royal honour on the poet in the last stage of his life and to leave his signature in a royal lotus seal. On the morning of 25 Baishak, 'Rabindra Jayanti Bisesh Durbar' was held in the durbar hall of Ujjayanta Rajprasad. According to convention, when the Maharaja enters the durbar hall with his courtiers, the pandits start reciting sacred Vedic hymns and benedictory words. With the permission of the Maharaja, Brajendra Kishore said in his speech:

> In no part of India has a poet's birthday ceremony been held in the special royal durbar of a king. I think it is a matter of pride for Tripura to earn this distinction ... many such days had passed in my life when the message of Rabindranath lit my way towards truth and justice. His advisory letters are one of my invaluable treasures.

In the concluding part, Brajendra Kishore added: 'Today, the king of our country, on the eightieth birthday of that very Rabindranath, has decided to celebrate his Jayanti festival in a royal style at durbar hall ... I pray this auspicious ceremony will augur well for our state.'

Then, the chief secretary of the Maharaja read out the *robkari* (proclamation) pertaining to Rabindranath. Kabiguru Rabindranath Tagore was adorned with the title of 'Bharat Bhaskar' (Sun of India) honouring his contributions to the Indian subcontinent. The name of the great poet was proclaimed as 'Bharat Bhaskar' by an announcement of the *nakib* (usher) and published in the government's administrative gazette.

The memorable proclamation bearing 'No. 252/Durbar', embellished with royal insignia, the royal lotus seal and the signature of the king of Tripura in Bengali, were as under:

Durbar/ Winner of Deadly Wars Mahamahoday Fifth Srijukta Maharaja of Tripura Captain His Highness Maharaja Manikya Sri Bir Bikram Kishore Deb Barma Bahadur K.C.S.I. Area— Independent Tripura state.

Narapateradeshohayang Karakbargeyshu Prachratu Paramashya Birajitey-Capital–Hastinapur– end-25 Baishak, 1351 (Tripura).

As the party this side is desirous to celebrate the eightieth birthday of the world-famous poet Srijut Rabindranath Tagore Mahoday, who is the pride of Bengal, for that matter of India as a whole:

The search for nectar is the highest goal of human life on earth—*"Martyoha Mrita Bhabati Etabadanu Shashanam."* Thus, the saints have given an opportunity to the world to realize the spirit of God through poetical works. The revelation of this immortal light in Rabindranath's blossoming compositions had attracted the then king of this kingdom, Maharaja Bir Chandra Manikya Bahadur, a qualified and witty person, and great grandfather of the party this side—it was he who had acclaimed a young Rabi with a royal felicitation—

The great poet had prayed ceaselessly for the welfare of this state in his literature, poetry and thought, and had developed a close friendship with Maharaja Radha Kishore Manikya Bahadur, grandfather of the party this side who was the torchbearer of a new age in Tripura state—

As the party this side was obliged to have the honour to participate at the seventieth birthday ceremony of the great poet in Calcutta, it is the duty of Tripura state to felicitate the great poet on his eightieth birthday with all the reverence due in his matured stage of a talent and toward he who is the lighthouse of Indian culture and art—

Jyotsna-bhirahata mahadbudayandhakaram.

Therefore,
To make this birthday ceremony worthy of being
Remembered forever
Poet Srijut Rabindranath Tagore Mahoday
Is adorned with the title 'Bharat Bhaskar'
And
Let God by His blessings Give the poet a hundred years of good health.

It is a matter of great regret that there is no mention in the history of Bengal or anywhere else about the first and the last honour conferred on the great poet by Tripura. A handful of intellectuals might be aware of this information, but most people are not. The so-called Indian intelligentsia frequently glosses over the honours given to the poet by his own country and instead always celebrates the accolades that came from abroad. Rabindranath, therefore, did not accept the felicitation of the people who came all the way to Shantiniketan from Calcutta to congratulate him after the receipt of the Nobel Prize. Nobody knows better than Rabindranath about the character of the Bengalis, for that matter of Indians in general. But the poet with all humility always accepted the honours given to him by this small state, Tripura. He mentioned it so many times, but none paid heed to it because the country's own honours weren't deemed as significant as those conferred on him by institutions in Europe. To speak frankly, most people even today don't even know where Tripura is. They think that Tripura is part of Assam, and that Agarpara and Agartala are the same. They, therefore, thought it prudent not to attach any importance to the honours given to Rabindranath by the tiny state of Tripura. We have not come across any literary compositions where Rabindranath was acclaimed as 'Bharat Bhaskar'. No one ever tried to understand the implications of Rabindranath's long continuous friendship with the four generations of Tripura Maharajas.

It might have made some readers curious as to why, in the proclamation of 'Bharat Bhaskar', the name of the capital was written 'Hastinapur' instead of Agartala. From time immemorial, in the charters of Tripura, the name of the capital has been mentioned as Hastinapur although the physical location of the capital has shifted multiple times. In ancient times, Hastinapur was the capital of the Pandavas and Kauravas. Does it mean that the mention of Hastinapur as the capital of Tripura instead of a real location indicates the royal dynasty's descent from the Pandavas and the Kauravas?

This topic, though not a part of our subject of discussion, demands clarification now that the question has been raised. According to the Puranas, Druhya, the banished prince (and a successor of the Kurus) was directed to go to Gandhara and then towards the north. Why Gandhara? Gandhara then referred to the Unnan province of China. Does it mean that the motherland of the Pandavas and the Kauravas was in China or Tibet? A reading of the eighty-first chapter of *Kalika Purana* reveals that the river Kapil originated from Brahmabil of the Kamakhya mountains. Druhya advanced from Unnan to Kamakhya along the banks of the river Kapil and established his kingdom in Trivega. The *Rajmala* mentions that the forefathers of the Tripura kings: 'Durhya established a city at the place Trivega/ The seat of the king was on the banks of the river Kapil.'

In the book, *The Background of Assamese Culture*, R.M. Nath had given a different explanation for Durhya's establishing his kingdom at Trivega:

> The Tipperahs have a tradition that Durhya, one of the sons of Yayati, the renowned king of the lunar dynasty of Delhi, married a Bodo princess against his father's wishes and was disinherited. He preferred to live with his beloved in her hilly home amongst her relatives, and his progeny became a ruling race. The ruling class of Tipperahs ascends from this traditional episode ... Whatever

might have been the origin of the royal dynasty, it is traditionally believed that once Pratordon came over to Assam and established a kingdom named Trivega in about 1900 BC, with his headquarters on the bank of the Kapil River in the present Nowgong district, and the dynasty ruled for fourteen generations.

A question thus arises whether the Pandavas and Kurus were Mongols or not. In this context, several scholars have proved that the Pandavas and Kurus hailed from a clan of Tibetans. The reasons given by them are as under:

1. Draupadi's marriage to multiple brothers was part of a custom in vogue only in Tibet and not in India.
2. Arjun was not caught red-handed in the garb of Brihannala for years together as most of the Tibetans do not have moustaches and beards. Some of them, though of age, have no facial hair.
3. The practice of enticing a man with the desire to beget a child was not prevalent in India at that period, but it was very much in vogue in Tibet.
4. The crossover of the Himalayas was the path of the Pandava's voluntary journey to the land of death. It means the Pandavas returned to their motherland, Tibet.
5. A dog had accompanied the Pandavas on their way to the last journey, which is a Tibetan custom.

The pundits all over the world admitted that the Mongolians in ancient times, much before the birth of Christ, came to India and established kingdoms. Tripura was one of them.

Now, let us return to our subject. The poet was bedridden at that time. He was unable to walk. The poet, whose handwritings were like pearls, could now not even hold the pen to write his signature.

His mind conjured up dozens of songs and poems, but he could not give them a home on the page. It was a terrible situation for any writer. At that point of time, Bhupendra Chandra Chakraborty, as a representative of the Maharaja, had appeared before the poet at Shantiniketan to hand him the letter proclaiming him as the 'Bharat Bhaskar', along with royal presents such as white silken stole, gold coins and ornate dresses. On 30 Baishak (1941), Rathindranath wrote to Brajendra Kishore:

> It is decided that the proclamation of the Maharaja will be given today to Baba Mahashay in the evening. The matter will end as per Nandalal Babu's advice by arranging a function for a small time. You will come to know the detailed report of the function from Bhupendra Babu. The honour conferred to Baba Mahashay in this way is befitting to the Maharaja of Tripura and it has touched all our hearts.

The love and affection of Rabindranath towards Tripura did not deter him despite his severe illness from doing the last ritual duty of his life. If the honour bestowed on the poet was another insignificant matter, he could have received it in his sickbed. However, he did not do that. He was unable to write and, therefore, the proclamation was embellished with a signature of his trembling fingers. On 30 Baishak, the poet, sitting on an invalid's chair, came to the meeting at Uttarayan and accepted the address of honour given by Maharaja Bir Bikram Kishore Manikya with great love and affection.

Rabindranath Tagore had received countless honours, mostly from abroad. As a mark of protest against the Jallianwala Bagh massacre, he had also returned the Knighthood given by the British Government. For a person of his stature, who received several laurels and honours and above all, the highest honour of literature, the Nobel Prize, he should not have cared about honours conferred on him by a small state like Tripura; but the cordial relationship that he shared with the state was evident in his long speech. He did not underestimate this local honour in comparison to his many international accolades. Rabindranath had given a glorious place to Tripura in the history of the world. In his speech, as usual, Rabindranath expressed his respect and gratitude to Maharaja Bir Chandra and Radha Kishore. The poet was not in a position due to his illness to read out the speech and, therefore, Rathindranath Tagore, the poet's son, did so on his behalf:

> I once received an unexpected honour from the royal family of Tripura; the time is ripe now to remember it specially and make it memorable. This sort of an occurrence is rare in this world… It is difficult to find in the history of literature instances of such a spontaneous and open friendship between a king and a tender-aged poet doubtful of his own road to fame … Yet, there is a special and far greater reason for my happiness—when I learned that the present Maharaja, with unusual generosity, had given shelter to countless oppressed and distressed people, the news filled me with joy and pride. I understood that his hereditary title of the king has been engraved in the minds of all the people of Bangladesh. Bengal's deity of fortune has blessed the royal lineage … Now my health is weak; let my feeble voice join the people of the country …

The poet remembered the refuge given by Maharaja Bir Bikram to the oppressed people of the Raipur riots. Rabindranath once wrote a song to felicitate Maharaja Radha Kishore. The lyrics of the song ran like this: 'Thy deft hands relieve the sufferings of the distressed/ Thy assurance of safety dispels fear of the weak.'

The history thereafter was mournful. Maharaja Bir Bikram, after joining the Standing Committee of the Chamber of Princes, was going from Bombay to Bangalore by train. On the morning of 23 Shaon, the train stopped for some reason near Guntakal. Dwijendra Chandra Dutta got down from the train and was startled to read the headlines of the newspaper in the hands of a co-passenger. The poet had passed away. He was called by a summons unknown on 22 Shaon at noon. When the train reached Guntakal, Dutta Mahashay purchased a newspaper and went up to the Maharaja's compartment to inform him. The Maharaja said, 'I came to know this a while ago. The sun (*Rabi*) had risen in the sky of Tripura's fortune at an auspicious time.' After the lamentation was over, he directed Sri Dutta to send a letter of condolence to Rathindranath Tagore by telegram and to immediately send directions to the minister to close all offices, courts and schools as a demonstration of respect for the departed soul.

In a benumbed Tripura, a day of condolence was observed. The death of an intimate friend created an outcry in the royal family. Everybody was dumbstruck. The procession of mourning reflected how much Rabindranath was loved in Tripura. Although the poet had embraced death, he was and is still alive. That was why he wrote '*Maran Re Tunhu Mama Shyam Saman*' (Death, you are like Shyam to me). Shyam is another name of a god who is omnipotent and deathless.

Maharaja Bir Bikram was a person with a modern outlook. He wanted to establish a harmony amongst all religions. His farsightedness could visualize that after India's independence there would be no existence of native states. He had a strong desire to merge with the stream of the common Indian populace. Till his death, he was the main spokesman to advocate the union of Tripura with India. He understood that the development of a small state would not be possible without its integration with India. Tripura therefore was the first native state that officially announced its desire to be an integral part of the Indian dominion.

Maharaja Bir Bikram was not only a thoughtful political administrator, but also like his forefathers, he nurtured his interests and practiced literature and music. He was a maestro of dramaturgy. He wrote two dramas, *Chand Kumudini* and *Sri Radha-Krishner Leela Bilash*. In the year 1934, the play *Sri Radha-Krishner Leela Bilash* was staged at Tripura House, Calcutta, and earned the applause of the critics and connoisseurs. He was quite proficient in classical music. He was adept at playing the sitar and esraj. He recorded the raga Malkosh in sitar. He did not allow the Record Company to market it despite repeated requests. Many musicians, instrumentalists and dancers—Ustad Alauddin Khan, Enayat Khan, Mazafar Khan, Majid Khan, Adam Boksh, Munna Khan and dancer Alokananda, to name a few—adorned his royal court. His natural attraction towards music and his respect for the musicians had earned the praise of all. Ustad Alauddin Khan and Anil Krishna Deb Barman used to play sarod and sitar for hours together. Ustad Alauddin Khan was in the royal court as an instrumentalist for many years. How much respect Bir Bikram used to command in his eyes would be evident from a letter he had written to Anil Krishna Deb Barman: 'By the blessings of Maharaja Bahadur, I have gained affection and fame.'

In another letter he wrote: 'Pay my crores and crores of pranamas (respects) to the auspicious feet of Srijukta Maharaja Bahadur …I am his worthless son and therefore, praying his forgiveness for the lapses committed by me.'

Although Tripura was in turmoil due to various kinds of political movements and agitations, the progress in arts and culture remained unhindered during the regime of Bir Bikram Kishore. Rather, his period of reign was marked as a 'New Age' in Tripura. He wanted to introduce a new educational system and modern ideas in culture. His contribution to art, culture and religion has not been properly evaluated up to now. He was not only a patron, but also an adept player in the field of literature and music. As Holi and Basanta Utsav were national festivals of Tripura, there were hardly any Maharajas, queens, princes and princesses who did not write any poem on this subject. Bir Bikram was no exception. From his book of poems, *Holi*, let me quote one small lyrical piece:

Oh beloved, the round mark in your forehead
Is like a reddish nimbus in the sky.
That round mark flashes lightning,
The rumbling clouds assemble for an
Ostentatious show. Who is
Sprinkling coloured water now, oh beloved!

After his world tour in 1939, Bir Bikram wrote a travelogue titled *Memorandum of World Tours*. He recorded the ideas that had germinated out of his experience with different climatic conditions, environments and natures of human beings in various places. He even wrote an introduction to this book with the desire to publish it, but unfortunately the book could not be published due to his immature death. Sri Bikach Chowdhury, in his book, *Rabindra Sannidhey Tripura*, mentioned that he found the book in the custody of Nirmalya Dutta, son of the late Dwijendra Chandra Dutta, who was a companion of the Maharaja on that journey.

On 17 May 1947, Maharaja Bir Bikram Manikya left the earthly abode at the young age of thirty-nine. He was the last king of Tripura.

5

Rabindranath and Maharaja Kumar Brajendra Kishore

This was a most astonishing relationship. Brajendra Kishore, son of Maharaja Radha Kishore, was Rabindranath's spiritual son. Rabindranath came into view as a shining pole star in the life of this prince in the year 1901. No matter the circumstance, Rabindranath wrote innumerable letters to Brajendra Kishore to keep him informed of his whereabouts and to enquire about Brajendra's well-being.

Towards the end of October 1901, the poet was invited to Tripura by Maharaja Radha Kishore. He stayed in one of the joint bungalows. Brajendra Kishore had set aside these bungalows for his personal use. Reflecting on his first meeting with the poet, Brajendra Kishore wrote:

> I was then twelve or fourteen years old. At that time, I was fortunate to have an interview with Rabindranath. That high placid appearance with long curly hairs looked very graceful. The deep impression he made on me is still vivid in my memory after all these years. He seemed new and strange ... Once, I told the

poet unhesitatingly to adopt me as one of his family members ... The legacy of my royal lineage hadn't even occurred to me. The poet took me close to him with great joy and said, "Surely, I will do so; all arrangements will be made." From that very day, I have been fortunate enough to have bonded so affectionately with the poet.

Rabindranath lived up to his words. After the establishment of Brahmacharya Ashram in 1901, he made all arrangements for Brajendra Kishore to come to Shantiniketan for his education under his guidance. He even got the permission of Radha Kishore, but the British Government and royal rules and regulations stood in the way. The British Government established Mayo College in Ajmer for the education of the princes of native states. Rabindranath and Radha Kishore had no faith in the imitation of the English and European style in daily life and conduct. Rabindranath wanted to inspire the princes with the ideal of ancient India. While the admission of Brajendra Kishore was almost certain in Brahmacharya Ashram at Shantiniketan, political interventions foiled the attempt and Rabindranath's earnest desire could not be fulfilled.

On his return from Agartala, Rabindranath, with Radha Kishore's permission, took Brajendra Kishore along with him. He had a mind to acquaint Maharaja Kumar with the environment of Shantiniketan. The poet first went to Shilaidaha from Agartala and thereafter to Calcutta and then to Shantiniketan. In the collection, *Rabindranath O Tripura*, it is mentioned that Brajendra Kishore got so much care and affection from the poet's wife at Shilaidaha that he remembered it throughout his life. However, Rabindranath's letter, written to Thakurdas Mukhopadhyay on 19 November 1901, suggests that it was at Shantiniketan and not at Shilaidaha where Brajendra Kishore was received by the poet's wife, Mrinalini Devi. When Mrinalini Devi died, Brajendra Kishore, in his letter of condolence, mentioned her motherly love and affection: '...The musk of our false aristocracy faded away before the strength and depth of her affection. I'm greatly pained by her absence.'

In his response, Rabindranath wrote to Brajendra Kishore on 4 December 1902:

> You have already been touched by her love in such a short time. Her nature was full of motherly warmth and in her eyes, you were like her child. She had been waiting eagerly for you to come here to the Vidyalaya. If you were with her, you would not have felt the absence of your mother even for a moment.

Rabindranath understood that the inclusion of the prince of Tripura in the list of students at Shantiniketan would enhance the prestige of the institution and set an example for the princes of native states to be educated in the ideals of ancient India. On 17 November, he wrote to Brajendra Kishore:

> I have written a letter to the Maharaja; I hope there will be no difficulty for your coming here. Rathi has been eagerly waiting for you. While coming, bring your instruments like those of carpentry and fretwork with you. You may bring your bicycle and books for reading at home. I will start the work of the Vidyalaya after you arrive here. Do not allow December to pass by.

Even after all this, nothing happened. Though Tripura was an independent state, yet the British Government exerted considerable influence over it. They were suspicious of the rather patriotic and egalitarian atmosphere at Shantiniketan. Besides the antagonism of the courtiers further prevented Brajendra Kishore from being educated at Shantiniketan. The school had been established on 22 December 1901.

Rabindranath could not ever forget the pain of not being able to accommodate the prince of Tripura as a student at his academy. Upon hearing that he'd been admitted to a school in Comilla, run by the British Government, Rabindranath wrote in an undated letter:

I am sorry to hear that you have been enrolled at a school in Comilla. I can very well understand that it will be oppressive for you. The uncivil arrogance and hateful conduct of this barbarian race are quite distressing ... Those who hate our whole nation, how they will respect me? And even if they do, why should I accept it? There cannot be any scene more shameful than this, where an insulted nation tries to gain the love of the English Sahebs. However, bear it out and save the independence of your mind. If you can, you will be able to protect your valour even in adverse conditions. May God always save you from all falsehoods!

Rabindranath had the unusual ability to nullify his own anguish. All his poems were instances of it. A supernatural self-confidence gave him the strength to deal with distress. In a letter dated 7 April written to Brajendra Kishore, he wrote: 'It is perhaps better for you not to come to my school, because I intend to do my work in seclusion, out of the purview of public discussion. If you come here, thousands of words will be spoken creating a hullabaloo. My peace of mind would naturally be hampered by this.'

His affection for Brajendra Kishore, made Rabindranath akin to the blind king Dhritarashtra of the Mahabharata. He had always forgiven Brajendra Kishore's vices and lapses; otherwise, how could he go out of his way and support Brajendra Kishore when he got married the second time? In Tripura, it was customary for the princes to have more than one queen, and plenty of concubines. The concubines were called Kachchha Rani. When Brajendra Kishore, in the presence of his first queen, got married again, the people of

Tripura of course accepted it, but why did Rabindranath approve of the same on the pretext of custom and convention? Affection can be a very dangerous thing. Rabindranath coolly ignored the insult and harm done to the first deprived queen of Brajendra Kishore. This incident proves beyond doubt that Rabindranath as a person was blinded by affection. What was normal in Tripura was unacceptable to the poet; why then did he not prevent Brajendra Kishore from this unjust, inhumane act? Instead of recognizing the second marriage, he could have succeeded in preventing Brajendra Kishore from carrying on with it, as Brajendra Kishore immensely respected the poet and could not have turned down his words.

In a letter to the prince, Rabindranath for the first time announced the ideals of his Brahmacharya Ashram. Recalling the ideals of ancient India, he advised the prince to stand with vigour and valour:

> ... Keep it firmly in mind that there is no disgrace in poverty, no shame in wearing loincloth and no incivility at all in the absence of furniture. Those who advocate abundance of riches and wealth, trade and business, collection of material objects as a symbol of civilization—they merely emulate barbarism in the name of civilization ... The English teacher will try in many ways to tarnish your natural valour ... Let your valour increase against that effort. Let the blessing of India save you, let the hands of God's assurance save you, and let your own talent save you. Remember that it is better to die than to accept the customs and practices of alien *mlechchhas*. "*Swadharmey Nidhanang Sreya Paradharmo Bhayabaha*" (It is better to die in the practice of one's own dharma because imitating those of others can be dangerous).

Rabindranath's literary intentions of this period could be surmised from the letters written to Brajendra Kishore, with whom the poet shared his thoughts and inspirations. In the June issue of *Bangadarshan*, 1902, his article '*Brahman*' was published. An English master had kicked one Maharastrian Brahmin and the matter had gone to High Court. There was terrible agitation in the indigenous newspapers when the judge dismissed the incident as an insignificant one in his verdict. The incident formed the subject matter of the article '*Brahman*'; Rabindranath expressed his opinion about the modern application of the ideals of ancient India. He opined that the Brahmans of the modern age had fallen from the grace of their ideals and had become an object of ridicule. The article was criticized for its rather orthodox perspectives.

It was written in June 1902, but if read along with a letter dated 20 April of the same year, written to Brajendra Kishore, one might detect Rabindranath's line of thought, which he shared with the prince well before the article was published:

In India, there is a scarcity of real Brahman and Kshatriya societies. Being affected by distress, we all have become Shudras (the lowest cast in Hindu society). If these two societies can be revived, only then may India regain its name. I have set about trying my best to re-establish Brahman ideals. Feeling the spirit of the Kshatriya inside you, nurture in your heart a strong resolve to propagate that ideal in your society. You are not expected to embrace the peaceful, meditative and dispassionate nature of the Brahman. Who will then preserve strength and valour in society? Where is the footing of Brahmans in the absence of valour and prowess of the Kshatriyas? On whose immobile strength will the peace of Brahmans be preserved? The glory of Kshatriya valour lies in giving shelter to the highest ideals of religion in society, protecting it from tyranny and hindrances. It is not the glorious Kshatriya religion, where one misuses power or gets lost in waywardness, luxury, and corruption, or is misled into empty egotism by the flattery of the courtiers. In this way, our Kshatriyas, having lost their original virtue, are now immersed in all kinds of sinful merriment. Those who were protectors of the whole society are now leading the disgraceful lives of brutes. Is not death better than this?

In the same letter, Rabindranath made an intense attempt to arouse Kshatriya pride in Brajendra Kishore! The letter goes on:

> Son, never, ever forget you are a Kshatriya. Any education and company should not trounce your valour, vigour and reverence. It is the duty of Kshatriyas to save the country and society from injustice, outrage, irreligiousness and immoral practices. There cannot be any other such pure and noble duty. You must take the responsibility to brighten again the ideals of the Kshatriya dharma in India by giving up fear, despising death, embracing sorrows, ignoring poverty and keeping your self-respect unimpaired. To accept that responsibility, you will have to keep your valour burning in the secret cave of your heart like a sacrificial fire.

Distance played a vital role in Rabindranath's relationship with Brajendra Kishore: it fastened them in an unbreakable bond. The exchange of numerous letters strengthened their relationship. Indeed, Brajendra Kishore was not known to have made any critical decision without the poet's consent.

Rabindranath was more of a father to Brajendra Kishore than Radha Kishore was. Brajendra Kishore, inspired by Rabindranath's exhortation to preserve the valour of Kshatriya dharma, wanted to join the Imperial Cadet Corps; he wrote a letter to Rabindranath to get his opinion on the subject. In reply, Rabindranath wrote on 16 Shaon 1309 (1902):

I am happy to receive your letter. I am glad to think that you will get the kind of education befitting a Kshatriya child in the Cadet Corps. Most of the princes of our country, in the company of English teachers, have sacrificed their nationalism and even their humanity ... I know undoubtedly that this sort of madness will never overwhelm you ... Without paying heed to anyone's praise or censure, patiently keep the sacrificial Kshatriya fire perennially burning with all sorts of fuel in your heart ... Amid all the dust and filth around you, like a son of heaven soaking in the river Ganges, you will move with untarnished purity, and without fear or hesitation.

Rabindranath had second thoughts after writing this. He thought, in the camp of Englishmen, an exhibition of the valour of Kshatriya dharma might have adverse consequences. A paternal Rabindranath, being stricken with the thought of danger threatening his child, cautioned Brajendra:

In whatever condition you're in, do not allow in any way the ideals of India to be erased from your heart. Always keep in mind that the barbarians of Europe, without understanding the true greatness of India, ridicule it. Do not grant any importance to this contempt. Surrender yourself wholeheartedly in all respects to India with calm reticence and unflinching discipline.

However, Brajendra Kishore could not stay up to the end. Adhering to Rabindranath's advice, he was staying there on his own, aloof, keeping his independence intact. He did not even pay heed to the Europeans jeering at him. His staying aloof and refusing to mix with others were considered a reflection of his haughtiness and, therefore, the English military teachers and the probationers started to insult him right and left. He was accustomed from his birth to be drenched in respect from all and sundry as the son of a king. After coming here, Brajendra Kishore was greatly perturbed by the insulting words of the English military teachers. All of them treated him as an uncultured woodman coming from the hilly forests of Tripura. Ultimately, even though he protested, the situation worsened beyond his tolerance and he returned home to avoid further clashes. He realized for the first time that the respect that comes out automatically in Tripura couldn't be expected beyond its borders. This experience had done him good and made him humane in future life. But his protest did not go in vain—because of his protest, disgraceful rules and regulations were changed. Brajendra Kishore was cheered by the kings of native states for this act.

Rabindranath felt sorry about what he'd read in Brajendra Kishore's letter, but he was also proud. The prince, whom he loved as his son, did not tamely accept the orders of the Englishmen; he held his head high by protesting against them. How affectionate Rabindranath was towards Brajendra Kishore and how persistently he would think about improving the young man's life can be seen from the letter dated 1 Kartik 1309 (1902): 'Accept my earnest blessing. I have always cherished this desire for you to be great; you will be a hero, and you will repay the debts of our Aryan forefathers ... I pray to God to make your life successful.'

The poet was in Giridih when Brajendra Kishore came back to Tripura from the Cadet Corps in a state of broken health. Rabindranath's health had improved considerably at Giridih. He was staying there as a guest of Srish Majumdar. On 11 November 1904, he wrote a letter to Mohit Chandra Sen: 'I am miraculously doing very well; this sort of incident never happened to me before.' He called Mohit Chandra to Giridih to recover his health. In the above letter, he wrote further: 'Next Monday, Jati is coming here along with the prince of Tripura; I have arranged a house for them.'

Rabindranath was worried about Brajendra Kishore's health, and he wrote a letter to Maharaja Radha Kishore requesting him to send Brajendra Kishore to Giridih so that he might recuperate and stay with the poet for a few days. Jatindranath Basu, accompanied by prince Brajendra reached Giridih on 12 September. Brajendra Kishore's reminiscence about his tour of Giridih is produced here in brief:

> Almost the whole day, the poet would charm everyone with his recitals of English or Bengali books ... During the period of our stay, the famous poem "Shivaji" was written. (This is not a correct statement, 'Shivaji Utsav' was written on 11 Bhadra, i.e., the last week of August; Brajendra Kishore was not at Giridih at that time.) He recited the poem before all and the same was sent to *Bangadarshan* for publication. The day it came, after getting printed, the usually calm and quiet Rabindranath grew suddenly furious. The issue was nothing but a negligible printing mistake. His friend Srish Chandra was the target of his wrath, but Srish remained silent. Rabindranath had the habit of doing everything immaculately... Suddenly, Mohit Chandra made his appearance. Seeing him at an unexpected time, the poet became somewhat suspicious. Although he sat with everyone to have food, the poet touched his body and exclaimed, "My God! He has got fever; as no food was given at the Calcutta house, he ran away from there and came here." He did not allow him to eat food; a sick diet was arranged. The poet with good humour told everybody about Mohit Babu's excessive fondness for food. The wretched professor kept sitting there with his head down; he did not utter a word. Walking along with the poet was another joy in Giridih ... While walking, he would speak about everything, the nearby trees, soil, flowers and leaves. No subject would be left untouched.

Though small, the waterfall Ushsri attracted everyone. The poet gave it a new name: "Asru (tears)". He gave so many explanations for that.

During his stay at Giridih, Rabindranath came to know that Sister Nivedita was planning to visit Bodh Gaya with a group of intellectuals. He wanted to join this tour with all his companions. The reason for planning this travel was not highlighted by Maharaja Kumar in his reminiscence. One should know that there was a purpose behind it. After the gradual decline of Buddhism owing to Islamic invasions, the Buddhist shrine of Gaya came into the possession of the Hindus. A Shaiva mahanta was looking after the shrine. However, Dharmapal from Sri Lanka, claimed that the shrine should be handed over to the Buddhists. As a result, there was a difference of opinion among the Hindus. Nivedita supported the Shaiva mahanta. While Dharmapal, taking advantage of the British laws, tried to re-establish Buddhism in India. In this dispute, Governor General Lord Curzon sympathized with the Buddhists. Nivedita took the initiative to increase the number of supporters in favour of the Hindu mahanta and, therefore, planned to visit Bodh Gaya with the topmost intellectuals.

On 8 October 1904, the afternoon of Mahalaya, Rabindranath, with his friends and followers, set out for Bodh Gaya. The passengers, in fact, were much greater in number than that of the list given by Rabindranath to Srish Chandra. Brajendra Kishore's reminiscence revealed:

> After spending a few days in Calcutta, Maharaja Kumar, with his teacher Mokshada Kumar Basu, joined the poet on his way to Bodh Gaya—it was during the last week of Aswin. The gang of companions was quite large—Jagadish Chandra Bose with

his wife, Sister Nivedita, the historian Jadunath Sarkar, two daughters of Ananda Mohan Basu, Rathindranath and Santosh Majumder, among others. He thought, even Mahim Chandra might be the one of the associates. He could only remember that there was some difference of opinion among the Buddhists and the journey was undertaken to settle the issue.

Jadunath Sarkar in his article, 'Nivedita as I Knew Her', had given an account of this journey. He wrote: 'Everyday, some passages from Warren's book *Buddhism in Translation* were read out, and off and on from Edwin Arnold's *Light of Asia*. The poet from time to time would sing or recite poems.'

Jadunath wrote about a Japanese fisherman who, with great hardship, had saved money to visit the place where Buddha attained enlightenment. In the evening he would sit under the Bodhi tree and chant mantras—*'Namo Namo Buddha Dibakaraya'* (Salute, Salute the sun-like Buddha). After that, Jadunath remarked: 'It is noteworthy that the poet remembered this mantra and put it as an utterance of Srimati in *Natir Puja*.'

Later, Rathindranath Tagore penned the experience of his visit to Bodh Gaya:

Darkness was imminent; the lamps were lighted in the windows of the temple. Silence was all pervading and amidst that the whirling of the Buddhist-mantra, *Om Manipadmey Hum*, in a low and deep sound reached the ears. Some of the Japanese pilgrims reciting the mantra repeatedly were going round the temple with incense. What a peaceful appearance they had and how deep was their devotion! How simple was their method of worship! ...Jagadish Chandra, Sister Nivedita and my father used to discuss the Buddhist religion and Buddhist history till late at night. Nivedita went on raising arguments one after another and Rabindranath tried to reach a fitting solution. The rest of us were absorbed in listening to their questions and answers and altercations. I believe this visit to Bodh Gaya had attracted my father to Buddhist religion and literature in the latter period. Coming back to Shantiniketan, he gave me the task to memorize *Dharmapada* from beginning to end. The reading of Pali (an ancient language) was also started by an order of my father, and I was engaged to translate the *Buddhacharita* of Ashvagosha.

Kumar Brajendra Kishore witnessed all these incidents and scenarios. During this visit, he met the topmost intellectuals of Bangladesh who showed him the path to excellence. As against them, he came to recognize his own shortcomings.

Many facets of Brajendra Kishore's life had already been discussed in the chapters of Maharaja Radha Kishore, Birendra Kishore and Bir Bikram Manikya. After the death of Radha Kishore, he became the prime minister of Maharaja Birendra Kishore. Rabindranath advised him to stand beside his elder brother in all circumstances. He left the prime minister's role within no time following the incidents of the Tripura Sundari lottery. After the death of his elder brother Birendra Kishore, he took up the prime minister's post again during the reign of his nephew, Maharaja Bir Bikram Manikya. Meanwhile, the poet came to Tripura for the seventh time. Tripura saw in him not only a poet, but also a politician and economist. The poet's versatile character was in full bloom only in Tripura and nowhere else. Thinking about the welfare of Tripura, he considered brotherly affection as paramount and, therefore, analyzed the responsibility of Brajendra Kishore's post: 'The general people should have unflinching faith in your natural justice. They should understand that the rules and regulations you will establish can be violated in no way by you or the king or any others.'

At the invitation of Brajendra Kishore, the poet visited Tripura for the last time in 1926. At the felicitation given to Rabindranath by Kishore Sahitya Samaj, Brajendra Kishore spoke with deep emotion about the poet's greatness. In response, the poet movingly said about Brajendra Kishore:

> I might not have done any other good to Tripura, but if I have been only able to improve Brajendra Kishore's character in the discharge of duty, then I will be proud to feel that I have done perennial good for this state. On this occasion, I bless him wholeheartedly. The memories associated with this place saddens me at present. My only joy is to see Brajendra Kishore here. I have come here at his invitation, overlooking my health and work. I enjoy the same cordial reception at his hands that I had once received from his father and grandfather ...

A few days after his return from Agartala, the poet got an invitation to visit Italy and England. The poet wanted Brajendra as his companion for this last visit. On his previous trip, Somendra Chandra had accompanied him. Rabindranath knew very well that Brajendra Kishore would get an opportunity to elevate his self by traveling abroad. In 1912, the poet had written to Brajendra Kishore: 'It comes to my mind again and again that you will profit by traveling to Europe for one or two years. Do not leave it as an absolute impossibility—whatever way it can be, at least once you should travel to this side.'

Rabindranath, therefore, was determined this time to have Brajendra Kishore as one of his tour companions. Having no alternative, Brajendra Kishore had to go. Taking leave from the administrative council for a few days, he set out for abroad for the first time on an Italian ship. It was Mussolini's regime in Italy. Rathindranath, Pratima Devi, Gourgopal Ghosh and Brajendra

Kishore accompanied the poet. The poet never got down from the deck of the ship. He would sit on the deck engaged in meditation, listening to the waves, or stayed locked away in his cabin, absorbed in writing. Describing Brajendra Kishore's experience, Satya Ranjan Basu wrote:

> One day, Brajendra Kishore tiptoed over very cautiously and stood behind the poet's seat. Without turning his head, Rabindranath said, "Prince, have you come? ... Well, sit down, let me talk about those past days." He discussed many things about Bir Chandra and Radha Kishore; his face was then lit up with joy. Maharaja Kumar said further, "... He did not forget to talk about what he had said a hundred times before, which was about the royal modesty and the courtesy of Bir Chandra at Kurseong. What great reverence for Bir Chandra the poet had!" That day, a meeting was held to felicitate the poet ... After his lecture in the overcrowded meeting hall was over, everyone thronged the poet for his autograph. He was exhausted after the long lecture. Being surrounded by the crowd; he could not find his way out of the hall. Seeing his condition, Brajendra Kishore went near him. Pushing almost everybody aside, he took the poet out. He desisted the autograph-collectors saying, "no more autographs, please." The poet also breathed freely and said, "How one can protect Brahmans without being a Kshatriya?"

Having experienced the culture of Europe, Brajendra Kishore returned alone after a few months to Tripura. Let us hear his experience: 'I perceived, in Italy, how the foreigners had accepted Rabindranath; when the boys and girls, old men and women respectfully kissed the dress worn by the poet, my heart was filled up with pride. I had heard that this sort of honour was reserved only for popes and emperors.'

Wherever Brajendra Kishore went, once he introduced himself as an Indian, the foreigners would start talking about Rabindranath. Brajendra Kishore said, 'I was enchanted by their awe, respect and reverence; I was beside myself with wonder …'

Two months after his arrival in India, Rabindranath and Brajendra Kishore met again. The poet at that time was spending his days in solitude at Barrackpore. After making several enquiries, Brajendra Kishore and his uncle Samarendra Chandra went there to meet the poet. The poet in utter astonishment said, 'It is impossible to hide from Lalu. People say it's a ghost house, that's why I got it very cheap. I'm staying here secluded from the public and limelight.'

Days went by. The last meeting was at Kalimpong. One day, Brajendra Kishore along with his queen, went to meet the poet. Let us hear from him the memories of that last meeting:

After getting down from the car, I saw him sitting in an easy chair. Illness was evident on his pale face. He jumped as soon as he saw me and embraced me very tightly; I would never forget that moment. He did not even allow me the time to touch his feet and do the pranam. After that, so many words were spoken … He started pestering me to stay with him there; he said so many things, like the water of Darjeeling was not good for my stomach trouble and that the oozing waters of Kalimpong was very beneficial and so on. Ultimately, he insisted that I stay there. But when he heard that I had come alone with my ailing queen and it was not possible to leave her alone, he was apologetic. He said: "you always have some or other excuse. I shall also have to go for the work of the Vidyalaya.' I said, "What is this? How can you go without recovering your health?" The poet remained silent. It was also not possible for me to spend more time. The Maharani was left alone in the car. When I was about to leave, the silent, fervent glance of the poet made me quite restless. I came out with my head down, leaving him alone. Who knew at that time that it was going to be the last meeting!

People of Rabindranath Tagore's stature is quite rare in this world. Fortunate were the royal families of Tripura. The soil of Tripura was gratified by the radiation of his God-given talent. This great man is beyond criticism. To understand such a multi-faceted personality is not an easy task. He was a great poet, a saint and a remarkable human, all in one, whose measure of greatness is perhaps the vast endless sky.

Maharaja Kumar Brajendra Kishore, ninety years old then, spoke about the humane Rabindranath in a deeply respectful tone:

> I saw Rabindranath in many different forms ... He used to drive away the blemishes of the human mind with his sweetness. I did so many wrongs to him, but never had he behaved harshly with me. The expression of his anger was drenched with affection, not with hatred. Whoever got the touch of his hand knew that it was an ointment of peace on a restless mind. I do not have the right language to make you understand what I intend to mean. I forgot the bereavement of relatives and friends, but I could not forget his passing away. I have been stricken with grief and sorrow many times throughout my life, but the very thought of him had always helped me overcome all my miseries.

6

Rabindranath and Colonel Mahim Chandra Deb Barma

In the history of Tripura, Mahim Chandra was a disputed character—caught in a conflict that was started by the poet himself. They were friends well before Maharaja Bir Chandra came into the picture. The deterioration of their relationship had begun in the regime of Radha Kishore. It went up to such a stage that Rabindranath marked him as a villain. He did not even hesitate to caution Radha Kishore about Mahim Chandra's selfish motives. And when no action was taken against him, he shot a letter directly to Mahim Chandra:

> I would try to say every word very clearly ... This Shandiz has got the high royal post and indulgence with your favour ... I find that you, Shandiz and Amiya (the doctor) are bounded by a close friendship. It is also seen that you people are handling the taking of debts and repayment of debts ... Thorough study of all these matters has led me to believe that though you do not pray for the great harm of the Maharaja, yet whenever you find a chance,

you cannot leave the temptation of causing him harm. For this weakness, despite your wish to do well to the state, it is becoming impossible for you to do so. I am mentally disturbed thinking of the plight of Tripura, and then I cannot help but to cry fie upon you all ... despite your ideals, your weakness of character means you cannot take charge of the welfare of the state ... you all are self-seeking.

So, Rabindranath labeled Mahim Chandra, among other targets, as a 'self-seeking' person. On the other hand, history is the witness: Mahim Chandra never uttered even a single dishonourable word about Rabindranath. Until his death in 1923, he remained respectful toward Rabindranath. Otherwise, had he uttered any ignominious words against Rabindranath in reply to his letter, it would have come to light in no time. However, Rabindranath wrote passionate letters to both Radha Kishore and Mahim Chandra to acquit himself from the charge of a 'self-seeking' person that the courtiers leveled upon him. Once, the poet wrote 'I don't want my friendship with the Maharaja to be such that people label me as self-serving ... Thus, I've decided not to take any financial help from the Maharaja for the job I've undertaken.'

After that, he wrote to Mahim Chandra: 'I sought the Maharaja's help to lead *Bangadarshan* without considering what was before or after. It was comprehended for various reasons that you all construed it as selfish... you courtiers are suspicious of everyone.'

After going through Rabindranath's next letter, it was evident that Mahim Chandra gave a reply clarifying the ill repute imputed to him. Rabindranath wrote thereafter: 'Don't mind anything. Keep faith in me that my heart is very eager to work for the homeland... After getting your kind letter, I've driven away all the doubts from my mind.'

The root cause of these misunderstandings was an apparent communication gap. The flow of words changing their appearances took different shapes. Some time or other, Jatindranath or Ramani Mohan would place before the poet the deliberations of the royal court. There was a time when Rabindranath saw only conspiracy all around the kingdom. As a result, he had sent letters to Radha Kishore, by registered post or by the hand of Jatindranath Basu. A thorough psychological analysis perhaps becomes indispensable to unearth the reason for this sudden crack in Rabindranath's relationship with Mahim Chandra. There is no doubt that Rabindranath sincerely wished to do good for Tripura. Those who perceived selfishness in his relationship with the four generations of Maharajas for a period of sixty years exposed nothing but their own narrow-mindedness. It was not possible for ordinary people to understand the glorious duty he had undertaken and the sacrifices he'd made for the country. Before the publication of *Bangadarshan*, Mahim Chandra was in charge of managing the bounties of the Royal Court; Rabindranath, instead of writing directly to the Maharaja, thus placed his prayers to him through his letters to Mahim Chandra. If Mahim Chandra considered Rabindranath as selfish, he would have opposed the charities given to him right from the outset. Rabindranath complained to Radha Kishore, blaming Mahim Chandra for his desire to paint Rabindranath as a self-seeking person. Maharaja Radha Kishore did not pay any heed to this accusation and wrote to Rabindranath: 'Agartala is an irresponsible rumourmonger's place. The only reason for this is that worthless people coming from outside have settled here. If you intend to accept the meaning of their abusive words, it will be an injustice done to me.'

Maharaja Radha Kishore had no doubt in his mind about Mahim Chandra's faithfulness.

It could not be denied that there was a sense of grievance in Tripura about the bounties being given to Rabindranath. In the prevailing pecuniary crisis of the state, when it was deep in debt, Mahim Chandra also being a well-wisher did not support the charities being donated outside Tripura. He might have been against charities, but that he deemed the poet 'selfish' was beyond imagination. Even now the intellectuals and others in Tripura think in the same vein. Rabindranath should not have given any importance to them. Particularly, he should not have thought otherwise about his long-standing friend who adored him and tried his very best to help him in distress. He acknowledged his mistake and expressed his regret. Why did it so happen? Rabindranath had no hesitation in asking for money for Jagadish Chandra, but when it was for his own cause, he could not take the same stand and was often quite hesitant. Thus, when he heard whisperings of antagonism toward the assistance to be given for *Bangadarshan*, he was furious and wanted to prove that he was not motivated by selfishness. It was not at all necessary; he should have ignored it completely as *Bangadarshan* was related to literary activities and not connected in any way with personal matters. Mahim Chandra became a villain in his eyes for no reason.

No relationship can survive in an atmosphere of selfishness. In that long relationship, never did there appear a crack between the Maharajas and Rabindranath. In fact, one should understand that mutual respect, affection and love form the basis of any relationship. It is quite natural to share a give-and-take dynamic. Those who judge in their selfish ways what the Maharajas paid to Rabindranath and what they got in return are simply vitiating the history of the sweet relationship that the poet shared with Tripura. We should not forget Rabindranath is not a person, but an institution. And nobody should dare disrespect such an institution as he is.

It is pertinent to note that in his letters written to Mahim Chandra, Rabindranath did not blame Mahim Chandra singularly, but always said, 'you all' framing him along with a set of other courtiers. The letter relating to *Bangadarshan* was an innocent letter from a sensitive poet. A part of this letter, which was not quoted before, is reproduced below:

> In fact, ordinary people tend to look at everyone who befriends the Maharaja with suspicion. Even your present minister Umacharan (Umakanta) Das, before he got into service, said suspiciously to one of my friends, "Why does a person like Rabi Babu visit this place so frequently?" ... I hear that your minister cherishes that idea even now.

From this letter it transpires that though it was written to Mahim Chandra, the target was Umakanta Das. Of course, Mahim Chandra was implicated in the word 'yours'. But deep within Rabindranath knew very well that Mahim Chandra was a kind-hearted person and that he never had the intention of accusing Rabindranath as 'selfish.' That was why their friendship remained steady till Mahim Chandra's death in 1923. For this reason, a repentant Rabindranath once wrote to Radha Kishore:

> Although doubt had crept into my mind again and again about the mean-mindedness and weakness of Mahim Chandra, I didn't leave him as a friend ... As it was a heinous breach of trust on my part, I'm suffering the punishments for that from the Almighty ... I would request the Maharaja to kindly show this letter to Mahim. Had I had respite I would have someday or other expressed clearly my mind's whole regrets and apprehensions before Mahim, but I did not get such an opportunity.

Those who sacrifice their lives for the country are patriots. No selfishness can be ascribed to this self-sacrifice. The question of selfishness arises only when a person wants something for his own advantage. Rabindranath never intended to have anything for his own benefit; he took the beggar's bowl for the welfare of the country. From a sapling, Visva Bharati has become a banyan tree now. Tripura has become an object of gratitude to all of India for the charities donated to Shantiniketan. In the language of Rabindranath: 'the more thou had accepted what I gave, the more I became indebted to thee.'

Mahim Chandra was not an extraordinary person, neither was he an ordinary one. He was a man of equal merits and demerits, who, like every other human being, wept in sorrow and was serene in happiness. He was a practical man of the soil of Tripura. It would be wrong to assume that he was completely above selfishness, but certainly he was a true patriot of his own state. And here lay the difference of opinion between him and Rabindranath.

A true devotee of the king, Mahim Chandra was vehemently opposed to sharing the king's absolute powers with the minister in any circumstances. On the other hand, Rabindranath was in favour of transferring absolute power to the minister for he had no faith at all in the efficiency of the Maharajas of Tripura to run the administration effectively. He, therefore, wrote to Mahim Chandra: 'It seems, a fear also works in all of your minds that if the king himself becomes competent in the future, your influence will be curtailed.'

Rabindranath no doubt loved Radha Kishore as a friend, but he didn't rely on his intelligence. Rabindranath, therefore wanted to assign complete powers to the minister. Mahim Chandra vehemently opposed this move. To him, the Maharaja was sovereign, and a transfer of power meant the weakening of the king's position. In Mahim Chandra's opinion, such a situation was deemed an insult to the Maharaja and the state. Even after his retirement, his patriotism shone bright, as evident in his letter to Birendra Kishore:

In Bangladesh (Bengal) one word is widely circulated that the minister with an imaginary power, named Karnama, can handle the post of the minister in Tripura. Nobody will now have this temptation. Lord Sinha was not interested in accepting the post of the minister during the regime of the late Maharaja without having absolute power for five years. No Bengali will give *achalnama* (a state of immobility) without getting *sachalnama* (a state of mobility). On the other side, at the time of appointing a person with a salary of twenty rupees in a student's boarding house at Cooch Behar, the sentence "subject to H. H's approval" exists even today.

Truly speaking, Mahim Chandra did not look kindly on the import of ministers and high officials from outside the state. A sharp man like Rabindranath also could not help praising Mahim Chandra for his intelligence, as evinced by a letter written to Radha Kishore: 'Whenever I discuss matters relating to the state with Mahim, my respect for him grows even more ... Mahim is very bright and sharp, his ability to conceive an idea is very strong and he is also keen to improve the welfare of the state.'

Mahim Chandra was efficient enough for the post of minister, but the cruel treatment of the Bengali courtiers from the beginning of his career made his life miserable. If the sons of the soil are not engaged in the higher posts of administration, the result often does not bode well for the original inhabitants: states like Gujarat, Maharashtra, West Bengal, Assam, Manipur, etc., have suffered because of this problem. The situation was same in Tripura at that point of time. Young Mahim Chandra had to suppress even his great love for reading. Let us go through the diary of Mahim Chandra, dated 16 Chaitra 1302 (1892): 'Many English daily papers would come to the Royal Palace. However, the Bengali officers refused to give them to me. They behave with us in an unrestrained way; it is astonishing to see how they look down upon us ...'.

This was an incident in 1892. At that time, Rabindranath had not entered Tripura's political stage. If this incident is ignored, the root cause of unrest among the original inhabitants of Tripura will remain beyond comprehension. For the last two hundred years up till today, the educated Bengalis were charged with the administration of Tripura. Their hostile behaviour and non-consideration of Tripuris as human beings and the general exhibition of contempt toward them had gradually ignited this fire of insurgency. This attitude of the Bengalis did not escape Rabindranath's notice. Rabindranath wanted the Bengalis to plunge into the mainstream with the native inhabitants, leaving their arrogance behind, and to establish Tripura as a developed native state. His dream was not fulfilled. In reality, it was found that the Bengalis maintained their exclusivity as a community and created disturbance in the equilibrium of the state, neglecting the Tripuris. Mahim Chandra, in his article, *'Tripurar Darbarey Rabindranath'*, wrote about Rabindranath's expectations from the Bengalis of Tripura:

> Rabi Babu was hurt ... The shortcomings of a state run by Bengali employees indicated the disgrace of the Bengalis themselves. Rabindranath cherished the idea that the Bengali talents fully blossomed should be utilized for the welfare of the state to create an example for all other states to follow ...

Mahim Chandra was highly educated, though in terms of formal education he had only passed the entrance; he was a man of political acumen with a modern outlook. He was engaged in the royal service for a very long time from the regime of Maharaja Bir Chandra to Birendra Kishore and proved his mettle with his vast experience and sharp intelligence in running the administration; yet his talent was not adequately recognized. He was fluent in both English and Bengali. His articles were published in many newspapers and magazines. Fascinated after reading his article published in *The Daily Mirror*, a reader had asked him the name of the college he had attended. In reply, Mahim Chandra said modestly, 'I have never been to any college and thus I do not claim to have any special knowledge.'

Every wise, practical man wants to have a place in the corridors of power. And Mahim Chandra was no exception. Among the courtiers, he was the only person who met the topmost intellectuals of Bengal and refined his learning and intelligence through gradual nourishment. His closeness with the Tagore family of Jorasanko was nurtured much before Maharaja Bir Chandra came into the picture. He acknowledged Rabindranath as his Guru: 'I was fortunate to have some part of Rabi Babu's friendship. I have started to practice writing in Bengali only after his remarkable encouragement.'

In the misunderstanding between the guru and his disciple, some Bengali officials played an important role. They were the people who spoke to Rabindranath secretly so as to prejudice him against Mahim Chandra.

In a letter, that is now torn and difficult to read through, dated 22 April 1907, Acharya Dinesh Chandra Sen wrote to Mahim Chandra:

I had an elaborate discussion with Rabindranath about Agartala. He had no hand in the reappointment of (U.D) Mahashay. He said that after settling the matter, Sri Srijut Bahadur had informed me ... that much. Ramani Babu and his minister Jati

Babu ... They are hearing so many things ... This is the quality of Agartala ... Shutting others' mouths, so even those who are thoughtful now pretend to be silent ...

Is your political sky clear by now? How is— Rai Bahadur ...? Tear my letters ...

This letter has got an immense historical value. U.D and Rai Bahadur are one and the same person—Umakanta Das, the state minister of Tripura. Mahim Chandra often disagreed with ministers Ramani Mohan Chattopadhyaya, Umakanta Das and the Maharaja's personal secretary Jatindranath Basu, over issues related to the state; therefore, their relationship had been damaged beyond repair. The minister of state Ramani Mohan and the Maharaja's personal secretary Jatindranath Basu had been appointed in royal service at Rabindranath's recommendation. They prejudiced Rabindranath on many occasions, saying all sorts of things against Mahim Chandra, and they succeeded in creating a poor impression about him in the poet's mind. It was evident from his letters that Rabindranath was entangled all over in the politics of Tripura. The reason for the deterioration of his relationship with Mahim Chandra was due to the malice of the courtiers. Having no recourse to verifiable information as he lived far off from Tripura, Rabindranath had to rely on reports he heard from others, which were often misleading and malicious in intent. In one of his letters, he admitted to Radha Kishore:

> I come to know from different people about the problems that arise in the discharge of royal duties. As I stay far off, it is difficult for me to make a right decision. Yet I cannot remain stoic. It will be unrighteous on my part if I do not inform the Maharaja for his own good that which is manifested in my intelligence.

As truth always reveals itself, the friendship between the poet and Mahim Chanra was later re-established with all its glory. Misunderstanding ended in goodwill. Rabindranath confessed to Radha Kishore in a letter dated 16 Shaon 1312 (1905): 'You know for sure that I've been eagerly discussing the development of Tripura for a long time. For that matter, suspicion had grown in me about Mahim Chandra for heresy and other reasons.'

In the same letter, after a long discussion on Mahim Chandra, a repentant Rabindranath wrote:

> The impression I had about Mahim was entirely baseless and keeping in mind this fact, it was not difficult for me to keep the friendship with him protected ... About Mahim, I am ashamed of myself. The Maharaja may kindly clear the fact and drive away my feeling of shame. I could not reply to some of his letters because of this deep sense of shame.

Broken glasses, even if joined together, leave a mark. Something of that sort persisted though their relationship healed; otherwise, Rabindranath should have saved Mahim Chandra in the Tripura Sundari Lottery Case. Before we proceed further, it should be kept in mind that Brajendra Kishore had resigned from the ministerial post on account of Mahim Chandra's acquittal from the lottery scandal case during Maharaja Birendra Kishore's reign, thereby disputing the royal proclamation. Brajendra Kishore had accordingly informed Rabindranath. After the death of Radha Kishore Manikya, Rabindranath had written to Brajendra Kishore: 'You must stand with your heart and soul in favour of the man on whom the burden of governance has been bestowed ... Now, you are to protect your new Maharaja ... At present, you are his closest relative ...'

However, in lottery scandal case, Rabindranath conveniently forgot his advice to Brajendra Kishore and in fact, approved his decision to leave the royal service. He neither recognized the royal order nor stood by his friend Mahim Chandra. How could he forget that, at that time of dispute over the right to the throne between Bad Thakur Samarendra Chandra and Birendra Kishore, he had strongly supported Radha Kishore, saying, 'I do not know royal aristocracy—I only know that the sin of disrespecting a Maharaja sitting on the throne should not be indulged by any means...' How could he then forgive Brajendra Kishore? As if this was not enough, he also worried about Brajendra Kishore's financial condition after his resignation. He wanted to know time and again whether his resignation would create any difficulties in his family and, furthermore, he supported Brajendra Kishore's move to settle his family allowance with the help of the British Government. How could he believe, after long years of friendship, that Mahim Chandra could even think of doing such a nasty thing? Rabindranath was blind in his support towards Brajendra Kishore, just as the blind monarch Dhritarashtra, under all circumstances.

Maharaja Birendra Kishore and Mahim Chandra knew all about their relationship. When Brajendra Kishore withdrew behind the scenes after the resignation, Birendra Kishore came to the forefront. He invited the poet to Tripura as a royal guest. During his visit, Tagore also accepted Mahim Chandra's hospitality and stayed as his guest for a day. They sat and discussed the manuscript of *Deshiya Rajya* that Mahim Chandra had written. This was the last time they met. Mahim Chandra left for his heavenly abode in 1923, but before that the fog of misunderstanding between him and Rabindranath had disappeared completely.

There was no mention of any opposition by Mahim Chandra in any other letters in the cases of bounties given by the Maharajas to

Tagore for various purposes, except in case of *Bangadarshan*. Rather Rabindranath himself had expressed his gratitude and thanked Mahim Chandra for getting him the assistance granted by the Maharajas. Acharya Dinesh Chandra Sen wrote to him: 'Your debt can't be paid; my strength fades if I intend to say something about it. The favour you have done to me and are doing still, I cannot even come to think of how to return that.'

In the same terms, Sarala Devi also expressed her gratitude to Mahim Chandra. A grant of 50 rupees per month was fixed for *Bangadarshan*. It is hard to believe that Mahim Chandra would oppose such a small grant for *Bangadarshan*, while he recommended charities involving thousands of rupees. Jagadish Chandra was a friend of Mahim Chandra and a revered man. He wrote many letters to Mahim Chandra. The major beneficiary of Maharaja Radha Kishore's donations was Acharya Jagadish Chandra Bose. However, Mahim Chandra never objected to the assistance given to Jagadish Chandra. What does it mean? The answer is very simple. The Bengali high officials were always treated with special honour and respect in Tripura. The policy of appeasing the Maharajas took centre stage. Mahim Chandra, on the other hand, had a tremendous sense of self-respect. He was not a person to yield for nothing. By the grace of the Maharaja, he had lots of power, and no instance could be cited of its misuse. Eventually, the enemies got the upper hand as they grew more numerous. For instance, toward the last part of his royal service, he was oppressed and defamed for not allowing the police superintendent, Ananda Mohan Guha, to enter the royal court in ordinary dress. Even if Ananda Mohan was permitted, he would have been shown the exit door forthwith. This was the rule of the royal durbar. The harassment he had to face at the hands of the enemies to protect the rule of the durbar remains a miserable episode in the history of Tripura. It was these people who misled

Rabindranath through their petty rumour-mongering. And what the poet heard, he brought it to the notice of Maharaja Radha Kishore. But the latter had no doubt at all about Mahim Chandra's loyalty to the throne.

No one ever before had thought about tribal identity crises. Mahim Chandra was a pioneer in this regard. He could perceive the destruction of the Tripuris under the excessive appeasement of the Bengali community. He always had to fight at every step with the Bengali royal officials to preserve the national identity and existence of the Tripuris. Rabindranath marked him as selfish. And he indeed was as he resolved to protect the national and ethnic identity of Tripuris against all odds. Rabindranath did not see any difference in the culture of Bengalis and Tripuris. Moreover, he addressed the Maharaja of Tripura as the Maharaja of Bengal. His magnanimity did not differentiate between Bengalis and Tripuris. No doubt, it indicated how great his heart was. But those Bengalis who had settled in Tripura prior to independence, either being engaged in government services, business or otherwise, and later the millions of Bengali refugees who came to Tripura from East Pakistan after independence, gradually changed the demographics. In their own states the Tripuris became a minority community. Historically, the Bengalis had never accepted the original inhabitants of Tripura as their own. The racial divide and discrimination is still even now firmly rooted and rather strong. Mahim Chandra waged a war against this racial discrimination to preserve the state's ethnic identity; Rabindranath, however, failed to detect this racial discrimination. He therefore thought of Mahim Chandra's opposition to bestowing absolute power to the minister as one born out of selfishness. Mahim Chandra was vociferous against passing any kind of law that would hinder the development of the Tripuris. At that time of taking the loan from the bank and during its repayment, he had no unfair collaboration with Shandiz and Dr Amiya as suspected. He wanted not only the well-being of the king but also of the state and the people. From this standpoint, he was no doubt selfish, but his selfishness would not ever tarnish his image. On the other hand, this nuance aspect of his character had escaped the poet's notice, who in his idealism never thought of the Bengalis and Tripuris as different. They were wholly one to him; they were all human. He thus wanted the overall development of Tripura irrespective of whether the people benefiting were Bengalis or Tripuris. For a poet who believed in universal humanism, he could not visualize a situation where the two peoples were to be treated separately, because he believed in 'oneness' and not in apparent differences. A faithful devotee and believer of the ideals of ancient India, Rabindranath had a deep hatred for any sort of racial and religious discrimination. He even initiated Maharaja Radha Kishore to the idea of an ideal king, citing passages from ancient scriptures such as the *Manusamhita*. He used to believe, like Swami Vivekananda, that 'all the inhabitants of India are my brothers'. For those who thought on such a wide scale, the petty boundaries of racial discrimination had no place in their worldview. From this standpoint, Rabindranath then did nothing objectionable in labeling Mahim Chandra 'selfish'. Mahim Chandra's role in the scenarios where he was present have already been discussed elsewhere in this book. Before I conclude the history of Rabindranath's relationship with Tripura, let me quote a part of an undated letter written to Mahim Chandra:

> I look upon you again and again for the welfare of Tripura. My relationship with this state is religiously fixed. As much as I wish, I cannot make my mind indifferent towards it ... Your life will be successful if you can perform this responsibility bestowed

on you ... God has given you enough intelligence and strength. And you have high ideals in your mind ... Therefore, you are to accept this duty to contribute to the welfare of your state—it is of course a hard, uphill task, but if you can engage yourself without thinking of loss or gain and comfort, then nothing is unachievable.

Epilogue

In world history, there may be instances of certain poets having a close bond with one or two kings, but it is improbable to find a trace of one poet having an extremely close, and continuous relationship of sixty years with four successive generations of kings. Tripura was the witness of this astonishingly rare situation. And he was not a poet of any sort, but a poet of the world, indeed the first Indian who won the Nobel Prize: the pride of the world, Kabiguru Rabindranath Tagore. It is a matter of shame that most Indians are not acquainted with this glorious history. If this episode is not known, the history of the commencement of his great activities will remain forever unknown and misunderstood. In the act of giving a concrete shape to the ideals of Rabindranath, the contribution of Tripura was no less. An old king of Tripura, in the time of Rabindranath's youth, had conferred on him the honour of 'Great Poet'. In his reminiscence, Rabindranath recollected:

> I was then quite young, and my writings were very few. Most of the readers of the country sarcastically named them "child's pleasure" ... It is difficult to find in the history of literature an account of such a spontaneous and open friendship of a king

with a tender-aged poet whose road to fame was then totally uncertain and doubtful.

By the grace of Rabindranath's *Rajarshi*, *Mukut* and *Bisharjan*, Tripura's name has become immortal in the history of literature. But, despite that, I regret that the portrait of an unusual Rabindranath—beyond poetry, literature and art—has not yet been wholly unveiled. This unprecedented relationship remains outside of popular knowledge. In my earnest endeavour to draw a sketch of Rabindranath, I find it to be an impossible task as he is an elusive beauty. I do, therefore, intend to conclude with two lines borrowed from one of his poems:

That she wanders in a flush, averts her gaze, can't be bridled,
That if she is within reach, flees with a push, dazzles the eyes.

A Glossary of the Manikya Dynasty of Tripura

1.	Chandra
2.	Budh
3.	Pururaba
4.	Aayu
5.	Nahush
6.	Yayati
7.	Durhya
8.	Baru
9.	Setu
10.	Anartya
11.	Gandhar
12.	Dharma (Gharma)
13.	Dhrita (Ghrita)
14.	Durmad
15.	Pracheta
16.	Parachi (Satyadharma)
17.	Parbasu
18.	Parisad
19.	Arijit
20.	Sujit
21.	Pururaba II
22.	Bibarnya
23.	Purusen
24.	Meghbarna
25.	Bikarna
26.	Basuman
27.	Kirti
28.	Kanian
29.	Pratisraba
30.	Pratistha
31.	Shatrujit
32.	Pratiradan
33.	Pramatha
34.	Kalinda
35.	Kromo (Krath)
36.	Mitrari
37.	Baribaraha
38.	Karmuk

39. Kalanga (Kalinga)	67. Sriman (Srimanta)
40. Bhishan	68. Lakshmitaru
41. Bhanumitra	69. Tarlakshmi (Rupaban)
42. Chitrasen (Agha Chitrasen)	70. Mailakshmi (Lakshmiban)
43. Chitrarath	71. Nageshwar
44. Chitrayudh	72. Jogeshwar
45. Daitya	73. Ishwarjag (Nildhwaj)
46. Tripur	74. Rangkhai (Basuraj)
47. Subrai (Trilochan)	75. Dhanraj Fa
48. Dakshin	76. Muchung Fa (Harihar)
49. Taidakshin	77. Maichang Fa (Chandrasekhar)
50. Sudakshin	
51. Tardakshin	78. Chandraraj (Tabhu or Taruraj)
52. Dharmataru (Dharmatar)	
	79. Tarfalai (Tripali)
53. Dharmapal	80. Sumantra
54. Swadharma (Sudharma)	81. Rupabanta (Sreth)
55. Tarbang	82. Tarhum (Tarham)
56. Debang	83. Khaham (Hariraj)
57. Narangeet	84. Katar Fa (Kashiraj)
58. Dharmangad	85. Kalatar Fa (Madhav)
59. Rukmangad	86. Chandra Fa (Chandraraj)
60. Somangad (Sonangad)	87. Gajeshwar
61. Najugrai (Nagjag)	88. Birraj II
62. Tarjung	89. Nageshwar (Nagpati)
63. Tarraj (Rajdharma)	90. Shikhiraj (Shikhyaraj)
64. Humraj	91. Debraj
65. Birraj	92. Dhusrang (Durasha)
66. Sriraj	93. Barakirti (Birraj or Biraj)

94. Sagar Fa	118. Jujru Fa (HamtarFa or Himti)
95. Malay Chandra	
96. Surya Rai (Suryanarayan)	119. Jangi Fa (Rajendra or Janak Fa)
97. AchangFanai (Indrakirti)	120. Partha (Debrai or Debraj)
98. Bir Singha (Charachar)	
99. Hachang Fa (Achang or Surendra)	121. Shibrai
	122. Durgur Fa (Harirai or Adidharma Fa)
100. Beemar	
101. Kumar	123. Kharung Fa (Kurung)
102. Sukumar	124. SengFanai (Nrisingha or Sing Fanai)
103. Tuisarau (Bir Chandra or Taksha Rao)	
	125. Lalit Rai
104. Rajyeshwar (Rajeshwar)	126. Mukund Fa (Kunda Fa)
105. Nageshwar (Michhliraj)	127. Kamal Rai
106. Tuichhang Fa (Tejang Fa)	128. Krishnadas
107. Narendra	129. Jash Fa (Jashoraj)
108. Tunda Kirti	130. Muchung Fa (Udhyav)
109. Biman (Paimaraj)	131. Sadhu Rai
110. Jashoraj	132. Pratap Rai
111. Banga (Nabanga)	133. Bishnu Prasad
112. Ganga Rai (Rajganga)	134. Baneshwar (Banishwar)
113. Sukurai (Chitrasen or Chhakrurai)	135. Birbahu
	136. Samab
114. Pratit	137. Champakeshwar (Champa)
115. Michhli (Marichi or Maruchhum)	
	138. Meghraj (Megh)
116. Gagan (Kathuk)	139. Sengkuheg (Dharmadhar)
117. Kirti (Nawraj or Naba Rai)	
	140. Sengthum (Kirtidhar)

141. Achang Fa (Rajsurya, Kunjaham Fa)	163. Govinda Manikya
	164. Chhatra Manikya (Nakshatra Rai)
142. Khichang Fa (Mohan)	
143. Danger Fa (Hari Rai)	165. Ramdev Manikya
144. Raja Fa	166. Ratna Manikya II
145. Ratna Fa (Ratna Manikya)	167. Narendra Manikya
	168. Mahendra Manikya
146. Pratap Manikya	169. Dharma Manikya 2
147. Mukul Manikya (Mukunda)	170. Mukunda Manikya
	171. Joy Manikya
148. Maha Manikya	172. Indra Manikya II
149. Dharma Manikya 1	173. Bijoy Manikya II
150. Pratap Manikya II	174. Krishna Manikya
151. Dhanya Manikya	175. Rajdhar Manikya II
152. Dhaja Manikya	176. Ramganga Manikya
153. Deb Manikya	177. Durga Manikya
154. Indra Manikya I	178. Kashichandra Manikya
155. Bijoy Manikya I	179. Krishna Kishore Manikya
156. Ananta Manikya	
157. Uday Manikya	180. Ishan Chandra Manikya
158. Joy Manikya (Luktar Fa)	181. Bir Chandra Manikya
159. Amar Manikya	182. Radha Kishore Manikya
160. Rajdhar Manikya	183. Birendra Kishore Manikya
161. Jashodhar Manikya	
162. Kalyan Manikya	184. Bir Bikram Manikya

The correct chronology could not be maintained in all cases as the names of several Maharajas could not be recovered.

Appendices

Note on the Budget of Tripura placed before Maharaja Radha Kishore by Rabindranath Tagore

A humble petition to the Maharaja about certain principles before an elaborate discussion on the budget—

Before the changes in the present situation, the governing of the state by the council for some time and by Umakanta Babu at other times had already been tested. There is no doubt that the test, having failed, created critical conditions in Tripura.

The reasons for which the previous tests could not be successful have to be determined.

The main reason for this in my consideration is that there was no undivided harmony in the administration of the state. There were self-contradictions in the administration. Those who were at the helm did not get the opportunity to steer the state's affairs in the correct direction to hit the mark. As a result, the norms they adopted became estranged and distracted. However, they thought it was enough to somehow continue the present work in these disordered conditions.

The consequences of this have been disastrous. Harmony in all the state's affairs must be restored without delay to protect the state from this horror—the state should be fastened by an unbendable administrative system.

In that case, the royal power of the Maharaja has to be concentrated. In reply to this, the Maharaja may say, I've given independent charge to the present minister to run the government. But then the obstacles to take over the independent charge must be removed. I intend to discuss the process as to how they can be removed. I hope the Maharaja will forgive my impertinence.

There are two natural divisions in the state. One relates to the Maharaja's personal domain, and the other is for the state. If both remain together, they may start striking each other—on this pretext, great harm might be caused— and there is every possibility of the growth of evil conspiracies at the juncture of these two divisions.

Ministers or other courtiers should not be given the right to set their hands on the Maharaja's personal division, which includes domestic affairs, his own funds, his travelling expenses, attendants etc. The personal division should therefore be independent of the minister's right, only the full charge of the state division should be given to the minister.

If the boundaries of the Maharaja's personal and state division are fixed, then the minister being aware of the extent of the revenue and strength of his departments will do the needful accordingly, and those who are sheltered by the Maharaja and seeking shelter will turn their greedy eyes away knowing that the state division is not a place for realizing one's own interest.

If the extent of the Maharaja's personal expenditure is fully determined, then with the remaining part of the revenue, the minister can repay the debt and carry on the expenses for state administration.

Those who assert that the Maharaja should curtail his own power by bestowing the charge of the state on the minister are in fact his most dangerous enemies. Being self-restrained by one's own rule, keeping a watch on the welfare of the state befits a king—it is the duty of a king. If the Maharaja intends to take full charge of the state, then the minister may be appointed only for counselling; otherwise, the welfare of the state will by no means be possible and discipline will collapse. Whenever the minister is deemed unfit for taking the charge, he should be relieved that very moment; but as long he holds the post, do not disgrace your royal power by belittling him in any way before the public.

I humbly submit to the Maharaja that he should make his attendants confide in him. Moreover, many people, out of a desire to do well, criticize the royal administration before the Maharaja. The outcome of all these discussions should not be kept hidden. In all doubtful matters, big or small, listen to what the ministers say—do not nourish even the smallest thorn in the corner of your heart. If the Maharaja's relation with the minster is completely open, then there will never be any regret for this.

There is no man who does not occasionally err in his work—Ramani also will do the same. But the only way to prevent mistakes is not to allow such work in the first place. Therefore, if the mind of the Maharaja remains unperturbed even in the face of sincere and insincere criticism—if it does not get burdened by suspicion, hesitation and hindrances, then the state will function unimpeded.

All India Regency Conference
(A draft proposal submitted by Rabindranath Tagore to Maharaja Radha Kishore)

The British government's reluctance to defray the costs of worship will be evident from the account of Hunter Sahib in his book *Orissa*.

Recently, Srijut Anand Charlu Mahashay raised a proposal in the ministerial committee to introduce a new law for temple maintenance, but the government disagreed.

The government generally avoids interfering in social affairs. Whenever there's any interference, the people resent it. The public gets dissatisfied whenever an alien sovereign tries to tamper with religion and society. It was perhaps for this reason that there was so much agitation against the law of consent to cohabitation. But against the traditional customs of marriage, the royal rule that has been introduced in Mysore is accepted by the Hindus there. It testifies to the greatness of the British Government that it hesitates to intervene in such matters. Nevertheless, whenever any sort of disorder appeared in religion and society or any rectification was called for, the kings, being attentive towards their duty, would issue rulings. Ballal Sen, although not a Brahman, introduced the Kulin system in Brahman-society when he was sitting on the royal throne; it is in vogue even today. If any perversion arises in this high descent, who will rectify that now?

Rectification is not possible by many people, because different people have different interests and different opinions—it is difficult to come about through an agreement by all or by the majority. In that case, the opinion and influence of the person who is the head of the country are effective.

With the advancement of knowledge and education in the British regime, the views and ideas of people are also rapidly changing. But the change in behavioural and social patterns is happening in secret. These changes, like a thief entering through a tunnel, are digging the foundation of society. In educated society, treacherous behaviour and chicanery tend to predominate. The only reason for this is that the right social changes are not getting the approval and assistance of the Hindu king. There is no one to propagate the rule—for the sake of convenience and comfort, therefore, people break the ancient customs and conventions. But they do not have the courage to admit their infractions.

Let us take an example. If a Bengali, after his return from England, does not expiate to be reclaimed in the fold of his caste, then it depends on the intelligence of the judge to determine whether this son will have the right to his father's wealth and his marriage in Hindu tradition will be considered as legitimate. It is not possible to determine the opinion of the judges. Nonetheless, at present, it has become necessary to go to England for the advancement of knowledge, education and worldly wisdom. In this place, going to England, if it is considered as a sin, there cannot be bliss in society. But who will give the ruling that the journey to England does not destroy Hinduism? The British government is reluctant to take up this responsibility. It is also impossible to estimate public opinion.

In such a situation, there is only one honest way out. An assemblage of the Hindu kings of India will have to take a decision. Whatever custom they will consider as befitting to Hindus, if the government admits it as Hindu rites, then there are no reasons for any hesitation and in this way the society too won't remain stagnant.

First, the regency conferences will have to be divided into five divisions, because the dissimilarities of customs in different lands of India are too great: Bengal, Bihar, Orissa are one, North and West form the second, Punjab and Sindhu comprise of the third, Gujarat and Maratha are the fourth and Madras forms the fifth division. Whether my divisions are rightly done may be considered later, but it must be kept in mind that if the small provincial dissimilarities are excessively focused on, everything will become futile.

In a specific conference hall of the government, if the kings of each division assemble in a particular month in winter, and work together even for fifteen days a year, then I expect something good will surely occur. The kings may employ worthy ministers or representatives to suitably express their own opinions. The government will decide the code of conduct at the meeting.

The more the right of the native kings will be widened for the welfare of homeland, the greater will be their responsibility and self-respect. The more they are associated with glorious deeds, the more will their power of judgment, multifold observations and pride be augmented. The king must think about the welfare of the people, their unity and pay close attention to his duty to ensure their well-being—that is what determines his greatness. The practice of supremacy, daintiness and foppery and waywardness—all these constitute a perversion of kingly duty. It is difficult to attain true excellence in this regard. But if the burden of India's general welfare is in the hands of kings and if they are to perform it by deliberation and counselling in full public view, then their intelligence, judgment and self-restraint must all be strengthened.

The proposal is made in a general way. If it is appropriate, then it is left to wise men to make it faultless and complete.

Rabi, Year II, Issue IV, 1332 Bengali Era

Speech of Rabindranath Tagore at the felicitation given by the Kishore Sahitya Samaj at Agartala

My first introduction to the state of Tripura was as a teenager. I had just returned from England and only one of my books of poetry was published at the time. It was not reprinted as it was a writing of my youth, full of shortcomings and imperfections.

In those days, very few people knew about me and my writings. My identity was confined to only near relatives and friends. Once, at that time, a messenger from the Maharaja of Tripura, Bir Chandra

Manikya Bahadur had sought an interview with me. I was very young and I welcomed him with a lot of hesitation. Many of you likely knew his name—he was Radha Raman Ghosh. The Maharaja had sent him from far-off Tripura especially to convey the message that he wanted to felicitate me as a poet. For this unexpected incident, the young poet was surprised no end.

After that, he gave me all kinds of advice on different occasions and had sent me in particular selected Sanskrit excerpts from *Rajmala* after having them printed at the time of my writing *Rajarshi*. From that, I came to know the true account of Govinda Manikya.

At the time, when he was going to Kurseong, he invited me to go along with him, and I went. Every evening, he used to listen to my writings and request me to sing songs. His affection and cordiality had drawn a permanent line in my soul.

Maharaja Bir Chandra was a maestro extraordinaire of music. It can be easily understood how hesitant I was, as an inexperienced young man, to sing before him. I got the courage only because of his indulgence and affection.

It was not that he had exempted me after listening to my recitations and songs; he tried to use my strength even in his worldly affairs.

In my immature beginnings, his wisdom could foresee my future, and that was why he honoured me as a great poet at that time. The fame that I now have, he was the first person in the world to predict it. A person who stays on the peak can see what is not normally visible; Bir Chandra likewise could identify what made me distinctive.

Just before his death, when I was enjoying his hospitality, I had various kinds of discussion with him on literature. He had resolved to collect the whole of Vaishnav Padabali as far as possible and to publish it, with a budget of 1 lakh rupees. But his sudden death came in the way of that resolve.

Bir Chandra's son, Radha Kishore Manikya, maintained the legacy of his father's affection towards me. He had drawn me close to him. He had kept his same respect for me even when my name was disgraced by rumours. He treated me as a friend, as a brother. The relation was such that he did not expect me to be false with him at any time. I remember, he told me once: 'Rabi Babu, you will even protect me against my wishes and nature.'

I came to Tripura repeatedly during his reign, drawn by his sincere love and affection.

Those days are no more. By the grace of God, I have received several honours—even from the royal hands of Europe—by the dint of my good fortune. But the honour I received from the kings of my home and homeland, the value of that in my personal life remains much higher. For that only, my relations with Tripura are not those of a transitory guest. This relation was entangled with the memories of the father of the present king, his grandfather and great-grandfather. I earnestly pray for the welfare of the state. I was charmed by the qualities befitting a king and the sense of humour of the two Maharajas of this state, whom I was fortunate to know very closely. This sort of courtesy, benevolence and large-heartedness are rare to find.

In this royal family, from time immemorial, the Bengali language has been receiving a glorious treatment. In fact, the history of all countries reveal that the country's language is not only the mother tongue but also her royal language. As the duty of a king is to protect and preserve the subjects, so he must also protect the language. The kings of the country should not be moved by the pomp of foreign customs and shirk this noble responsibility. I have keenly observed deep respect and attachment for the Bengali language and literature in this family. My relationship with the family has become strong and steady because of this common attachment.

I have seen very few letters written like those by Radha Kishore and Bir Chandra. Those letters were self-restrained, polite and savoury. Such an adroit use of the mother tongue is a part of their royal courtesy. These witticisms, the capability of appreciating the country's music, art and culture testify to their glory. I have observed that their natural humility is indicative of the utter loftiness of their souls.

Brajendra Kishore was a boy when he came to me. He occupied the place of my nearest relative by his behaviour and conduct. He used to write letters to me from his boyhood. I am greatly pleased to see that it has not been proved futile. I might not have done any other good to Tripura, but if I have been only able to inculcate a firm sense of duty in Brajendra Kishore's character, then I will be proud to feel that I've rendered a great service to Tripura. On this occasion, I am rendering my wholehearted blessings to him. The memories of this place at the present moment cast a shadow of sadness in my mind. My only joy is to see Brajendra Kishore here. I have come here at his invitation, overlooking my health and work. The warm reception that I had received once from his father and grandfather, the same I am enjoying even today through his hands. For that, now in spring, when the beautiful forests of Tripura send the invitation of the floral festival, whose fragrance is carried by the southerly winds in every corner, I have come to accept that garland from him as a friend of his father—a garland that his father and grandfather used to keep adorned for this affectionate guest.

I pray for his wellbeing and with the same desire I hope that, by the glory of his character, the welfare of Tripura will be expanded.

On this occasion, I intend to express my special gratitude to the kings of Tripura for another reason. I have been running a school at Shantiniketan for more than twenty years. Amongst the people of the country, I have received regular assistance for a long time only from Radha Kishore Manikya. He had gladdened and honoured us by accepting the hospitality of the Ashram. At that time, this institution of mine was poverty-stricken and virtually unknown. Nevertheless, Radha Kishore at that time not only helped this auspicious work with an annual grant, but also sent many boys with student scholarships to Shantiniketan for the purpose of learning. His son, Birendra Kishore, also not only continued the grant up to the last, but also donated 5,000 rupees for constructing a medical hospital there and also agreed to pay another 5,000. Their respect for my deeds right from the outset is, for me, a matter of immense gratitude.

Lastly, I wish to express my gratitude today to Kishore Sahitya Samaj and the people of Tripura for this felicitation, and I take leave with a salute in return to Srijukta Shital Chandra Chakraborty Mahashay for his salutations to me. Let me convey my last words to you all that I have not come here today as a famous poet to receive honour; the love and respect that I have received in my youth as the friend of the late Maharajas, that very lasting flavour of relationship, I wish to enjoy that at present in these last stages of my life and say, *'Sarba Starato Durgani Sarbo Bhadran Pashyatu'* (May there be prosperity and welfare are for all people).

Rabi, Year II, Issue IV, 1332 Bengali Era

Speech of Maharaja Bir Bikram Manikya at the inauguration ceremony of Rabindra Shilpa Pradarshani O Mela organized on Tagore's 70th birthday

You all have fastened me with the string of gratitude by appointing me as a conductor of this great ceremony. It is inevitable for a person like me to hesitate to lead a felicitation of a poet adored all over the world. Yet, the very existence of the unending affection between

Tripura and the poet has inspired me. Today, I do not intend to behold the luminous brilliance of *Rabi* (Sun) shining in its full glory. I feel honoured being invited by you and to be associated with the birth ceremony of my grandfather and great grandfather's affectionate friend. I feel fortunate to be here today.

By the grace of God, the royal family of Tripura from time immemorial were the devotees of art and culture. That was why my great grandfather, the most reverend late Bir Chandra Manikya, was attracted in an auspicious moment to the rays of the young rising *Rabi* (sun). From then onwards, we had a special relationship with the great poet. My father Birendra Kishore Manikya had also maintained that relationship.

The influence of the poet on the royal family of Tripura is not insignificant. On the other hand, Tripura, adorned with mountains and waterfalls, flowers of the forest, natural beauty of the green hills, the achievements of Govinda Manikya, etc.; a distinguished literary culture, music, dance, paintings and the art of weaving—about all of which Tripura is extremely proud—also attracted the great poet immensely.

Forgive me please, I have selfishly mentioned my personal relations with the poet. But Rabindranath, who is the poet of Bengal—the poet of India—the poet of the world—to him, I pay my tribute as the 'Poet of Tripura'.

But it should not be forgotten that the sphere of the great poet's work and influence is not limited to only the world of literature. The expectations and longings of the people of the world have played high and deep in the strings of his *veena*; but he does not stop there. He toils tirelessly to fulfill them. For him, even the daily life of an ordinary person is not a matter of neglect, and he should not be deprived of the chance to peacefully integrate himself with the world at large. That is the ideal that he always propagates before everyone through his advice, works and lifelong activities. Thus, he never thought of art and culture as something to be enjoyed solely by the elites. We have learnt from him how to integrate the art and culture of our own country with a true spirit of truth and goodwill. All the doors of the divine house of artistic beauty have been opened before us only after being initiated by him. Even in this matter, the people of Tripura have an unbounded good fortune, because the foremost of his articles, '*Deshiya Rajya*', relating to the country's art and culture, was first read in the Sahitya Sammelani of Tripura, twenty-six years ago. Today, on the one hand, the profound tune of *Gitanjali* echoes constantly in the hearts of our Vaishnava family; on the other, the great words of '*Deshiya Rajya*', teaches us how to improve our administration—all his works gratify us with a sense of divine direction.

I do not intend to take your time anymore. Come; let us all, together, on the seventieth birth anniversary of the great poet, pray at the feet of God to give the poet a long life, to enable him to propagate worldwide God's eternal promise. With the desire to have the blessings of the great poet, I now inaugurate the Shilpa Pradarshani.

Reception accorded to Maharaja Bir Bikram Manikya by Rabindranath Tagore at the mango grove of Shantiniketan (22 Poush 1345 Bengali Era)[7]

Sri Sri Maharaja Bir Bikram Kishore Manikya
To
You who deserve all affection,

My heart, like the setting sun today, is dispersing its blessings to you from the western horizon of my life. The light of that previous day's auspicious union enkindles my union today with you; I am happy to have an opportunity to inform you of that incident. At that time, you were not born, and I was a young man. Then, your great grandfather Bir Chandra Manikya had sent his minister to Jorasanko only to convey that he wanted to honour me as a great poet. This was the first time I received a felicitation from the country. It was not expected, and the days were far off then to be worthy of receiving this highest honour. Thereafter, while going to Kurseong to recover his health, he called me up to accompany him. He was rather older than me, but he used to discuss literature with me like a friend. He had an extraordinary knowledge of music, but he listened with indulgence to my rather amateur compositions, no doubt expecting great things of me in the future. It was as if, on the canvas of his imagination, he could see what lay ahead for me. It is amazing, of all things, to remember that the Maharaja used to discuss all his views on Bengali literature with me, and he proposed to take me as a literary associate. After a short time, he returned to Calcutta and died; I thought my relationship with this royal family had been suddenly broken then and there. But it was astonishing for me to see that it did not happen. The seat of friendship that went vacant in his absence in Tripura, Maharaja Radha Kishore occupied it; and called me to Tripura without delay. The true and earnest friendship he gave me was a rare thing indeed. Today, I have the right to say these words to you with pride: the poet of India, now lauded worldwide, was once rather unknown—and the royal family's care and concern for so unknown a poet indeed destines them for immortality. I hope you have understood that this union is historically precious. Culture and elevation of mind, which are indispensable to the soul of a country, the kings of this land had once considered them as the main features of royal splendour; your forefathers kept this in their minds. My relationship with them was fastened by this appreciation of culture and it was a true and deep relationship. Today, your arrival has brought the south wind of the happy memories of those days. You have given to this present day the offering of the past, and, on this occasion, accept my loving heart's gift that I had offered to your forefathers, and my wholehearted blessings.

Affectionately yours,
Rabindranath Tagore

Speech of Rabindranath Tagore after accepting the title of 'Bharat Bhaskar' at Uttarayan

With Best wishes for your well-being—

To the highly esteemed Sri Bir Bikram Manikya Deb Bahadur

Now, I want to reflect on an unexpected honour that I once received from the royal family of Tripura. This sort of an unexpected honour is rare in the world. When Maharaja Bir Chandra Manikya sent his ambassador to me to convey that my work held great promise for the future, it was impossible for me to accept that with full assurance. I was then quite young, and my writings were very few. Most of the readers of the country sarcastically dismissed them as 'child's pleasure'. Bir Chandra knew about that and felt sorry for me. For that, he had proposed to buy an independent press at 1 lakh rupees where an ornamental edition of my poems could be published. At that time, he was visiting the Kurseong hills. After his return to Calcutta, he died within a few days. I thought this death had put an end to my relations with the royal family. It was quite amazing that it did not happen. The flow of affection and respect of his father towards the young poet continued ceaselessly even during Maharaja Radha Kishore's reign. In fact, at that time, he was preoccupied day and night with severe personal problems. But he did not forget me even for a day. Afterwards I continuously enjoyed his hospitality. And his love and affection towards me had never ceased, although the royal retinue was always suspicious and unwelcoming. He constantly feared that I would be thwarted by their simmering hostility. He even frankly said to me, 'I wish you could come to me with a sound mind, despite the resistance of my courtiers.' Thus, for the short period he was alive, I did not pay any heed to the rising antagonism. It is difficult to find in the history of literature instances of such a spontaneous and open friendship between a king and a tender-aged poet doubtful of his own road to fame. This present title conferred by the royal family has illuminated the horizon of the last few days of my life. Yet, there is a special and far greater reason for my happiness—when I learned that the present Maharaja, with unusual generosity, had given shelter to countless oppressed and distressed people, the news filled me with joy and pride. I understood that his hereditary title of the king has been engraved in the minds of all the people of Bangladesh. Bengal's deity of fortune has blessed the royal lineage. This glory, higher than others of this lineage, has been fully revealed at this bright moment, and the titles and offerings that I have received from the hands of the king—I accept them gloriously and hope that fortune rewards the Maharaja for his piety with great success. Now my health is weak; let my feeble voice join the people of the country in his praise. As a poet, I now only long for peace and quietude for the final days.

30 Baishak 1348
Your well-wisher,
Rabindranath Tagore

Letters of Historical Importance
Letter from Rabindranath to Maharaja Bir Chandra Manikya

Om

23 Baishak 1293 Bengali Era

With due respect and humble submission,

I have heard that your royal family and our family have been long acquainted. For this I've ventured to write this letter to the Maharaja. My intention is simply to remind the Maharaja of our old association.

The Maharaja might have heard that I'm writing a novel called *Rajarshi* set against the background of the royal history of Tripura. But I could not be entirely true to history, because it was not available to me. I crave your indulgence for it. It is too late now, but if the Maharaja graciously sends me the detailed history of the reign of Maharaja Govinda Manikya and his brother, I will try my best to make changes accordingly. It would be a great help to me if I may come to know in what condition and in what places Maharaja Govinda Manikya was at Chattogram during the period of his exile. I would be benefited if it may be possible to get the photographs of the old capital of Udaypur and other places in Tripura.

I will consider myself most fortunate if I get a response to this letter and an opportunity to converse with your majesty.

N0. 6, Dwarkanath Tagore Lane
Jorasanko, Calcutta
Yours humbly,
Sri Rabindranath Debsarman

Letter from Bir Chandra Manikya to Rabindranath Sri Hari

To
The man of all good qualities,

I am greatly delighted to receive your letter. You have written that the main purpose of your letter is to recollect the relationship between our two families. I did not forget that happy association. I am most obliged to you for your coming forward again for its glorification. I hope I will keep getting such candid and thought-provoking letters from you.

I have already read both the articles *Mukut* and *Rajarshi*. The errors relating to historical events can be easily rectified by you.

There is one chronological history of the Tripura dynasty in Sanskrit, named *Rajratanakar*. The compilation of this book was started in the regime of Dharma Manikya. Dharma Manikya assumed the throne of Tripura in the Era (TE) 868. Now it is TE 1296. In the *Rajratanakar*, there is a mention of another *Rajmala*, written in an ancient Sanskrit language, but that ancient *Rajmala* could not be found anywhere. The *Rajmala* written in Bengali verse, which is in vogue now, is a short version of the *Rajratanakar* and collected therefrom. The second *Rajmala* was written with the intention to help the ordinary people understand easily while reading it. It starts from the life-history of Maharaja Daitya. The history of many kings prior to him is missing. I have met the writer of the second *Rajmala* in my childhood. Apart from it, there exists one historical account in Bengali verse based on the character of Maharaja Krishna Manikya—the name of the book is *Krishna-Mala*. There is a custom among the people born in the hills that they compose songs based on some special incidents that happened in the lives of the Maharajas and sing them in their own dialects. So many narrations can be derived from these songs. It is understood that there is an advantage to collecting various incidents of history from the slabs of temples and charters.

I am ever grateful to you for taking care of the history of Tripura while writing your novels. Wherever you need help regarding this history, I am ever ready to collect the material from the aforesaid originals. This is my earnest desire that, in your commendable articles on various subjects, the interpretation of history should be proper and accurate. If some particular historical information is needed within a short time, then whatever is available in *Rajratanakar* only can be sent. Otherwise, if there's enough time, then efforts can be made to collect the information from the local sources. Probably, the last method will be more satisfactory to you.

My forefathers, apart from Udaypur, had their capital at Dharma Nagar, Kalyanpur, Amarpur, etc. One can also find the mementos of glorious deeds in these places. If it is necessary for you, the historical data of all these places will be made known to you.

I would send you a few photographs of Udaypur after writing an account on each of them. The way the character of Govinda Manikya and his brother Chhatra Manikya are depicted in *Rajratanakar* have already been copied and endeavours are being made to get them typed immediately. It will be sent after having them fully typed up. The places in which accurate history was not preserved in *Rajarshi* can be understood while going through the quoted parts of *Rajratanakar*.

I have taken an initiative to get *Rajratanakar* printed; all arrangements are not complete as yet. If, by the grace of God, it is done, I will send one copy to you.

In *Rajratanakar*, there are two parts—mythological and historical. The mythological parts consist of the biography of Maharaja Daitya, etc., and the historical parts consist of the period when Bengal was under the occupation of Muslims—numerous and various portions of that period are simply beautiful. If you write a novel based on this portion, I believe, it will become comparatively more praiseworthy.

We are well; write to me to say you all are doing.

18 Jyeshtha 1296 Tripura Era
Yours humbly,
Sri Bir Chandra Deb Barma

Rabi, Year II, Issue IV, 1332 Bengali Era.

Letters from Rabindranath to Maharaja Radha Kishore Manikya

Om

Shilaidaha
Kumarkhali

With my due respect and humble submission—

It gives me immense pleasure to receive your Majesty's affectionate letter today after a long time. Yesterday, I sent one copy of *Kahini*[8] to your Majesty's address—I hope the Maharaja may find some pleasure in it, if not for its poetical excellence, but for his magnanimity.

Here at my end, as there is no scourge of cholera or plague or even the scorching heat of summer, I am passing my days in tranquility and, therefore, I request your Majesty to send Mahim Chandra[9] so that he may stir us up to be wakeful and restless for some time. The loss I suffered by not being able to go to Tripura to enjoy the festival, I wish to somewhat appreciate its flavour by hearing stories and discussing with him.

Pandit Mahashay[10] after his return from Tripura this time is eulogizing your majesty and has become an admirer of Mahim Chandra.

14 Chaitra 1306 Bengali Era
Yours affectionately,
Rabindranath Tagore

Om

Shilaidaha
Kumarkhali

With due respect and humble submission—

I am delighted to receive the letter expected for many days. The persons[11] I have selected for the prince[12] and princess are from a decent family, and they have good characters. I earnestly hope that they do not bring me any shame before the Maharaja. I have counselled them again and again about their responsibilities, yet for some habitual demerits if they are found to be not a bit suitable for the posts, the Maharaja should not have the slightest hesitation in removing them immediately. Kindly keep in mind that, compared to the bond of friendship I have with them, the welfare of the prince to me is much more important. In fact, it is very difficult to get a suitable, educated, and confident Hindu lady as a confidante for the princess. Good girls are available from ordinary Brahmo Samaj, but in conduct and behaviour they may cause inconveniences in the inner mahal—for this reason, I have informed Mahim Chandra about Jati's wife, the only Hindu lady that I could find at the moment. I'll be totally free of anxiety if they can prove themselves worthy for the tasks assigned.

If the money for Jagadish Chandra is sent to me, I will dispatch the same gladly to the right place at the right time. In the meantime, I went to Calcutta for a couple of days—I had an elaborate discussion there with Jagadish Babu. I was delighted to go through all the most enthusiastic letters, which he recently received from the scholars of England. They wrote: 'Your new discoveries are really wonderful.'

We are well. My best wishes to Maharaja and his family.

21 Baishak 1307
Yours ever,
Sri Rabindranath Tagore

Om

Shilaidaha

As I was at Khulna at the invitation of Lokendra Palit, the affectionate letter of the Maharaja reached me late. It is through his large-heartedness that the Maharaja has drawn me as a near relation of the royal family within a short period of acquaintance. I openly say that the welfare of the Maharaja and the progress of Tripura is what I long for; lest you deem it an exaggeration, I cherish it silently in my heart and only off and on I get the pleasure of discussing it with Mahim Chandra.

I am happy to learn about Jati's wife and his mother-in-law from the Maharaja's letter. It is my firm belief that they will gradually earn the Maharaja's favour.

I did not bring to the notice of the Maharaja their one request and one childish insistence, as I had been waiting for the Maharaja to become favourable towards them.

After my first discussion with Mahim Chandra about Jati[13], I brought Jati immediately to Shilaidaha. I vindicated all the pleas and objections they had of going to an unknown state for doing the job. At last, they informed me about their other objection: a short time before, Jati's mother-in-law was in a well-to-do condition; they were from a decent and gentle family; even after a change of fortune, they refused to consider the request of many high families to accept jobs. They have abandoned their hesitation only after I told them about the Maharaja. In consultation with Mahim Chandra, I have decided that 200 rupees should be enough to provide for their food, clothing and shelter; besides, if the Maharaja transfers this palace in the name of Jati and extricates the ladies from linking their names, then a special request of mine gets fulfilled and I shall attain salvation from a promise made to them. For doing so, do not think that there may be some sorts of deficiencies in their performance of duty; have faith in my friendship; I am taking that responsibility.

I have a mind to go on travelling. I am thinking of going to Kashmir with Lokendra Palit. I have an invitation from Jati's mother-in-law to go to Tripura—even her invitation to go to Shimla has been pending. I have three options. Ultimately, I will be where I'm supposed to be.

Meanwhile, is there any resolve of the Maharaja to travel somewhere?

Everything is fine here—all the best wishes to Maharaja.

20 Bhadra 1307 Bengali Era

Yours ever,

Sri Rabindranath Tagore

Om[14]

Jorasanko

With due respect and humble submission,

I am happy to receive an affectionate letter from the Maharaja after a long time. I am going to Muzaffarpur tomorrow, escorting my daughter to her husband's place—I am worried about that.

In *Manusamhita*, the chapter on the 'duties of a king' outlines the ideals of the duty of a king over his domain. The king must perform his duties only, and he has no right over his riches—this becomes clear from the custom of the handover of the charge of the kingdom to his son at an old age and going to the forest for spiritual meditation. The duty of a king is fixed in each part of his life—the burden of the kingdom is only a manifestation of it. In Europe, the kingdom is everything to a king. In ancient India, the realm of a king is regarded as his social and personal duty and not as an embodiment of pleasure and power. The king used to fight not to protect his wealth but to save the social laws and religion from all sorts of invasions and transgressions. The duty of the native kings to maintain the ideals of their indigenous societies has been intensified as India is now under the occupation of an alien emperor. The Hindu society at present has been crippled by foreigners. What catastrophe is on its way is uncertain. If the kings are wakeful and keep the qualified sagacious persons awakened, only then may Hindu society prosper. The kings should attract learned men in the royal court and, for the welfare of the society, make all sorts of deliberations on religion and implement effective welfare schemes. Work in Mysore has been started almost in a similar fashion, and on reading the articles of the late Mahatma Ranade, an inhabitant of Bombay, one comes to know that the Peshwas of Maratha were in fact heedful towards society. In my article 'Hindutva', to be published in the next issue of the month Shaon in *Bangadarshan*, I have shown that the society operates along Hindutva (practices and rites and sacraments of Hinduism) and the king, Brahmans, businessmen and low castes are there to make the society progress in different directions. At the first stage of life, the Brahman, Kshatriya and Vaishya have to prepare for many years to undertake brahmacharya (a mode of life marked by devoted study of the Vedas and other scriptures, and by complete abstinence from sexual and secular pleasures). It will be very pleasant if the Maharaja discusses something about Hindu rajdharma (a Hindu's royal duty)—he may omit the unnecessary parts and discuss only those parts which still hold relevance. I hope the Maharaja is well; I have sent hundred pieces of mangoes and sweetmeats; has the Maharaja tasted them?

Yours ever,
Sri Rabindranath Tagore

Om

With due respect and humble submission,[15]

I am glad to receive the letter of the Maharaja after a long time.

I don't want my friendship with the Maharaja to be such that people label me as self-serving. My capability is minimal, but my goal remains the welfare of the people. Thus, I've decided not to take any financial help from the Maharaja for the job I've undertaken. Noble deeds have no value without hardship and sacrifice. I would feel proud if I can cross the limit of whatever capability I have in the running of *Bangadarshan*. In this matter, I have become more assured after going through the letter of Jagadish Babu this time. Since there's a wonderful union of Jagadish Babu's talent and large-heartedness, I greatly value his opinion in all matters. He wrote:

> At first, I was sorry to suppose that you would again waste your time by taking the change of an editor. Thereafter, I was extremely happy on receiving two issues of *Bangadarshan*. I have become very hopeful noticing the new ideas in all the articles. Nothing more is expected. If, after so many days, we remove the cover from our eyes and understand our real humanness; It will be great. Your work should spread all over India. In addition, you should be able to attain the goal you have undertaken. My foremost grievance is that we have forgotten our real pride and got attracted to false displays of pomp. Now, as I have had a good look of all these countries, I have understood that in no other country has civilization spread to even the lower strata of the society. Which other race could convert the non-Aryans to Aryans? In which place, virtue was extended to the lowest below? Nowadays, civility and incivility are judged on the basis of knowledge. I have heard these words not only from foreigners but also from compatriots that 'you are fool, you can only imitate'. All the people of the country have become spellbound by these words. You have, for the sake of your affection, unnecessarily praised me a lot. If anything is praiseworthy, it is that I have liberated myself from the bondage of this splendour. I am telling the truth that what others had done and whatever height they might have achieved, it is not impossible for us to attain. Bless me all of you, so that I can sever the bondage of falsehood for good.

The letter of Jagadish Babu is a reward to me. He understood what I tried to say. I will be gratified if 'what is the real pride of the Hindus' and in 'what direction lies the actual way forward for the upliftment of Hindus' are discussed properly in *Bangadarshan*. I am gradually trying to show 'what is Hindutva' and, with this, I'm asserting that what is called 'national greatness' in Western civilization is in fact not the ideal of greatness. Our vast social ideals are much larger and higher than this. If we allow these ideals to be destroyed due to inertia, then in Europe's opinion we will never evolve as a nation; at the same time, being detached from our own nature, we will become disabled and weak.

This is the time to do something for Jagadish Babu. A critical time of his research work has arrived. If he is impeded in his progress, there will be no end of grief and shame for us. Maharaja, let me tell you frankly—if unfortunately for the indiscretion of others, I had not been entangled coup-a-pied in the net of debt, I would not have stood at the door of anyone for Jagadish Babu; I would have taken his full charge. My main grievance is that being in distress, I can do nothing but excite others to act for the welfare of the country. The Maharaja is large-hearted, benevolence is natural to him, and for these qualities I am thoroughly attracted to the Maharaja. Thus, I am willing to canvas directly before the Maharaja for Jagadish Babu. I cannot depend on Mahim, etc.; I have gradually lost faith in them. They may be experts in royal service, but they have never let the Maharaja's magnanimity manifest in its entirety. They are not suitable assistants of the Maharaja so far as noble resolve and lofty intentions are concerned. And for this, I intend to enter the solitary private durbar of the Maharaja; I might create extreme trouble for the Maharaja, but I will not be prevented by his ministers. The courtiers of the Maharaja may say so many things; suspecting various kinds of motive, they will harass me, but I shall bear it on my head. This is my prayer to the Maharaja in advance. I have told everything unhesitatingly as I cherish true respect for the Maharaja. Please pardon any impertinence. And, after forgiving me, please look favourably on my intentions of earnest welfare.

Today is the marriage ceremony of my daughter Srimati Renuka. As the bridegroom is suitable, the marriage has been fixed within two or three days. Mahim has arrived on the right day.

With best wishes to the Maharaja.

Yours ever,
Sri Rabindranath Tagore

N.B. I am sending an English paper by post, where you will find sketches done by some of the famous artists of Paris.

An undated letter from Rabindranath Tagore[16]
(Please destroy the letter once you have read it.)

With due respect and humble submission,

All the conditions that revealed themselves before me, I will try to describe them to you with utter frankness.

That the Maharaja should take a loan from the government has become a matter of special interest for some people there. The person whom the government will appoint for the recovery of the loan, I have heard that he belongs to the planter's class—it will not be difficult for a man like Shandiz[17] to bring him under control.

If it happens, the state will be thoroughly bound by a nagpash and if the selfish employees of the Maharaja gain power over the person appointed by the Government, the Maharaja will become weak.

Taking the Maharaja in seclusion in Calcutta, they will keep the Maharaja engaged there in this matter.

If there was no such plan, a man like Shandiz would not have proposed to me to request the Maharaja to go to Calcutta to attend to his medical needs. He does not come to anyone just for the sake of courtesy.

It is a doubtful proposition that the loan will be available from the Bank of Bengal[18] and, therefore, the loan must be taken from some other private bank. It is easy to establish a secret selfish design with a private bank. It is not impossible even in the case of a high-ranking officer of the government.

Some of the people here have come to know that I have given the proposal to appoint Ramani Mohan[19] to assist the Maharaja.

To make me happy and to take me to their team, they are saying it is a good proposal. They are also saying that everything will be settled if Ramani is appointed with the consent of the government for arranging the repayment of the loan. It is easy to take steps so that the government does not nominate Ramani.

Ramani is an efficient officer, but the government knows that Ramani and Nilambar Babu[20] troubled the government during the reformation work done in the municipality.

In the performance of Ramani's duty, if the slightest mistake was discovered, then they would have sacked him immediately—but there is no officer more efficient than Ramani.

However, I do not know how much favour Frazer[21] has for Ramani.

Genuinely speaking, the Maharaja needs such a person whom those with selfish interests will not be able to coax, through force or friendship, to join their own camp. That person in all circumstances will stand by the side of the Maharaja. This is the only way to save the Maharaja from conspiracies.

I feel very hesitant in naming Ramani. It is not because he is my relative; it is a very delicate matter to shoulder the responsibility of nominating someone's name like this at such a crucial juncture. I have tried to overcome this hesitation, thinking only of the duty of a friend. I surely know that if Ramani is appointed there, I must accept a lot of disgrace.

If not Ramani, some other person, determined and efficient, must be appointed as minister.

If the Maharaja is forced to abide by the conditions of the government for the purpose of taking a loan, and also to accept the person from the government for the administration of zamindari, then the Maharaja should appoint an efficient man of his choice as minister—kindly do not mix them up.

It is my feeling that a vicious net is being weaved—thus, without an iota of further delay, the Maharaja should make up his mind; do not hesitate at all—make an arrangement to tear asunder this net. The more you delay, the weaker you will get.

Yours faithfully,
Sri Rabindranath Tagore

Om

With due respect and humble submission—

I am writing this letter to place before the Maharaja a prayer for Professor Bose. Professor Mahashay has invented an instrument for measuring the growth of plants. At present, he is engaged in discussing the theory of plant growth.

The thin bamboos that grow in Tripura exhibit very rapid growth in their infancy stage. The saplings of this tree are urgently necessary for his experiment. It will be most beneficial for him if the Maharaja gives an order to immediately send freshly sprouted saplings of thin bamboos to his address; it will be necessary to put the trees with roots on soil in pack-boxes with a cage cover above so that the saplings do not die on the way. For the time being, he will require twenty to twenty-five trees. If these trees die because of the experiment, there will again be a need for fresh saplings—the Maharaja can then give an order once again. As the trees cannot be located in nearby Calcutta, his experiment remains incomplete.

In a registered letter I wrote some important matters to the Maharaja—the Maharaja has probably received it.

I am in Calcutta dealing with some property matters—hope I will be able to finish it within a weak and have some respite for a few days for the time being.

I pray for the well-being of the Maharaja.

2 Ashar 1312 Bengali Era
Yours ever,
Sri Rabindranath Tagore

Om

With due respect and humble submission[22]—

I am writing this letter from a ship—it will be sent to you from Goalnand in an envelope addressed to Jati[23].

I have seen the letter of the magistrate (of Tripura). The Maharaja's intentions were not communicated clearly to the magistrate. It was not brought to the notice of the magistrate that the Maharaja was trying on his own to get the loan disregarding the help of the government; it is not necessary to mortgage the whole of Chakla Roshanabad in the hands of a new man for the repayment of the loan. It seems that the magistrate was conveyed that the Maharaja wants to keep one part of the estate. But all the efforts of the Maharaja to engage with the government is proving to be wholly futile due to differences of intentions of the people involved. Furthermore, they are trying to project the Maharaja before the authorities as an object of displeasure. I could clearly see that, with the intention to sack Srijukta Sarat Basu[24], an effort is going on to dislodge the Maharaja from the control of his zamindari. I know nothing about Sarat Babu—the Maharaja himself should consider whether it is beneficial to dismiss him, but for a trifling matter like this, a conspiracy of such magnitude cannot be given latitude. The eagerness of a group of people to give the post of manager of Roshanabad to their own man has now become quite evident.

I am indeed wondering how the Maharaja will continue talking to the government before the appointment of a faithful and an efficient person. Those in charge are against it.

Whether the Maharaja should come to Calcutta, I shall write about it after a consultation or send a telegram. I am afraid of those who will accompany him—I do not know what they will say to the authority and how they'll say it!

If a loan is unavoidable and the conditions of the government are to be accepted, then do not give the responsibility of this job to them. The amount of ten lakh rupees, receivable as commission, should come to the Maharaja's own treasury. First of all, appoint a good man and then take up this job.

If you decide to appoint Ramani[25], then he will need to apply for leave. Inform me whatever you decide—never think that I will be hurt if Ramani is not appointed. I know everything of the Maharaja's impediments—he has to work after considering different sides; despite one's will, it is not possible in politics to turn one's intentions swiftly into reality.

I will write to Maharaja after reaching Calcutta.

Yours ever,
Sri Rabindranath Tagore

Om

With due respect and humble submission—

I am apprised of Maharaja's intentions from Mahim's letter. I talked to Ramani after coming to Calcutta. I will be able to engage him in the Maharaja's service on two years leave with a salary fixed for the post of minister. He does not want to improve his pecuniary situation. He will be gratified if he can efficiently achieve discipline and development in the kingdom of the Maharaja and be respected for doing so. In fact, he is indifferent to moneymaking. He even wants to leave his job after three years and be entitled for a pension.

However, if the Maharaja so decides, Ramani must apply for leave now. It may take three months to get the leave. My other request is: handover the task to Ramani Mohan, so that he does not fail in any part and finds a place to exert his full expertness. He claims that he has never failed in any task that he has undertaken till date. He is thus doomed to failure if limited power is bestowed on him in Tripura. The Maharaja will have no regrets if the proper workload is allocated to Ramani.

I will reach Calcutta on Saturday morning. I shall have to stay there occupied for a few days. If, in the meantime, the Maharaja comes for a welcome visit there, all the issues may be discussed. If it takes time, wherever I may be, I will come immediately after getting the news. I feel as if God has conferred on me a vow that the system in the kingdom of the Maharaja will have to be settled. My heart is eager to take leave from service, but I have clearly understood that this work must be accomplished by me. I am religiously bound by it; even the Maharaja will not be able to set me free from this. In the midst of all my present problems related to property settlement, the thought of the Maharaja's kingdom does not leave me. It is not for the

Maharaja only; I shall have to apply my mind to the Maharaja's work to release myself from anxiety. The connection that my grandfather had in the history of Tripura, I shall have to maintain that—perhaps it is, for that purpose, that by the will of God, the late Maharaja, all of a sudden, had bound me with Tripura.

28 Ashar 1312 Bengali Era
Yours ever,
Sri Rabindranath Tagore

Om

Jorasanko

With due respect and humble submission—

I have received the Maharaja's letter from Jati.

All these days, I have discussed each moment with Ramani, the account of which you will have from Jati ... For the time being, I am informing the Maharaja in a nutshell about the appointment of Ramani.

He gets here 1,250 rupees at present. He expects 1,500 from the Maharaja.

The full charge of administration, defence, judiciary, etc., and all other tasks should be handed over to him.

After his consent to these two proposals, the moment the Maharaja invites him to join his work with a signed letter, he will apply for leave. There will perhaps be no hindrance to get the leave, but it may not be possible to have it before November.

After Ramani's leave is sanctioned for two years and he joins the service, the Maharaja will then come to know entirely about his efficiency. If nothing disadvantageous happens in the meantime, there will be no reason for the Maharaja to hesitate in releasing him. From Ramani's side, he shall be unconcerned if it is admitted that the Maharaja will require him only for two years in service.

If the Maharaja is satisfied with his work during the two years, the Maharaja may consider and make arrangements to keep him permanently in his service—but for now there is no need to think of all that. The matter of taking a loan may be kept pending so long as Ramani is not appointed. For if this is done now, the Maharaja might have to sustain a loss from those who are greedy and avaricious.

I am informing the Maharaja again that if Ramani is appointed to royal service, the Maharaja will be satisfied and unperturbed in all respects by his faithfulness, efficiency, farsightedness and magnanimity. I shall be gratified if I can totally secure the Maharaja from the danger of disguised enemies.

May God keep the Maharaja free from danger!

9 Shaon 1312 Bengali Era
Yours ever,
Sri Rabindranath Tagore

Om

With due respect and humble submission[26]—

Leaving aside all hesitation, I am about to raise some topics to bring them to the Maharaja's attention. Please forgive any impertinence on my part.

I know about all sorts of problems that may arise in the course of royal duties. I stay far away; it is difficult for me to arrive at a right decision—yet I cannot remain stoic. And it will be irreligious for me if I do not convey to the Maharaja what I am able to grasp through my intelligence.

At present, the proposal of taking a loan has become the most important subject of discussion in the state and I have heard a debate of all the parties in this respect.

I have heard that it will be beneficial to take a loan from the government and repay the whole miscellaneous amount and the small standing debts. Based on the said proposal, the administration of zamindari and to some extent the control over income and expenditure will have to be handed over to a government-nominated English supervisor.

On the other hand, it is apparently not impossible to arrange a good settlement of repaying the loan through regular payments by persuading the creditors to agree. The creditors especially do not have an opportunity to claim a higher rate of interest.

I have no courage as such to come to a decision only based on such contradictory hearsays. The Maharaja, no doubt, has taken into consideration all these facts. My only resort is supposition: yet, on the possibilities of its working in favour of the Maharaja, I could not help but narrate all the facts.

Right from the outset, the word British creates a fear; a carefree surrender to this class is by no means warranted. Nothing to say, of course, if one is compelled to do so. Those who, even after thwarting the authority of the Maharaja up to this level, are very eager to repay the whole debt in one go, then their eagerness should be held suspect. Is it true that if the repayment of the loan is not done immediately, then an interest has to be paid at 12 per cent? Is it also true that the creditors will not agree if the debt is repaid within five or six years by regular payments? Are there any other ways for them not to agree? As such, in case the debt is repaid by taking a loan from an institution and if any of the employees of the Maharaja expect rewards from the creditor, then one has to wonder if there's any reason for alarm. The last words I uttered may be entirely baseless—I have no substantial proof before me to suspect anyone, but in the matter of royal duties even the slightest suspicion is worthy of discussion; for this, if I may commit any injustice toward an innocent, then I plead for your forgiveness immediately.

But as I am not able to say anything emphatically, I only humbly submit this much, that in order to help the Maharaja in the governance of the state, a person who is an efficient, farsighted and resolute economist needs to be appointed on whose intelligence and sense of duty the Maharaja can wholly rely. The heart of the Maharaja is quite soft, and therefore to save himself from his own virtues of forgiveness and magnanimity, he is badly in need of an able assistance from a proficient minister. I have noticed that constant hostility and conflicts among different parties trouble the Maharaja at all times; it is feared, lest the trap becomes gradually more complicated, and the Maharaja gets entangled in some kind of disrepute. It is proper to bind oneself rigorously by one's own rule rather than being bound by the bondage of others. I remain worried for I have observed that the health of the Maharaja has been deteriorating for a long time now. I earnestly pray to God to relieve you from sickness and disturbances. It is my belief that instead of being mentally disturbed by the pull of different people, the Maharaja will regain peace and health provided he bestows his full faith on any one person. I am not requesting the Maharaja to appoint the person whose name I have recommended earlier—my submission is that there cannot be discipline at all in royal duties if unconditional power is not given to one person. At present, the minister of the Maharaja is failing for he is insulted by the other employees working under him, and it is for this reason that the deity presiding over the Maharaja's state feels dishonoured. If the Maharaja wants to keep him as a minister, then the Maharaja by his unwavering royal power must put him firmly in his own post; otherwise, misfortune will be intensified—kindly pay heed to the humble words of an affectionate friend and forgive all his impertinence. I hope what I said is driven by faith and reason.

N.B. After you have read the letter, destroy it without delay.

Yours ever,
Sri Rabindranath Tagore

Om

Shantiniketan
Bolpur

With due respect and humble petitions—

For some days, I've felt a growing sense of shame, so I am writing this letter to the Maharaja today to try and drive it away.

After getting Mahim's letter and telegram with the Maharaja's letter, I've felt a deep pain in my heart.

You know for sure that, for a long time now, I have eagerly discussed the development of Tripura. In this connection, I grew suspicious of Mahim for various reasons. Once, at Darjeeling, I clearly expressed this suspicion.

But all these suspicions did not get a firm foothold in my mind. The reason was that I did not know all the real incidents pertaining to Tripura through my personal experience. I have got no right to bear in mind any adverse impression about Mahim—particularly when I have never worked with him.

Another reason is: whenever I have discussed with Mahim any matters relating to the state, I have only come to respect him more and more. I have understood that Mahim is very quick and sharp, his ability to conceive an idea is very strong, and he is indeed enthusiastic about the welfare of the state.

Whenever Mahim and I discussed the advancement of Tripura, Mahim would start lamenting about the various obstacles against this advancement. I wondered whether he knew that one of the greatest obstacles against this advancement was his own weakness. He possesses an extraordinary spirit of intelligence and willingness to work and that has the potential to bear good results for Tripura.

The cordial relationship that has been established with the Maharaja by the grace of God, I feel it now more and more intensely.

There are duties that needs to be performed within this relationship as well. And I believe it is wrong if these duties are not undertaken. Thus, I have decided this time that I will perform these duties leaving aside all hesitations for the welfare of Tripura.

Now it is not the right time for me to work. My mind often becomes impatient to wind up all the nets of the world. Right now, why God has drawn me even for a moment in the matters of the royal court, full of conspiracy and complexity, only He knows! The path of the work seems inaccessible and is strewn with thorns. I have tasted conspiracy as soon as I have set foot on this path.

Initially, seized with dreadful suspicion, I was nonplussed. I was anxious to find out from which direction the Maharaja had fallen into crisis. But I had no time and an opportunity at my disposal to understand the whole matter—because I am at the periphery of the Maharaja's circle. The hints that I got through momentary contact cannot be depended upon. But the places from where chances of danger could be inferred, I did not think it proper to keep them a secret from the Maharaja. The Maharaja knows much more than I do about the internal conditions—hoping that the Maharaja will consider and deliberate upon them, I have placed before the Maharaja whatever facts I came across. Really, I had no capacity to judge fully what was secret and what was open, what was significant and what was insignificant, and what the purpose was. For this incapability, I placed everything before the Maharaja to judge and consider.

Although doubts had crept into my mind repeatedly about Mahim's mean-mindedness and weakness of spirit, I did not leave him as a friend. I still share a faithful relationship with him. As it was a heinous breach of trust on my part, I have been suffering punishment for that from the Almighty. Hence, I would request the Maharaja to kindly show this letter to Mahim. Have I had respite,

I would have some day or the other clearly told Mahim my regrets and apprehensions, but I did not get such an opportunity. Thus, what needs to be said, let me say it today clearly.

I do not believe Shandiz Saheb at all. I have heard from so many sources that Shandiz extorts the Maharaja's money by means of different strategies. From when I have seen Mahim getting close to Shandiz Saheb, I have realized then that unselfishly working for the well-being of the Maharaja's state will not be anymore possible for Mahim.

When I did not understand the necessity to repay the Maharaja's loan of 10 lakh rupees in a lump sum but found Mahim and Shandiz to be quite eager in this matter, I was naturally suspicious and it would have been unjust for me to hide this fact from the Maharaja.

It might give Mahim solace, thinking that when the repayment of the loan is inevitable, then what is the harm in maximizing his own advantage along with the welfare of the state?

But I did not like the efforts being made to bring the Maharaja under the control of others on this kind of pretext.

Regarding this, Mahim might have convinced the Maharaja by claiming that if the Maharaja consented to being subjected under such an authority, then it would prove beneficial for the state's well-being. If Mahim himself was pure, firm and had done his duty without thinking of the result, then there was no need to play all these tricks.

After going to Tripura, I have seen that partisanship has become very acute there—in this condition, it is not possible for any party to stand for the Maharaja. Each party's top priority is to foil the other party and gain strength for one's own faction; as such, it is inevitable that the Maharaja should come to harm. It was thus impossible for me to identify the Maharaja's real friends! I could only discern that Maharaja is entangled in a net of a crisis. I did not have the courage to depend on Mahim to get rid of this crisis as I did not know what he had in mind. He might have wished well, but how far he himself was entangled with which camp was not known.

I also saw that Mahim, Shandiz and one or two other persons conducted all the conversations of the Maharaja with the government. If they so wished, they could misuse this power in such a way that it might have proven to be dangerous for the Maharaja—in such a situation, if there remains an iota of doubt, it is the duty of a king to be extra cautious. For this, I thought that the Maharaja then needed a neutral person, unselfish, well-educated and efficient. As far as I know, an efficient person like Ramani is rare and, therefore, I had recommended Ramani's name.

However, for that, I am no longer eager now. I feel it was irreligious on my part to have kept secret from Mahim all those doubts I harboured about him. Mahim will clearly understand my mental state if he reads this letter.

The impression I had about Mahim was mostly likely to be baseless, and keeping in mind this possibility of it being baseless, I was able to keep our friendship intact. However, for the sake of the Maharaja's work, even now, I would continue bearing this doubt in my mind about others who surround him in the court.

About Mahim, I am greatly ashamed of myself; the Maharaja may kindly clear the fact and drive away my feelings of shame. I could not reply to some of his letters because of this sense of shame. May God relieve the Maharaja from all disturbances!

16 Shaon 1312
Yours ever,
Sri Rabindranath Tagore

Om

With due respect and humble submission—

Amid the Calcutta crowd, I have become mentally and physically exhausted; I have thus decided to go to Bolpur today by the evening mail.

I have already expressed my opinions about the Maharaja's state administration yesterday.

Nowhere is work said to be done by the council. Keeping the council as an advisory body, one leader does all the work. In that case, the members of the council are bound to obey the leader. Otherwise, there would be no end of shrewd conspiracy, mutual antagonism and disorderliness. Does the Maharaja have real respect for the present courtiers? Do they have the capacity to shoulder such an enormous responsibility? Would the Maharaja surrender his well-being in their hands? The Maharaja by his constant indulgence has increased their strength; he should have slowly and steadily reduced that strength and liberated himself from the network of these selfish, and narrow-minded persons. Or should he handover the charge of running the state administration into their hands and make them practically invincible?

Another proposal is to appoint Macmean[27] Saheb as an administrator. There cannot be anything more lamentable to me than this … But you will not get him for good—such a permanent arrangement must be made so that there's no lapse at all in administration and no fear of humiliation by the authorities. If you are unperturbed, believing yourself to be safe, only then will danger draw near. My earnest request to the Maharaja is not to allow Tripura to be bound by obligations and thus be crippled. Now, it must be made to stand in a hard system. Those who are around the Maharaja are playing with his well-being—it is my belief that they are too eager to realize their own interests even at the cost of the fall of the kingdom. If this belief is untrue, may God forgive me. But whatever it may be, they are not capable of shouldering any kind of important responsibilities—because they are men of frivolous character; they may have sharp intelligence but no sobriety—for this only, I am earnestly requesting the Maharaja not to surrender to them now so that he may have to repent later. It is easy to create bondage, but hard to sever it. Now, if you do not consider the connected line of events, you will never get time later.

I do not know whether Ramani will be able to accomplish the tasks of the Maharaja; I cannot say whether he will be ultimately available. But at any cost, the Maharaja needs an able, God-fearing and earnest well-wisher—the state administration will have to be run with him in a position of absolute power. Such a person is needed who will work without fear and with a firm hand, having no connection whatsoever with the enemies of the state or with any of the local parties; and he must mercilessly repress those who need to be repressed. I am saying all this very frankly to the Maharaja. If any of my sayings come across as haughty, I beg to be pardoned. I pray to God to rescue me from any bondage; I have no excuse if I fail within my ability to do good for this relationship. I did not get an opportunity hitherto to let Maharaja know everything—today I have submitted it in my letter. Now whatever the will of God is, that will prevail. I can only pray for the Maharaja's well-being; I can do no more than that. I will never forget that I am indebted to the Maharaja's love and affection. Now, let the Maharaja permit me to go to my place of work and meditate in peace. May God favour the Maharaja!

14 Poush 1313 Bengali Era
Yours ever,
Sri Rabindranath Tagore

Letters from Maharaja Radha Kishore Manikya to Rabindranath Tagore

Sri Hari

My dear Rabi Babu,

I am happy to learn from your letter written to Sriman Mahim[28] that you are going to Darjeeling. I am not able to express how happy I would be during my stay there for a few days if I get your company in the glorious Himalayas. I suppose the impediments of Calcutta should not be there on the snow peaks.

I have taken two houses named Wood Vine Villa and Lounge. I shall leave on 6 Ashwin and reach there on 8. I will reach Kushtia on 7 by the Chattogram mail. Is it possible to meet you at that time?

We are well. Pay my respects to Maharshi. After going to Darjeeling, I will write a letter to him.

2 Ashwin 1309 Tripura
Yours ever,
Sri Radha Kishore Deb Barma

Sri Hari

My dear Rabi Babu,

We had planned to celebrate the marriage of Sriman Yubraj[29] on 8 Falgun, but as there was a scourge of cholera here, I was compelled to postpone the auspicious ceremony to 24 Falgun. I had a mind to fix the date for next winter, but the bride's side is unwilling to wait after *faldan* (a part of the marriage rituals that involves the giving of fruits). The ceremony of giving and accepting fruits was held on 3 Falgun. I thought of inviting the foreign gentry on this auspicious occasion but as it is now becoming very hot, it won't be possible. I would be happy if you, Jyoti Babu[30], Gagan Babu[31], Ashu Babu[32] and, if possible,

Jagadish Babu[33] are present during this auspicious occasion. It is borne in my mind that a laboratory needs to be built for Jagadish Babu.

I hope you'll be able to make it to the auspicious ceremony, and at that time I would be ready to do whatever decision comes out of our discussions. I pray to God and wish Jagadish Babu a long life so that he enhances the glory of India.

I am writing separate letters to Jyoti Babu etc. But, amongst them, those who will surely come, it will be convenient if they are informed a bit early.

You have expressed your desire to associate my name with *Kahini*; how can I say no to that? I would be happy if you could please send me ten or twelve copies of the book; the moment printing is over, I will distribute them to my friends.

I am well with my family; I would be happy to know if all of you are well.

15 Falgun 1309 Tripura Era
Always yours,
Sri Radha Kishore

Sri Hari

My dear Rabi Babu,

I was very busy looking after the arrangements of the marriage ceremony. Now I am somewhat at peace. I am sorry that you could not attend the occasion as your son had suddenly fallen sick. However, I am not perturbed now after having heard the news of his improved health.

I tried to have some rest in seclusion and went to the forest to hunt, but the virulence of the hailstorm was such that I had to return home fully drenched. I've never seen such a huge hailstorm before. Some of the hailstones were at least more than one fourth of a sher (a standard of weight measuring 1/4th of 1 kg).

I have received your clothes as a gift through Pandit Mahashay[34]. The cloth befits my daughter-in-law. I have given it to Badhumata (daughter-in-law) as a blessing of yours. Srimati has already used it.

Mahim is devising a clever means to get leave taking your name. What is your order about him? It is my wish to send him to your residence. He may create trouble. But at times, a slight disturbance is of course welcome. If your reply is favourable, he may pack his five hand-tools[35].

The weather here is fine; after the heat, it is a relief now. What about your place? I hope to hear news about you and your family.

11 Chaitra 1309 Tripura Era

Yours,

Sri Radha Kishore Barma

Sri Hari

My dear Rabi Babu,

I have received two consecutive letters from you. After receiving *Kahini* along with your first letter, I have started reading it in earnest. I could not get through more than half up to now. The end of the year is near. It's not right to read it in a hurry. One must savour the beauty of the text. At least, this is what I do.

Is there any point in showering unnecessary appreciation merely for the sake of friendship? You're naturally talented, and your poetry is thus profound and solemn. I am delighted by it. The chosen language is entirely appropriate to the theme. In the books written in modern times, based on ancient history or otherwise, I don't find language that skillfully expresses such solemnity. Your books are devoid of these demerits. I believe the aforesaid qualities, if properly maintained, shall greatly enliven the book.

Mahim will obey your order very soon. He will soon be with you after ensuring some peace here. He has with him a camera, gun, and other tools. I only fear that he doesn't start hunting human beings like those white English sepoys. Is it not better to prevent him from using a gun? I have heard that Mahim does compose songs; I have tried to read all his compositions once. But Sriman Mahim Chandra does not allow me to see them. Can you not ask him to show them to you? I have also heard that his compositions do not come to him if he is not possessed by a Yaksha (a class of demigods in mythology). Wretched as he is, because of the vices of the evil company he keeps, he is almost on the road to being utterly lost.

Storm and rain have started here as usual. The rain gods this time have probably arrived on horsebacks. I cannot say what the outcome may be; but the small mangoes have been ruined. Nothing is left to make some chutney (a condiment) or even *tak* (sour)! What a loss!

We are well. How are you with your family? Is it true that the plague is spreading in all directions? I am anxious about it.

21 Chaitra 1309 Tripura Era
An admirer,
Sri Radha Kishore Barma

Sri Hari

My dear Rabi Babu,

I have received both of your letters at the right time. As I was in a mess, I could not reply to even one of them—accept my apologies for the same.

I have met Jatindra Babu[36]. I've been happy talking to him. Since you have personally selected and appointed the person for Sriman and Srimati[37], I have nothing more to say. We'll have the desired result if Jatin and his wife are employed for the same purpose. Jatindra Babu has already gone. He will probably return with his wife. An arrangement has been made for their house. His work will start the moment he arrives.

The matter regarding Jagadish Babu is still in my mind. I will send the said assistance before he goes to England. I had had no discussion with Jagadish Babu on this subject. I would, therefore, like to send the money order in your name. Moreover, that I think will be a better arrangement.

Regarding the subject of a new theory of Professor Bose, I could understand only a little through Mahim. And I have also got a slight proof of it in a small instrument that he had sent. Can Mahim's explanations possibly satisfy my desire to know more about it?

I have a mind to go to Darjeeling once again. I am afraid; there should not be any kind of hindrances like last time. I shall write to you after fixing a date. The photographs taken by Mahim this time are not bad. I will send the copies after getting them sufficiently printed. After coming from your place, he continues with his endeavours here. It would have been better, if he could have remained there for a few more days. We are doing well. Hope all of you are in good health and spirit.

14 Baishak 1310 Tripura Era
Yours ever,
Sri Radha Kishore Barma

Sri Hari

My dear Rabi Babu,

I am happy to learn from your letter that you are keen to go to Darjeeling. After a long time, I could somehow manage to settle the issues over here. Now I want to rest well for a few days. I am excited by the thought that my leisure time will be spent amidst the beauty of the Himalayas and in the company of your poems and music. Please bring your notebook of poetry and a few books along with you. I am also taking a few books with me. However, now let Grihini Thakurani[38] answer your prayers. Otherwise, Mahim, without saying anything whatsoever, will trespass all of a sudden. I shall start from here on Monday, 23, and reach Kushtia station Tuesday afternoon, around four o'clock. From there, we can go together. The house taken on rent in Darjeeling can accommodate all of us.

The news of the republication of Bankim's *Bangadarshan* is very good. The enthusiasm of famous writers makes the news greater. In my opinion, without further delay and hesitation, you should take the charge of editorship. Just let me know what I have to do. I am ready to undertake its charge in all respects.

I have come to know from Jati's letter that you had a great quarrel with Chowdhurani[39] and that the affair also took place on the pretext of my letter. But do not forget, she is an intermediary between us. If you enrage an intermediary, that might risk the friendship.

On the advice of a political agent, I have not sent Mahim and Jati immediately to Ajmer. It is good. I will get an opportunity to discuss with you.

There are constant hailstorms going on here. There are only heaps of bricks, brick-dust, rubbish and mud all around the house. I am extremely disgusted.

We are doing fine. Hope all of you are well.

Yours ever,
14 Baishak 1311 Tripura Era
Sri Radha Kishore Barma

Sri Hari

My dear Rabi Babu,

I am staying here for a few days with Sriman Yubraj[40]. In the meantime, I was preoccupied with various tasks and, therefore, could not write a letter.

My daughter-in-law's education[41] has already begun. I found Jati's mother-in-law[42] and family very enthusiastic. I hope their efforts bring about a good result. Having bestowed all the responsibilities of my daughter-in-law on such gentle and intelligent women, I am at peace.

Meanwhile, I went home for two days to call on the relatives. I saw Jati's mother-in-law and Uma Rani[43] had good relations with my daughter-in-law. I did not find any kind of incompatibility between them. If you visit this place at some point, you can see it for yourself.

I have read your letter written to Jati. I am delighted at the sincerity reflected in your directions given to him on the method of education that would benefit Sriman. It is difficult to get a friend in this world who can exhibit such large-heartedness. It is commendable that because of your consistent efforts, Jati and his family are here now. I would help Sriman Jati Babu to see that your advice is rightly complied with. I shall go home after staying here a few more days. Then I can see them every day.

We are well. Write to me to say how you are.

13 Bhadra 1310 Tripura Era
Yours ever
Sri Radha Kishore Barma.

Sri Hari

My dear Rabi Babu,

I have got your letter written from Kushtia. I am happy to learn that you are well. I was only thinking that I should not be blamed by your better half[44] for your sickness, but I discovered that you have got the opportunity to realize your unreasonable demands with interest—it is a matter of joy for me.

I could not write in detail. Today again at three o' clock there will be a meeting with the Lieutenant Governor (LG). The LG has accepted your and Cooch Behar Maharaja's[45] opinions about the education of my son. But I had to make him understand a great deal. He advised me to appoint a good teacher from Cooch Behar. Accordingly, I have made a proposal to the Maharaja of Cooch Behar. He will most likely send a letter to England.

I had an interview with the said Maharaja for the initiative taken by you.

The result of the discussion with the LG. on royal matters proved fruitful. The present LG is candid and vastly experienced. The discussion today is in our favour and we expect a good result thereof.

I am going back home tomorrow. I will be happy to see you at Kushtia. It is not impossible that you may get my telegram before the arrival of this letter. I would request you to take care of yourself. The marriage is approaching. You should not fall ill at this juncture.

I am more than satisfied that Jati has taken care of you. He is young and inexperienced; thus his trouble needs to be tolerated.

I have left Mahim here. He will come later. Write to me after the date of marriage is fixed.

We are well. I should get your letter just after reaching home. I shall also write.

Yours ever,
Sri Radha Kishore Barma

N.B. Received Jati's letter day before yesterday. They are well. There are so many things in this letter.

Letters from Rabindranath to Maharaja Birendra Kishore Manikya

Om

Shantiniketan

To the esteemed Maharaja,

We are glad and grateful to the Maharaja for sending Buddhimanta Singh[46] to the Ashram. The boys are enthusiastically learning to dance from him. Our girls are also eager to learn Manipuri dance and art. If the Maharaja gives an order to send Buddhimanta Singh's wife here, our purpose will be served. It is our wish that the girls from respectable families practice works like cloth weaving. For this, one teacher from Assam is teaching cloth weaving to the girls here. But the art of the Manipuri women, which I have seen in Sylhet, is much better than this. I have made my proposal to Buddhimanta. He has said that if he gets the consent of the Maharaja to bring his wife, then arrangements can be made to teach Manipuri dance and art to the women here. About this matter and for this purpose I shall await the Maharaja's consent.

May God bless you.

19 Magh 1326
Your well-wisher,
Sri Rabindranath Tagore

To the esteemed Maharaja,

You are aware that Bolpur Vidyalaya has been receiving an annual grant from the late Maharaja. That generosity has saved this school in times of adversity—my gratitude to the late king is eternal, and I shall always remember his affection toward me.

I am writing this letter to know whether we can hope to get the grant initiated by the late Maharaja from your Majesty. We cherish in our hearts the hope that our relationship with Tripura will not be severed for any reason.

May God bless you.

26 August 1909
Your well-wisher,
Sri Rabindranath Tagore

Letters from Rabindranath to Prince Brajendra Kishore

Om

Bolpur

My dear,

My health is not good. I am sorry to hear that you have been admitted to a school at Comilla. I can very well understand that it will be oppressive for you. The uncivil arrogance and hateful conduct of this barbarian race are quite distressing. They do not want us, they neglect us, yet we follow and emulate them; this is an insult on our part. Those who hate our whole nation, how will they respect me? Even if they do, why should I accept it? There cannot be any scene more shameful than this, where an insulted nation tries to gain favour from the English Sahibs. However, bear it out, and save the independence of your mind; if you can do so, you will be able to protect your valour even in adverse conditions. May God always save you from all falsehoods. What is to be learnt, learn it, what is to be seen, see it quietly, and what is to be kept in mind, keep it forever! May God always save you from false illusions!

Friday (n.d.)
Sri Rabindranath Tagore

Om

Shantiniketan,
Bolpur

My dear,

As I was too busy, I could not write to you. I came to Shantiniketan yesterday with a cough and cold from Calcutta—I hope there will be no delay in my recovery after coming here. I have written a letter to the Maharaja—I hope there will be no difficulty for you to come here. Rathi has been eagerly waiting for you. While coming, bring your carpentry and fretwork with you. You may bring your bicycle and books as well. We are appointing one well-qualified professor of science who is skillful in all kinds of handicrafts—he is also aware of photography. I will start the work of Vidyalaya after your arrival here. Do not allow December to pass by. Our earnest blessings are to you.

1 Agrahayan 1308
Sri Rabindranath Tagore

Om

Shantiniketan,
Bolpur

My dear,

In whatever condition, companionship and education you are in, do not allow in any way the ideals of India to fade away from your heart. Surely, keep in mind that the barbarians of Europe, without understanding the true greatness of India, ridicule it. Do not give any importance to their contempt. Surrender yourself wholeheartedly in all respects to India with a calm and unflinching discipline. If your teachers condemn India, ignore them without giving any reply. It is perhaps better for you not to come to my school, because I intend to do my work in seclusion, out of the purview of public discussion. If you come here, thousands of words will be said creating a hullabaloo. My peace of mind would naturally be hampered by this.

Following the ancient ideal of Brahmcharya in India, I want my students to be in seclusion without worries and to become proper human beings, pure and clean—I intend to initiate them into India's graceful, holy humility, keeping them free of infatuation with all sorts of British luxuries. You, too, need that initiation in your heart. Keep it firmly in mind that there is no disgrace in poverty, no shame in wearing loincloth and no incivility at all in the absence of furniture. Those who advocate abundance of riches and wealth, trade and business, collection of material objects as a mark of civilization, they merely emulate barbarism in the name of civilization. Civilization is manifested in peace, pleasure, forgiveness, knowledge and meditation—having fortitude, self-restraint, purity, being in deep communion with oneself, ignoring the whole tumult and attraction of the outside world, get ready to become the true children of an ancient country, to be entitled as the heirs of the first civilization and to have the taste of true freedom from bondage. Do not spoil your strength unnecessarily by putting forth an oral counterplea. Surrender earnestly, calmly and silently to India with firm faith. As your present education is against this ideal, your firmness should be more than double in this tug-of-war. This opposition will foster your true education. I know, the natural glory of India dwells in your heart—she has so long saved you from many calamities. Even now she will not leave you. The British teacher will try in many ways to tarnish your natural valour and to extinguish it—let your valour be increased against that unfavourable effort and make you stand the test. Let the blessings of India save you, let the assurance of God save you and let your own talent save you. Remember that it is better to die than to accept the customs and practices of alien *mlechchhas*. 'Swadharmey Nidhanang Sreya Parodharma Bhayabaha' ['It is better to die in the practice of one's own dharma because imitating those of others can be dangerous.'] Write to me for that shall make me happy. In the coming New Year, take a vow to become the child of India and nourish this vow till the end of your life.

24 Chaitra 1308
With blessings,
Sri Rabindranath Tagore

Om

Shantiniketan

My dear,

Son, never ever forget you are a Kshatriya. Any education and company should not trounce your valour, vigour and reverence. If the foreigners deceive us into thinking of ourselves as mean, it will be our true failure. Our minds are gradually acquiring a slavish attitude because of the education of the British. For this, in our clothing, food and enjoyment, and in decorating our houses with luxury items, we are only using the leftovers of the English. It is the duty of a Kshatriya to save the country and society from injustice, outrage, irreligiousness and immoral practices. There is no other purer and nobler duty than this. Take the responsibility to brighten again the ideals of Kshatriya dharma in India by giving up fear, despising death, embracing sorrows, ignoring poverty and keeping your self-respect unimpaired. To accept that responsibility, you will have to keep your whole valour burning in the secret cave of your heart like a sacred fire. Bhishma, Arjuna and Karna of the Mahabharata are the perfect embodiments of the Kshatriya ideal. Accept this ideal. In the course of time, the Mahabharata has become bloated with inessential things. Leaving out all those trivialities, if you follow the main story, you will be acquainted with Kshatriya society. There's not an iota of doubt that the Mahabharata is the greatest epic in the world.

In India, there is a scarcity of real Brahman and Kshatriya societies. Being affected by distress, we all have become Shudras. If these two societies can be revived, only then may India regain its name and glory. I have tried my best to re-establish Brahman ideals. Feeling the spirit of the Kshatriya inside you, nurture in your heart a strong resolve to propagate that ideal in your society. You are not expected to embrace the peaceful, engrossed and dispassionate nature of the Brahman. Who will then preserve strength and valour in society? Where is the footing of the Brahmans in the absence of valour and the prowess of the Kshatriya? On whose strength will the peace of the Brahmans sustain itself? The glory of the Kshatriya's valour lies in saving the highest ideals of religion in society, protecting it from tyranny and disturbances. It is not the glorious Kshatriya religion, where one misuses power or gets lost in waywardness, luxury, and corruption or is misled into empty egotism by the flattery of the courtiers. In this way, our Kshatriyas, having their valour ruined, their intelligence cast off and their character lost, are suffering their own downfall and remain entrenched in sinful merriment. Those who were protectors of the whole society are now leading animalistic lives, languishing in disgrace. Is not death better than this? Is not this sort of life most disgraceful for a Kshatriya? What is there to live for if you live like this? Give to yourself and to society, valour, protection and assurance, and inflame yourself with a vow to preserve religion and relieve the distressed. Let your life be meaningful. Let God draw in His own hand on your forehead the mark of the Kshatriya glory.

7 Baishak 1309
Sri Rabindranath Tagore

N.B. Read my article '*Nababarsha*' published in *Bangadarshan*'s Baishak issue. It speaks about the Brahman's own mind. It was not meant for Kshatriyas; yet it will give you some food for thought.

Om

Almora

My dear,

I am happy to have received your letter. I am glad to think that you will get a proper education befitting a Kshatriya child in the cadet corps. Most of the princes of our country, under the influence of their British teachers, have sacrificed their nationalism and even their humanity—they have forgotten their own duties, lost interest in the homeland and fallen into neglect toward indigenous literature and art. They have made themselves vile by gambling day and night, drinking, dancing and moving frantically all the time in the pleasure-meets of the Englishmen—they are poisoning India's blood. I know, undoubtedly, that this sort of madness will never overwhelm you. Be self-restrained and unruffled, accept single-mindedly whatever is acceptable, but do not distract yourself in excessive association with the foreigners. Without paying heed to anyone's praise or censure, keep the sacrificial fires of the pure Kshatriya Dharma of India always burning in your heart with patience and quietude—attribute your valour only to God. Remain austere in your incantations. The valour of God that illuminates the three worlds and is dispersing light over the whole universe and the spirit of intelligence and consciousness that is luminous in your heart—recall that great spirit residing within you by the hymns of Gayatri in the morning and embrace the same in your heart. Every day you will be invigorated by that valour—may the rays of the sun you see in the early morning keep your inner self unblemished and bright; keep it stored in your body and heart for the whole day—no sin will ever touch you; no disgrace will attack you. Amid all the dust and filth around you, like a son of heaven, drenched in the river Ganges, may you move with an untarnished purity without fear and hesitation. Your glory will never fade; I earnestly pray to God for you.

16 Shaon 1309
With blessings,
Sri Rabindranath Tagore

Om

Shilaidaha

My dear,

I got your letter after arriving in Bolpur. And I was greatly delighted to read it. I had got a hint of that the matter, which you have mentioned, from Jati earlier; but even on hearing it, I did not harbour any sense of disrespect toward you. Today, after going through your letter, I came to know what you have done, and it is indeed what ought to have been done in those circumstances—for if it was not so, it would have been improper and unjust even though society might not have condemned you; you would have gone astray from the religious path. For that reason, my heart has in fact become joyous after reading your letter—when you have faith in virtue, God will never make you weak; he will certainly bless you, and he will do it in times of both joy and sorrow. Your well-being will blossom in your heart, and in your life. I am blessing you with all my heart—may you attain true humanity amid all earthy merits and demerits, profits and losses—be grateful to the favour of God.

I am staying on the river Padma with my family. I am doing all right. I have a mind to go to Bolpur from here next Baishak. Today, I have come to know from Mahim's letter that your marriage with that bride of Dholpur will be held very soon. Let God make your conjugal life happy in all respects—this is my earnest prayer.

13 Falgun 1314
Your well-wisher,
Sri Rabindranath Tagore

Om

Bolpur

My dear,

In your hardest times[47], your virtue itself will protect you.

'*Shukhang Ba Jadi Ba Dookhang*
Priyang Ba Jadi Ba Apriyang
Praptang Praptamupasita Hridayena Parajita'

That is, whether in happiness or sorrow, circumstances favourable or unpleasant—always move ahead with an indomitable will in your heart. You have that strength in your mind—protect your virtue with a stable mind under all situations. Know for certain, my mind is unperturbed about you. Now my advice to you is that you must stand with your heart and soul in support of the person[48] on whom the burden of governance has been bestowed—because the welfare of the state means the welfare of all of you. There are many enemies on all sides of the royal throne. At this time, you have to protect your new king from their false friendships; at present, you are his closest relative—the good relationship between you two should not bend even the slightest bit—if that happens, then the enemies will avail of this opportunity. They will, no doubt, try in many ways to create rifts between you two. I pray to God that these kinds of evil conspiracies fail in the days to come—nobody should at any time be able to create suspicion in the king's mind about your benevolence. You should win over all sorts of intrigues by your honesty and apply your strength to the welfare of your state.

You should be diligent in keeping your focus on the welfare of the people. In the course of events, so many improprieties will try to distract you—then your valour will prevent you from becoming self-oblivious. You are to endure all these blows silently while keeping a close watch on your duty. Try not to allow any weakness to attack your king and kingdom—and then gradually, as and when the opportunity arises, clear all the rubbish. You will have to be particularly vigilant to ensure that no sudden revolution of any sort takes place. My earnest desire is that being inseparably united with the king will help you accelerate Tripura's development. I have a strong belief that if you get an opportunity to apply your strength correctly, Tripura will succeed. As I am bound by the debt of true affection of your father and grandfather, I cannot remain stoic in matters related to Tripura. Though I live far away, I will never abstain from thinking about Tripura's welfare. My cherished wish will be fulfilled when I see you two brothers firmly united, glorifying the royal deity and ensuring a stable state, with happy subjects, peace prevailing all over and no sin around the throne. My blessings to you is let God keep you firm and sober in both joy and sorrow and make you unwavering in your duty.

10 Chaitra 1315
Your well-wisher,
Sri Rabindranath Tagore

Om

Shantiniketan

My dear,

There cannot be anything better than this for Tripura, if you will accept the post of minister. Of the various kinds of proposals that were made so long about running your administration, there is no doubt that this is the best of them all. You should finalize the arrangement beforehand so that unforeseen obstacles don't get in your way. All the rubbish of the ages that has been accumulated in the method of work and amongst the employees, get them all cleared firmly at an opportune time. Your state administration should be nourished as your practice of virtue; allow no slackness. All important work can be done only by sharp merit; it requires good conscience. The public should have an unflinching faith in your natural justice. They should understand that the rules and the regulations you establish can be violated in no way by you or the king or any others. You are to deliver justice as per the demands of the situation—don't let anger get in the way of your adherence to the law. He who has power must regulate it in line with the law.

There is no need to say all this to you—because I firmly believe that you will protect the truth without discrimination. I am eager to see one day that the system of government in Tripura will improve in your hands, and Bengal will be proud. The deity of fortune resides in the forests and soil of your land. Spread education and wealth. The duty that you have done towards your subjects for a long time, continue that with all your efforts; your life will thereby be successful.

Let God give you strength in the field of work, momentum on the path of welfare, courage in the practice of life. Your mind should not be disturbed by hindrances. Keep firmly in mind that your prayers will be answered if you do your work with perseverance, paying no heed to praise, slander, loss or gain; give all your works as offerings to God.

1 Falgun 1320
Yours affectionately,
Sri Rabindranath Tagore

Letters from Rabindranath to Colonel Thakur Mahim Chandra Deb Barma

Om

Shilaidaha,
Kumarkhali

Mahimarnav,

You might have received my letter before. In the meantime, I'm glad to receive your letter through Sarbananda.

I am sending through Sarbananda a sheet of woven silk fabric for the Maharaja. One sheet of matka (silky cloth) has also come for you from Rajshahi Shilpa Vidyalaya; I will send this present to you, and I will be very happy when you come to Shilaidaha wearing a suit made of this material. I do regularly purchase silk cloth from there to encourage the industrial institute. They cannot provide cloth in large quantities due to the paucity of manpower. These clothes are not simply my gifts to my friends; these are gifts of the country. I do, therefore, hope that you will not treat them with neglect.

30 Chaitra 1305
Sri Rabindranath Tagore

Om

My dear,

Don't mind anything. Have faith—know that my heart is eager to work for the homeland. In matters of certain welfare work, if I hear rumours that I'm being secretly driven by selfish motives, it becomes heartbreaking. If anybody strikes this doubt in mind, it is unbearable and, therefore, it so happened that I had once come to the verge of being turned away from you all. After getting your kind letter, I have driven away all those doubts from my mind.

I am very busy these days; in fact, I'm seeing my son-in-law off to America tomorrow. I am also trying to arrange for the establishment of a school at our Bolpur Ashram. I went out in the morning. After eating, I have to go out again. The car is ready. I have some information about a good professor. Atul Krishna Goswami is now undergoing a bit of a financial crisis. The money that he will have from you, if sent immediately, will benefit him. Send it to Majumder Co. without delay, otherwise they will have to take a loan and pay the money to Goswami Mahashay.

I shall write a letter to the Maharaja tomorrow. I will most likely go to Tripura soon. I have received letters from Jagadish Babu and Ramesh Dutta.

Sri Rabindranath Tagore

Om

My dear,

I have just received your letter and felt quite happy after reading it. It is very difficult for me to disbelieve you and, therefore, I look up to you repeatedly for the welfare of Tripura. My relationship with this state is religiously fixed. I cannot be indifferent. Sometimes, I'm repelled by the unhealthy atmosphere in the Maharaja's milieu because of all the conspirators working against him. However, God has bound me to the Maharaja in an unbreakable bond. At present, I do not see any possibility by which I may do some special kind of good to the Maharaja—I have got no ability, time or opportunity; my earnest request to all of you is that, despite your weaknesses, don't falter when it comes to serving your country. Your life will be successful if you can carry out this great duty. Not everyone gets such a grand opportunity to do so. God has given you intelligence and strength, and you have the ideal in your heart. Therefore, take the vow to serve your state—it is difficult, but if you get involved without any concern for personal gain, then nothing is impossible. I want to set your son free from the nagpash of pomp and grandeur and adorn him with manly qualities, so that after becoming an adult, he is not hindered by his own prejudices, which may make him shirk from his duties. I hope, when he becomes an adult, he will be an asset to your state.

6 Chaitra
Sri Rabindranath Tagore

Om[49]

Bolpur

My dear,

I will try to say every word clearly. I have been hearing so many things for so many days. For a long time, I had carried a certain impression in my mind about you ... but whenever I discussed about the welfare of the state with you and the Maharaja, I had to drive away all suspicions after having observed your opinion, good consideration and zeal. I have even told Ramani again and again to ignore any slanders against you. So many of my days were spent in hesitation, whether to suspect you or not, but I had no inclination to disrespect you. After proper discussion, I realized that the main cause of the present crisis was due to the burden of debt and extravagance. All of you know that, without rectification of this, there is no way out. All of you and even Shandiz verbally say so, but I found that in practice you people do exactly the opposite and in fact, worsen the situation. Shandiz and the courtiers have cleverly attracted the attention of the Maharaja about the large debts outstanding in English shops. This is surely true that the Maharaja himself is not aware about this. It is also well known that, taking advantage of his lack of awareness, he is being skillfully driven toward temptation. I saw that costly things were purchased in the name of the Maharaja, but in the next moment they were out of sight—I saw that the Maharaja's palace was enclosed for the residence of Shandiz and his furniture were brought from the household goods of the Maharaja. The Maharaja spends a lot on various occasions for his family members. This Shandiz has the high royal post and indulgence by your favour. Shandiz and Doctor Amiya flatter the Maharaja in his presence but show disrespect behind his back and extort his favour in different ways. I find that you, Shandiz and Amiya share a close bond. And that you people are also handling the matter of debt and the repayment of debt. I know you are eager to see that all the large debts are repaid. A thorough study of all these matters has given rise to an impression in my mind that though you (not Shandiz) do not pray for great harm to the Maharaja, yet you're tempted by various opportunities. For this weakness, despite your wish to do well to the state, it is becoming impossible for you to accomplish the same. I am disturbed thinking of the sorry plight and dreadful consequence of it in Tripura, and I cannot help but to cry fie upon you all. I know that you harbour an earnest desire to work for the king's welfare. I do not think this desire is untrue or deceptive. But due to the weakness of your character, you are not able to contribute to the welfare of the state.

You all have no real desire to protect the royal family in the noblest way. It seems you're also scared that your influence will be curtailed if the king becomes more competent. I do not find any ray of hope anywhere when I contemplate the future of Tripura if things continue in this way.

The Maharaja has bound me with the debt of affection. In the deepest recesses of his character, I have seen glimmers of his greatness. But his magnanimity is also getting gradually hampered because of the changing conditions, and thus the welfare of the state is becoming more and more of an uphill task. The way he has been entangled on all sides, my whole heart becomes restless thinking of him. He is a king of Bengal, and all that is happening to him is a disgrace for Bengal.

Firstly, when I see that the present Maharaja, for his education and habit, has become incapable in every way to run the government, then my heart cannot but become averse towards you. You all had never tried your best.

But you are an inhabitant of Tripura and an educated man, you are familiar with the scriptural ideal, you have been brought up with the favour of the Maharaja; have you ever tried earnestly to stop the current disaster in Tripura? Is that not self-seeking ...

Sri Rabindranath Tagore

My dear,

I am telling you everything quite frankly.

When *Bangadarshan* came to my hand, I was eager to make it a first-class paper in all respects. However, in my present condition, I could by no means meet the expenditure and the efforts that were required for the purpose. Thus, I sought the Maharaja's help to lead *Bangadarshan*, without considering what was before or after. It was comprehended for various reasons that you all imagined it to be my selfish motive. I thought that you all are courtiers; you do not have faith in the honest intentions of the people—you look at everybody with eyes of suspicion you all have obscured the usual magnanimity of the Maharaja.

In fact, ordinary people tend to look at everyone who befriends the Maharaja with suspicion. Even your present minister Umacharan (Umakanta) Das, before he got into service, said suspiciously to one of my friends, 'Why does a person like Rabi Babu visit this place so frequently?' I have a good standing amongst people in general—and I do hesitate to accept this bad name that I go and come to the door of the Maharaja as a beggar and self-seeking person. I hear that your minister cherishes that idea even now. The Maharaja is naturally inclined to treat people like me as respectable friends and behave accordingly. But I have heard that you people prohibit him from doing so and want to keep him away—therefore, in the eyes of the people, you tarnish my relationship with the Maharaja. For all these reasons, despite my earnest respect, love and affection toward the Maharaja, I have tried to gradually distance myself. In the matters related to Jagadish Babu, I do not care about dignity, insult or vanity—whatever people may say about me and as much resistance as I may get, I shall be gratified if I can free him from bondage—it is not a deed of friendship, it is a deed for the country. I would, therefore, stand before the Maharaja again without hesitation as a beggar. I am the son of a rich man, but I am not rich—I have no power in my hands to accomplish those good resolves that are put in my heart by God; it is therefore my duty to relinquish all egotism, which may hinder my actions. I shall give it up for Jagadish Babu. After that, if I can, taking myself away from all the songs of praise and reprehension of worldly life, I shall do my duty to the best of my ability and with a quiet heart.

I have full consent for the stand that you have taken in Bela's marriage. In fact, any other arrangement would not have been good by any means. You have done the right thing by being present at the right time.

Do not mind what I have written. Everyone's nature is not the same. Yet, I hope you understand what I feel. But if you do not, even then I shall not lament. It is not that a friendship develops because of similarities. Whatever love and respect you give me with your heart, I will accept that as a friend, and any part of me that you misunderstand, I shall accept it knowing that part remains beyond the reach of your comprehension and that is all.

I thought of going to your place for the puja. But at that time Bela and my son-in-law will be here. It is not possible to leave them and go then. Thus, I will visit you some other time.

Sri Rabindranath Tagore

[There are many more letters written by the Maharajas and Rabindranath. Here, only the important letters have been included.]

Bibliography

Bhattacharjee, Apurba Chandra. *Progressive Tripura*. 1930.

Bishi, Pramatha Nath. *'Tripurar Bhasha O Sahitya'*.

Basu, Satya Ranjan. *Tripuraye Rabindra Smriti*.

Chakraborty, Bhupendra Chandra. *Rajmala*. Teachers' and Co., 1947.

Chatterji, Suniti Kumar. *Kirata-Jana-Krti: The Indo-Mongoloids; Their Contribution to the History and Culture of India*. The Asiatic Society, 1951.

—*The Origin and Development of the Bengali Language*. Calcutta University Press, 1926.

Chattopadhyay, Gobinda Narayan, and Himangshu Gangopadhyay, eds. *Rabindranath O Tripura*. Department of Higher Education, Government of Tripura, 1961.

Choudhury, Achyut Charan. *Srihatter Itibritta*. 1916.

Chowdhury, Bikach. *Rabindra Shannidhey Tripura*.

Dainik Sangbad, Agartala, July 1, 2007.

Deb Barma, Mahim Chandra.

—Tripurar Durbarey Rabindranath

—Tripuray Bangabhasha

—Deshiya Rajya

Deb Barma, Nabadwip Chandra. A*barjanar Jhuri*.

Deb Barma, Shailesh Chandra. '*Rabitirtha Smriti*'.

Dutta, Dwijendra Chandra, and Suprasanna Bandopadhyay, eds. *Rajgee Tripurar Sarkari Bangla*. Siksha Adhikar: 1976.

Long, James. "Analysis of the Bengali Poem Ráj Málá, or Chronicles of Tripurá." Journal of the Asiatic Society of Bengal, 1850.

Mukhopadhyay, Prabhat Kumar. *Rabindra Jibani*. Shantiniketan Press, 1936.

Nath, R.M. *The Background of Assamese Culture*. Ananda Printing & Publishing House, 1948.

Pal, Prashanta Kumar. *Rabi Jibani*. Bhurjapatra, 1982.

Rajgee Tripurar Rajdhanir Sachitra Kathakatha (first part)— Rabindra Sengupta

Sarkar, Jadunath. 'Nivedita as I Knew Her'.

Sengupta, Kaliprasanna. *Tripurar Rajader Sahitya Seva*.

Singh, Kailash Chandra. *Rajmala O Tripurar Itihas*. 1896.

Tagore, Rabindranath. '*Deshiya Rajya*'.1905.

—*Jiban Smriti*. Adi Brahmo Samaj Press, 1912.

Notes

1. Sajanikanta Das, the clever Bengali poet and editor of *Shanibarer Chithi*, was famous for his funny and mocking poems.
2. 'Thakur' is the feudal title, which can be used as the last name.
3. Rabindranath Tagore is also known as 'Rabi Thakur'.
4. Reverend James Long (1814–1887) was an Anglo-Irish priest of the Anglican Church.
5. Poddar, Satyadeo (ed.), History of Tripura: As Reflected in the Manuscripts, 2016, https://www.namami.gov.in/sites/default/files/book_pdf/History-of-Tripura_0.pdf.
6. Dola Purnima is a Hindu festival celebrated particularly in Odisha, West Bengal and Assam, that celebrates the divine couple Radha and Lord Krishna. It coincides with the full moon of the Phalguna month.
7. This has been taken from the collection of Dwinjendra Chandra Dutta's writings.
8. *Kahini* refers to the book of poems written by Rabindranath Tagore.

9. Refers to Colonel Mahim Chandra Deb Barma.

10. Refers to Pandit Baikuntha Bachaspati.

11. Refers to Jatindranath Basu.

12. Refers to prince Birendra Kishore.

13. Refers to Jatindranath Basu, the son-in-law of the poet Akshay Chowdhury. Sarat Kumari Chowdhurani was his mother-in-law.

14. This letter was probably written at the end of Ashar, 1308 Bengali Era.

15. This letter was possibly written at the end of Ashar 1308 Bengali Era.

16. Though undated, the letter was probably written in the last part of 1311 Bengali Era.

17. Refers to Mr Shandiz, the personal secretary of the Maharaja.

18. However, the loan was ultimately taken from the Bank of Bengal.

19. The son-in-law of Dwijendranath Tagore, Ramani Mohan Chattopadhaya was a high official of Calcutta Municipality at that time. He later became the minister of Tripura during the reign of Maharaja Radha Kishore Manikya on the recommendation of Rabindranath.

20. Refers to Nilambar Mukhopadhyay.

21. Refers to Sri Andrews Frazer, Lt. Governor of Bengal.

22. This letter was probably written after 17 Ashar, 1312 Bengali Era.

23. Refers to Jatindranath Basu, the personal secretary of Maharaja.

24. Refers to the diwan of Chakla Roshanabad, Sarat Chandra Basu.

25. Refers to Ramani Mohan Chattopadhyaya, the son-in-law of Dwijendranath Tagore. He served as the minister of Tripura during the reign of Radha Kishore Manikya.

26. The letter was probably written in 1312 Bengali Era.

27. The manager of the Chakla Roshanabad zamindari, Mr C. W. McMinn, ICS, was retired commissioner the Chattogram Division.

28. Refers to Colonel Mahim Chandra Deb Barma.

29. Refers to prince Brajendra Kishore.

30. Refers to Jyotirindranath Tagore.

31. Refers to Gaganendranath Tagore.

32. Refers to Ashutosh Chowdhuri.

33. Refers to Acharya Jagadish Chandra Bose.

34. Refers to Pandit Baikuntha Bachaspati.

35. Refers to the various tools including the camera, gun, etc.

36. Refers to Jatindranath Basu who was the personal secretary of the Maharaja.

37. The prince and the princess respectively.

38. Refers to Tagore's wife, Srimati Mrinalini Devi.

39. Refers to Sarat Kumari Chowdhurani, the mother-in-law of Jatindranath Basu.

40. Refers to prince Birendra Kishore.

41. Refers to Maharani Prabhabati Devi.

42. Refers to Sarat Kumari Chowdhurani, writer and wife of the poet Akshay Chowdhury.

43. Refers to the wife of Jatindranath Basu.

44. Refers to Mrinalini Devi, Tagore's wife.

45. That is, Maharaja Nripendra Narayan Bhup Bahadur.

46. Refers to the Manipuri dancer, prince Buddhimanta Singh.

47. Referring to the death of his father, Radha Kishore Manikya.

48. Maharaja Birendra Kishore.

49. This undated letter was received by the courtesy of Kushankur Deb Barma, great grandson of Colonel Mahim Chandra Deb Barma. The letter was worm-eaten and, therefore, a sincere effort has been made to decipher it.

Index

Abarjanar Jhuri, Nabadwip Chandra Bahadur, 17, 19–21, 70
absolute power, xii, 88–89, 97–98, 100, 165–166, 210–211, 218, 267
administrative reforms, x, 170
Agartala, 18, 23, 34, 40—44, 46, 56, 64, 68, 70, 72, 75, 85, 91, 93–94, 110, 113, 117, 136, 139–140, 142–144, 149, 152, 154, 158–159, 165, 170, 180–181, 189, 201, 207, 213–214
Ahlstrom, Gunnar, 125
Akal Kusum, Bir Chandra, 19
Ali, Syed Mujtaba, 103
All India Regency Conference, 229–232
Alokananda, 186

Amiya, 205, 219, 289,
Ananda Biday, Roy, 127
Anangamohini Devi (daughter of Maharaja Bir Chandra), 117–119
Andrews, C.P., 120, 122
Anjuman-e-Islamia of Comilla, 168
antagonism, x, 36, 58, 65, 76, 79, 87, 93, 103, 142–143, 190, 241
Apollonius, 22
Arundhuti Mahadevi (Rajmata Maharani), death of, 176

Bachaspathi, Baikuntha, 55
The Background of Assamese Culture, Nath, 181
Bagchi, Jatindra Mohan, 62

Bain, Sarat, 19
Baksh, Kulandar, 19
Bandhopadhyay, Hemchandra, 47
Bandopadhyay, Binodlal, 133–134
Bandopadhyay, Jogesh, 76
Bandopadhyay, Panchkari, 127
Bandopadhyay, Surendranath, 112
Baneshwar, 11–13
Bangabhasha O Sahitya, Sen, 33
Bangadarshan, Bankim, 63–65, 76, 107, 193, 197, 206–209, 217, 249–251, 273, 291
Bangiya Pradeshik Sammelan, 94
Barshiki, 105
Bartley, J., 139
Basak, Ram Kumar, 19
Basu, Ananda Mohan, 38, 40, 199
Basu, Jatindranath, 56–58, 71, 79, 87–88, 102, 110–111, 196–197, 207, 214
Basu, Kshetra Mohan, 19
Basu, Mokshada Kumar, 47, 110, 198
Basu, Nagendranath, 47
Basu, Satya Ranjan, 30, 38, 40–42, 44, 70, 76, 132, 202
Bengali language, xiii–xiv, 13, 20, 31, 65, 74, 96–97, 104, 154, 234; Gupta on, 97; history in Tripura, 10; Mahabharata into 14; *Rajmala* in 11, 13: as royal language of Tripura, 8–9, 96–97, 166
Bengali literature, xi, 3, 15, 37, 127, 239; contribution of Tripura, xiii
Bengalis, 127, 154, 165, 180, 211, 213, 217, 219; in administration of Tripura, 212; art and culture, 1, 147, 166–167, 218; refugees from East Pakistan, 218, (*see also* refugees); Rothenstein on 127; use of English, 97; Tagore on, 212; in Tripura, 218
Bhagna Hriday, Tagore, ix, 2–6, 25, 30, 129
Bhakti Ratnakar, Ghosh, 18
Bhanumati Devi (queen of Maharaja Bir Chandra Manikya), 3, 19; death of, ix, 2

Index

'Bharat Bhaskar', royal honour, xiii, 7, 35, 178, 180–181, 183
'Bharat Rajanya Sabha', 85
'Bharat Sangeet Samaj', 61, 117
Bhatta, Jadu, 19
Bhattacharjee, Apurba Chandra, 22
Bhattacharya, Haridas, 152
Bhattacharya, Upendra, 76
Bhubanmay, Mitra, 18
Bichitra Prabandha, 102
Biharilal, 5
Bijay Babu, 156
Bisharjan, Tagore, 9, 14, 28–30, 61–63, 117, 153, 222
Bishi, Pramatha Nath, 28
Bogdanov, Professor, 103
Boksh, Adam, 186
Bose, Jagadish Chandra, xi, xiv, 40, 46–47, 50–55, 59–62, 64–66, 68–69, 72–74, 76, 80–82, 107, 159–162, 198–199, 208, 217, 246; beneficiary of Radha Kishore, 217; in England, 60–61, 70; and plants growth, 82; returning from England, 82; science lab for, 52; travel to England, 58
Bou Thakuranir Haat, Tagore, 9
Bradley, A.C., 120, 122–123
Brahmacharya Ashram, Shantiniketan, xi, 67, 75, 115, 189, 192
'Brahman', Tagore, 193
Brajabuli language, 2, 15, 19, 105
Brajendra Kishore (Maharaja Kumar Brajendra Kishore), 70–71, 75, 91–92, 102–104, 109–117, 119, 130–132, 134–140, 142–143, 149, 151–152, 154–155, 157, 165, 178, 183, 188–204, 215–216, 235; felicitating Rabindranath, 130; Kshatriya pride in, 194; Kumar, 70, 92, 102, 188, 200, 204; letter to Tagore, 130; return home, 196; Tagore letters to, 188
Brihannaradiya Purana in Bengali, 15, 106

Brihat Banga, Sen, 14, 33
British rule, 85
Brooke, Stopford, 120, 122–123
Browning, works of, 71
Burman, S.D., 17, 76, 113, 167

'Calcutta Photographic International' exhibitions 23
Camera Club of Tripura, 23
Carmichael, 139
casteism, 168
Chaitanya Charitamrita, 12
Chaitanya Mangal, Ghosh, 18
Chakaraborty, Amiya, 158
Chakla Roshanabad, 70, 86–87, 97–98, 113, 255
Chakraborty, Ajit, 121
Chakraborty, Bholanath, 19
Chakraborty, Bhupendra Chandra, 183
Chakraborty, Dwarkanath, 40, 134
Chakraborty, Narahari, 16
Chakraborty, Shital Chandra, 141, 153, 236
Chakradhwaj, 112

Champak Vijay, 15
Chandalika, 172–173
Chand Bai, 19
Chand Kumudini, Bir Bikram, 186
Chandra, Jadav, 132–134
Chandra, Mohit, 196–197
Chandra, Nabadwip, 17–20, 70, 76–77, 112–113, 119, 134, 142; on 'Bankim Chandra's *Durgesh Nandini*, 20
Chandra, Srish, 197
Chandra, Surendra, 112
Chandra Rakshit, Rai Bahadur Haran, 47
Charlu, Anand 230
Chatterjee (Chattopadhyaya), Ramani Mohan, 81, 84, 79, 87–88, 91, 93–96, 98, 100, 119, 143, 207, 214, 257
Chattopadhyay, Jadunath or Shailen (Shaliesh), 102
Chattopadhyay, Monoranjan, 94
Chelmsford, Lady, 148
Chowdhury, Ashutosh, 38, 40, 112
Chowdhurani, Sarat Kumari, 57

Index

Chowdhury, Akhsay Chandra, 56
Chowdhury, Bikach, 136–137, 187
Chowdhury, B.L., 100
Chowdhury, Sri Sudhakanta Roy, 174–175
communal conflicts, 168
Curzon, Lord, 40, 198

Darjeeling, 49–50, 56, 58–59, 203, 262, 268, 272–273
Daroga Babu, 132
Das, Brindaban, pseudonym of Radha Kishore, 105
Das, Sajanikanta, 5, 73, 127
Das, Umakanta (Rai Bahadur), 100, 209, 214
Dasgupta, Surendranath, 128
Deb Barma Bahadur, Bir Bikram Kishore, 179 183, 187
Deb Barma, Jadav Chandra, 132
Deb Barma, Kalachand, 70–71
Deb Barma, Kumar Surendra Chandra, 98

Deb Barma, Mahendra Chandra, 133
Deb Barma, Mahendra Kumar, 106
Deb Barma, Mahim Chandra, 8–9, 31–33, 36, 38–39, 42, 45–46, 48–49, 52, 56–57, 63–64, 67, 75–76, 83, 89–90, 101, 110, 132–134, 205–219, 245–247, 271; death of, 216; Radha Kishore on, 207; 'self-seeking' person, 206; Sen to, 213; Tagore letters to, 39, 49, 63–64, 67, 76, 90–91, 101, 205–210, 213, 216–217, 219, 286–292; Tagore on, 89
Deb Barma, Shailesh Chandra, 45, 174
Deb Barma, Somendra Chandra (son of Mahim Chandra Deb Barma), 101–102, 119–121, 128, 131, 135–137, 145, 172, 174, 201; death of, 174; education in America, 120
Deb Barma, Srijut Kalachand, 70

Deb Barman, Anil Krishna, 186
Deb Barman, Dhiren Krishna, 77, 159, 162
Debendranath, Maharishi, 40, 75
decency and indecency, debate on, 20
Deledda, Grazia, 124
Deshiya Rajya, Deb Barma, 48–49, 216
Deshiya Rajya, Tagore, 29, 83–84, 238
'Deshnayak', 94
Dev Burman, Somendra, 76
Dhaka Prakash, 170–171
donation, xi, 16, 55, 67, 73, 77, 107, 142, 155, 162, 217; of Maharaja to Brahma Vidyalaya, 78
Durgesh Nandini, Bankim Chandra, 20
Durlavendra, 12
Dutta, Dwijendra Chandra, 156, 175, 177, 185
Dutta, Dwijendranath, 41, 50, 153
Dutta, Mahim Chandra, 133
Dutta, Nirmalya, 187
Dutta, Rabi, 121
Dutta, Rama Prasad, 11, 13

earthquake, 35, 44; of 1897, 44; destroying royal palace, 78
'*Eh Bhara Badar, Maha Bhadar, Shunya Hridaya More*', 4
'*Ektuku Chhoya Laagey, Ektuku Katha Shuni*', Tagore, 4
Elmhirst, Leonard, 173
ethnic identity, 218

Faguet, Emile, 125
female education, 118, *see also* Ved Vidyalaya (Brahma Vidyalaya); Shantiniketan; *see also under* Tripura
festival, 42, 146, 178, 245; Basanta Utsav, 42–44, 149, 187, (*see also under* Shantiniketan); Dol Purnima, 40, 42–43; Holi, 44; Manipuri Rash, 44; of Rash Leela, 149
France, Anatole, 124

Index

Gangopadhyay, Nishikanta, 133
Ganguly, Jogendra, 76
Gazi, Shamsher, 14–16
Gazinama, Manohar, 15
Geet Chandroday,
   Chakraborty, 16
Geet Kalpataru,
   Chakraborty, 16
'Ghatey Lagaiya Dinga',
   Jatindranath, 57
Ghosh, Gourgopal, 201
Ghosh, Manmathanath, 49
Ghosh, Matilal, 40
Ghosh, Radha Raman, ix, 6–7,
   18, 31–32, 233
Ghosh, Rashbihari, 40
Ghosh, Shantidev, 151
Giridih, 196–198
Gitanjali, Tagore 120–122,
   125–127, 238
Goswami, Nabin Chandra, 19
Gourlay, 137
'Great poet', honour of, ix–x,
   6–7, 17, 25, 44, 129, 173,
   178, 221
Guha, Ananda Mohan, 133,
   134, 217
Gupta, Ananda Charan, 96

Gupta, Basanta Kumar, 67
Gupta, K.G., 119

Hallstrom, P., 124
Haridas, 19
Heidenstan, Carl Gustaf Verner
   von, 124
Hesh, Sashi Kumar, 67
hill tribes, 165–166, 170
Hori, Bir Chandra, 19
Hossain, Nisher, 18
humanism, 29, 219

Jallianwala Bagh massacre, 183
Janhavi Devi (queen of Krishna
   Manikya), 16
Janmangal Samiti of Tripura,
   170
Jatra Karanidhi, 14
Jhulan, Bir Chandra, 19
Jibansmriti, Tagore, 25
Jora Bungalow, 70, 83
Jorasanko, ix, 6, 40, 173, 213,
   239

Kabita Kadamba, Mitra, 18
Kabyatirtha, Krishna Kumar,
   141

Kadambari Devi/Heyketi (wife of Jyotirindranath Tagore), 4–5
Kahini, 50–51, 269–270
Kalika Purana, 181
Kanika, 118
Karigar, Alam, 16
Karnama, 211
Kashim, Meer, 15
Kedarnath, 121
Khan, Enayat, 186
Khan, Haidar, 19
Khan, Kashem Ali, 19
Khan, Majid, 186
Khan, Mazafar, 186
Khan, Meer, 15
Khan, Munna, 186
Khan, Ustad Alauddin, 186
Kheya, 90
Khudiram, 170
Khyati Akhyatir Nepathye, Mitra, 126
Kirtibus, 12
Kishore, Narendra, 153, 156
Kishore, Ranbir, 156
Kishore Sahitya Samaj, 30, 154, 201; speech by Tagore, 232

Kokborok dialect, 8, 10, 164–166
Krishna, Dhiren, 162–163
Krishnamala, 15; Sen on, 16
Krishna, Nil, 112
Kriyayogasara, of *Padma Purana*, 16
Kumar, Sisir, 40
Kumar Prafulla, S.D., 76
Kumar Ranbir, 153
Kunjaban, 41–42, 140–141, 152, 157–158
Kurseong, 30–34, 202, 233, 239–240
Kushtia, 49, 58–59, 268, 273–275

Lahiri, Durgadas, 47
Lavisse, Ernest, 124
Lawrence, 67
letter–writing, xiv
loan from government, xi, 80–81, 218, 252, 259
Long, Reverend, 11, 16
Loti, Pierre, 124
lyrics, 19, 24, 33, 122, 184
Lytton, Lord and Lady, 150

Index

Mahabharata, 13, 147, 191, 280; translated into Bengali, 14
Mahaddin, Sheikh, 15
Maharaja of Nator, 38, 40, 61, 91
Maharajas, financial help from, 64, 75, 102, 107–108, 206, 249
Maitra, Akshay Kumar, 39
Majumder, Prafulla Kumar, 71
Majumder, Santosh, 78, 199
Majumder, Shailesh Chandra, 41, 63
Manikya, Amar, 9, 15
Manikya, Bir Bikram, xiii, 35, 78, 101, 148–149, 158, 161, 163, 165, 167–175, 177–179, 181, 183–187, 200; accident of, 174; coronation ceremony, 159; death of, 187; donations, 174; reception to, 238–240; for refugees, 176; at Shantiniketan, 172; speech of, 236–238; world tour, 175, 187
Manikya, Bir Chandra (Maharaja), ix–x, 2–10, 17–28, 30–38, 54, 71, 84, 89, 104–106, 110, 113, 148, 152–154, 164, 173, 178–179, 184, 202, 205, 213, 232–233, 235, 237, 239–240; birthday on Wednesday, 44; Chandra Bahadur on, 18; composition, 71–72; death of, x; demise of, 35; letter to Tagore, 27–28, 242–244; lyrics by, 24–25; music maestro, 24, 31; period of reign, 1; photography, 22; poem in Brajabuli, 2–3; Sen on, 33; Tagore on, 6–7
Manikya, Birendra Kishore (Maharaja), 37, 55, 78, 104, 109–119, , 130–131, 134–135, 137–142, 144, 146–148, 154, 161, 164, 200, 211, 213, 215–216, 236–237, 275–276; death of, 149; donation to war fund, 148; marriage, 51, 55, 68, 161; marriage of prince, 55; paintings of, 145

Manikya, Chhatra, 16, 27
Manikya, Dhanya, 14
Manikya, Dharma, 10–14, 28, 243
Manikya, Govinda, 8, 15, 25–29, 153, 164, 176, 233, 237, 242, 244
Manikya, Indra, 15
Manikya, Ishan Chandra, 18, 70, 113
Manikya, Jagat, 16
Manikya, Krishna Kishore, 26, 243
Manikya, Krishna, 15–16
Manikya, Radha Kishore (Maharaja), x—xiv, 10, 34–40, 46–49, 52–54, 56, 58–61, 64–68, 70, 72, 74, 79–80, 84–85, 88–90, 92, 96–98, 99–108, 110–115, 118, 133, 140, 142–143, 146, 148, 152, 154,, 159–162, 165–167, 174, 179, 184, 188–189, 194, 197, 200, 202, 205–207, 209–211, 214–216, 218–219, 234–235, 239; assistance to Tagore, 107; bamboos saplings for Bose, 82–83;
for Bengali language, 65; budget note of Tagore, 227, 229; death of, 117, 162; donation by, 54–55, 68, 73, 162; donation to Victoria College, 77–78; felicitation to, 63; free college by, 77; on *Kahini*, 51; letter to Tagore, 55–56, 63, 268–275; meeting Tagore, 36; rock inscriptions, 106; for scientific advancement, 54–55; Tagore letter to, 59, 67, 76, 87, 207, 245–267; Tagore wrote song for, 185
Manikya, Rajdhar, 16
Manikya II, Ratna, 15
Manikyas, 1, 223–226
Manipuri dance, 144, 149–151, 157–158, 276; Rash dance, 144
Manohar, Sheikh, 15
Manusamhita, 66, 166, 219, 248
Matree Sangha, 169
Maynell, Alice, 122
Mayo College, Ajmer, 58, 189
McMinn, C.W., 98
'Memorandum of World Tours', Bir Bikram, 187

Milan Sangha, 169
Mitra, Keshab Chandra, 19
Mitra, Madan, 18
Mitra, Madan Mohan, 19
Mitra, Panchanan, 19
Mitra, Rajendralal, 40
Mitra, Ramesh Chandra, 19
Mitra, Sourindra, 126
Mongolians, 182
Morris, Hirji Bhai Pestanji, 152, 156
Moulik, Jatindranath, 133
Mrinalini Devi (wife of Tagore), 189
'*Mrityu Amrita Kore Dan*' ('Death confers immortality'), 2
Mukherjee, Shyama Prasad, 103
Mukhopadhyay, Prabhat Kumar, 5, 30, 78, 158
Mukhopadhyay, Pratap, 19
Mukhopadhyay, Rajendranath, 40
Mukhopadhyay, Sambhu Chandra, 18
Mukhopadhyay, Thakurdas, 189
Mukunda, 17
Mukut, Tagore, 9, 14, 25, 27, 222, 243
My Rabindranath, Jatindra, 57

Nag, Kunjalal 71
Nandalal Babu, 183
Nanua Devi (queen of Dharma Manikya), 14
Narayan, Nripendra, 40, 59, 60
Nath, R.M., 181
Natir Puja, Tagore, 158, 199
Nevinson, Henry, 122
'New Age' in Tripura, 186
Nivedita, Sister, 198–200
Nobel Prize for literature for 1913, 73–74, 120, 123–125, 127–130, 141, 180, 183, 221

paintings, 1, 23, 74, 104, 109–110, 141, 145, 147, 163, 168, 172–173, 237; exhibition at Paris, 162, *see also* photography exhibition
Pal, Prashanta Kumar, 38, 41
Palit, Lokendra, 40, 121, 246–247
Palit, Taraknath, 40
Panchali, Utkal Khanda, 14

partisanship, 92, 134, 143, 264
patrons of art, xiii, 1
people of Tripura, xi–xii, 16, 73, 100, 110, 130, 135, 142, 146, 165, 170–171, 236, 238; as military race, 16
people's revolutionary movement, 170
Perez Galdos, Benito, 124
photographers, 24, 38
Photographic Society of India, 22–23
photography, 17, 22; exhibition, 23, 173
political stage, xii, 79, 212
Pound, Ezra, 120, 122, 127
Prabhavati Devi (queen of Birendra Kishore [Maharani]), 146
Prasanta, S.D., 76
Pratima Devi (daughter-in-law of Tagore), 152, 162, 201
Prem Marichika, Bir Chandra, 19
Pret Chaturdashir Geet, 14
Progressive Tripura, Bhattacharjee, 22

Rabi Jibani, Pal, 41

Rabindra dance, 144
'Rabindra Jayanti Bisesh Durbar,' 178
Rabindra Jibani, Mukhopadhyay, 78, 158
Rabindranath O Tripura, 41, 189
Rabindranritya, 144, 149–150
Rabindra Sangamey Europe Prabahser Smritikatha, 120
Rabindrasangeet, 74, 163
Rabindra Sannidhey Tripura, Chowdhury, 136, 187
Rabindra Shilpa Pradarshani, 163
'*Rabitirtha Smriti*', Shailesh Chandra Deb Barma, 45
racial discrimination, 168, 218–219
racism, 168–169, 171
Radha Kishori, 146
Rai, Nakshatra, 25
Raipura riot, 176
Rajarshi, Tagore, 9, 14, 25–30, 153, 222, 233, 242–244
'*Rajmala O Tripurar Itihas*', Singh, 9, 11, 17
Rajratnakar, 27
Ramayana, 14

Ramganga, Pundit, 16
Rash Leela, 43, 149, 157–158
reflected glory, 69, 74
refugees, 176–177, 218; coming to Tripura, 176
religion, 14, 16, 29, 66, 85, 168, 171, 187, 193, 199, 200, 230, 248–249, 281
Rhys, Ernest, 120, 122, 126–127
Rothenstein, William, 120–122, 126–127, 162; letter of Tagore to, 125–126; stay at Shantiniketan, 127
royal durbar, xiii, 1, 14, 87, 91, 133, 178, 217
Roy, Anukul Chandra, 103
Roy, Champak, 15
Roy, Dwijadas, 141
Roy, Dwijendralal, 73, 127
Roy, Jagadananda, 67
Roy, Jagadindranath, 40, 61, 92
Russell, 120

Sachin Kartar Ganer Bhuban, 43
Samajpati, Suresh, 127
Samarendra Chandra, Bod Thakur, 38, 112–114, 203, 216

Sarala Devi, 40, 148, 217
Sarkar, Jadunath, 103, 199
secularism, 169
Sen, Dinesh Chandra, 10–11, 14–16, 33, 76, 107, 213, 217
Sengupta, Bidhubhusan, 177
Sengupta, Kaliprasanna, 16
Sen, Kshitimohan, 125, 142, 173
Sen, Nirmal Chandra, 40
Sen, Sukumar, 15
Shandiz, 80, 89, 205, 219, 253, 264–265, 289
Shantiniketan, xi, 44–46, 67, 76–78, 97–98, 101–102, 104, 114–116, 119–120, 127–129, 141–142, 144, 149–152, 155, 158, 167–168, 172–175, 180, 183, 189–190, 200, 235–236, 238, 277; Basanta Utsav at, 43; charities donated to, 210; school at, xi, 75, *see also* Ved Vidyalaya (Brahma Vidyalaya)
Sharma, Ramani Mohan, 146
Shelley, works of, 71
Shil, Ramkanai, 71

Shilaidahey Rabindranath,
   Jatindra, 57
'Shivaji', Tagore, 197
Shohag, Bir Chandra, 19
Shokagatha,
   from Anangamohini Devi,
   118
Shukreshwar, 11–13
Sinclair, May, 122
Sinclair, Upton, 120
Singh, Baikuntha, 158
Singh, Buddhimanta, 144,
   149–150
Singh, Golak Chandra, 9
Singh, Kailash Chandra, 9, 11,
   17, 25
Singh, Navakumar, 149–151,
   158
Singh, Satyendra Prasanna, 40
Sinha, Lord, 211
Sircar, Nilratan, 100
Spitteler, Carl, 124
Srimad Bhagavat, Ghosh, 18, 34
Sri Radha-Krishner Leela Bilash,
   Bir Bikram, 186
Sri Sri Chaitanya Charitamrita,
   32
Strangways, Fox, 120, 122

Sturge Moore, T., 74, 120,
   123–124, 127
'Swadeshi Samaj,' 94
Swamy, Kumar, 121

Tagner, Esaias Henrik
   Wilhelm, 120, 124
Tagore, Abanindranath, 38, 40
Tagore, Balendranath, 8–9
Tagore, Dinendranath, 152–
   154, 156
Tagore, Dwarkanath, 26
Tagore, Dwijendranath, 40, 79
Tagore, Gaganendranath, 40
Tagore, Jyotirindranath, 4–5,
   57, 113
Tagore, Madhurilata (Bela), 59;
   marriage ceremony of his
   daughter, 66
Tagore, Meera Devi, 120
Tagore, Rabindranath/
   Gurudev/ Kabiguru / Rabi
   Babu/Rabi Thakur, 6, 8, 27,
   30–33, 34, 42, 45, 47–48,
   53, 56–57, 74, 101, 163,
   172–173, 178–180, 209,
   212, 221, 227, 229, 232,
   234, 238, 291; to Agartala,
   158–159; allegations

against, 64; and Bir Bikram
Manikya, 101, 149; birth
anniversary, xiii, 163;
death of, 185; honourary
Doctorate in Literature,
128; letters to Birendra
Kishore, 115, 275–276;
letters to Brajendra
Kishore, 111, 131, 190–191,
277–286; letters to Mahim
Chandra Deb Barma, 8–9,
31, 36, 38–39, 45, 48, 52, 63,
67, 132–133, 209, 210–212,
286–292; letters to Bir
Chandra, 26, 30, 241–242;
letter to Jatindranath
Basu, 102; letters to Radha
Kishore, 245–267; mind
games, 71; to Mohit
Chandra Sen, 76–77, 196;
'poet of the Maharajas',
164, 167; 'Poet of Tripura',
163–164, 167; proclamation
of 'Bharat Bhaskar', 183;
relationship with Tripura,
2, 114–115, 140, 163, 167,
219; *robkari* (proclamation)
to, 178; songs of, 71, 159;
speech at Uttarayan,
240–241; visit to East

Bengal, 151; visit to Tripura,
83, 140, 152, 201; writing to
Jagadish Chandra, xiv, 59,
61, 69, 72; on youth, 3–4
Tagore, Renuka Devi, marriage
of, 69, 252
Tagore, Satyendranath, 40
Tasher Desh, 172
Thakur, Jatindranath, 40
Thakur, Radharamon, grammar
of Kokborok in the Bengali
alphabet by, 166
Tipperahs, 23, 160, 181
Trevelyan, Charles, 122
Trilochan, 12
Tripura: education in, 165, 167;
history of, xiii, 9, 15, 26–27,
166, 205, 217, 242–243,
258; recognition from, 8;
revenue of, 69, 86, 97
'Tripurar Bhasha O Sahitya,
Bishi,' 28
'Tripurar Durbarey
Rabindranath,' Mahim
Thakur, 31, 36, 212
*Tripurar Prachin Punthi
Prasangey*, Dutta, 13
Tripura Sundari Lottery,
132–133, 200, 215

'*Tripuray Bangabhasha*', Barma, 8

'*Tripuray Rabindra Smriti*', Basu, 30, 38, 40, 132

Tulshibati Devi (queen of Radha Kishore and Maharani), 105–106, 146

Uchchhash, Bir Chandra, 19
Ujir, Durgamani, 13
Ujjal Nilmoni, Ghosh, 18
Ujjayanta Palace, xiii, 45, 68
Ujjayanta Rajprasad, 41, 117, 152, 178
unitary system, 97
Utkal Khanda Panchali, 14

Vaishnavism, 14, 28
Vaishnav Mahajan Padabali, 33
Vaishnav Padabali, 16, 24, 32, 34, 233
Ved Vidyalaya (Brahma Vidyalaya), 65, 75–76, 78; Radha Kishore and, 77, 115, 155, 174
Verner, Carl Gustaf, 124
Vidyapati, 1, 14, 15

Vidyaratna, Ramnarayan, 18
Vidyarnava, Bhuban, 127
Vidyasagar, Ishwar Chandra, 8, 74
Vijay, Champak, 15
Visva-Bharati, 172, 175, 210
Vivekananda, Swami, 219

welfare system, 66, 170
Wells, H.G., 120
Williams, T.R., 60, 110
Woodburn, John, LG, 59
World War, First, 148; Second, 174–175; Tripura Rifles in, 176

Yeats, W.B., 74, 120, 122–123, 125–127
youth, 3–4, 25, 155, 221, 232, 236

zamindari, 70, 79, 81, 86–87, 254, 256, 260
Zebunnisa, Samarendra Chandra Deb Burma, Abanindranath Tagore, 38

ABOUT THE AUTHOR

Khagesh Dev Burman hails from the royal family of Tripura sharing the same heritage as the legendary Maharajas of Tripura. Born on 14 December 1940 in Agartala, Tripura, he was brought up in an environment conducive to art and literature. He loves to live away from the maddening crowd and is sternly against any kind of self-publicity and propaganda. Even his friends and near relatives are unaware of his writings.

An M.A. in Political Science from Calcutta University, he joined the Indian Revenue Service in 1967 and retired as commissioner of Income Tax. During his period of service, he hardly wrote anything but after retirement he plunged deep into literary activities. And his writings subsequently drew the attention of his readers.

About the Author

A poet, Khagesh Dev Burman is also the editor of *Prantik*—the first ever collection of poems from Tripura, published in the year 1962. He was also the editor of the bi-monthly magazine *Prantik Sahitya Patra* for thirteen years.

He was awarded the Sachin Samman by the government of Tripura for his book *Sachin Kartar Ganer Bhuban*. Tripura Rabindra Parisad honoured him with the Bijan Krishna Smriti Purashkar.

He is the author of *S.D. Burman: The World of His Music* (2013), and *R.D. Burman: Prince of Music* (2015).

He has also authored the following books in Bengali: *Tripuray Annya Rabindranath*, *Sachin Kartar Ganer Bhuban*, *Ganer Rajputra Rahul Dev Burman*, *Rajnandini*, *Aayanaye Nijer Mukh*, *Nasta Samay*, *Tritiya Nayan*, *Santan*, *Sandhey Belar Pratham Dupur* and *Chandra Prahar*. His works have been highly acclaimed by literary critics.

HarperCollins *Publishers* India

At HarperCollins India, we believe in telling the best stories and finding the widest readership for our books in every format possible. We started publishing in 1992; a great deal has changed since then, but what has remained constant is the passion with which our authors write their books, the love with which readers receive them, and the sheer joy and excitement that we as publishers feel in being a part of the publishing process.

Over the years, we've had the pleasure of publishing some of the finest writing from the subcontinent and around the world, including several award-winning titles and some of the biggest bestsellers in India's publishing history. But nothing has meant more to us than the fact that millions of people have read the books we published, and that somewhere, a book of ours might have made a difference.

As we look to the future, we go back to that one word—a word which has been a driving force for us all these years.

Read.